SISTERS OF CALIBAN

SISTERS OF CALIBAN

Contemporary Women Poets of
the Caribbean

A Multilingual Anthology

Edited by
MJ Fenwick

Azul Editions
MCMXCVI

Published by
Azul Editions
7804 Sycamore Dr.
Falls Church, VA 22042 USA
e-mail: azulpress@aol.com

Cover painting: *Black Venus* © Rufino Tamayo

ISBN 1-885214-09-X
Library of Congress Catalog Number: 96-86065

Printed in the United States of America

First Edition
First printing November 1996
10 9 8 7 6 5 4 3 2 1

CONTENTS

ACKNOWLEDGMENTS

I am grateful to the University of Memphis for its generous support of my research work in Caribbean area literature over the past fifteen years. The process of selection for Sisters of Caliban was made possible through two Professional Development Assignments, travel grants to libraries and conferences in the Caribbean, and funding for research assistants and translators. Significant additional research support came from the University's Interlibrary Loan Department under the direction of Elizabeth Buck.

Above all, *Sisters of Caliban* is the artistic creation of the poets. I am grateful to each of them for their work and, in many cases, their acquaintance and their suggestion.

—MJ Fenwick

INTRODUCTION

Cultural hegemony is a subtle and pervasive aspect of colonialism. The dominant nation seeks to impose not only its economic and political institutions upon the peripheral nation but also its social and artistic models. Although subtle, cultural hegemony is a basic component toward facilitating ultimate domination by the aggressor nation. Historically, the underlying premises in colonialism have been that the dominant culture is superior to that of the colonized nation in all aspects and that the progress of the colonized people will correspond to their obedience to the superior cultural orthodoxy. In the dialectical process that exists between history and the arts, if the artistic expressions are made to reiterate the dominant perspective of economic and political relations, the original cultural integrity will be gradually subverted.

Much of the European literature written during the early centuries of conquest shows us that the native inhabitants of the colonies were judged to be primitive, uncivilized, even barbaric and savage creatures without a soul. Shakespeare's Caliban, for example, from *The Tempest* (written in 1611-12) was characterized as a half-breed, subhuman, uncultured, uncivilized slave of Prospero, the intellectual Italian nobleman who took possession of Caliban's island. The narrative perspective of the play is sympathetic with Prospero. The audience shares Prospero's frustration as he attempts to train Caliban and to teach him the practical skills of language and servitude. In spite of Prospero's efforts to train him otherwise, Caliban's acquired verbal expression is only concerned with cursing his master. He is ungrateful for the training, rebellious to his master, and resentful of Prospero's claim on his island; but, as testimony for Prospero's presumed superiority and Caliban's presumed inferiority, Caliban is ultimately submissive. From Prospero's perspective, the story justifies colonization.

Culturally and metaphorically, Caliban came to represent the inhabitants of the colonies, territories conquered, settled, and ruled by the Spanish, British, French, Portuguese or Dutch from the sixteenth century through the nineteenth, and in many cases into and throughout the twentieth century. The patronizing position assumed by Prospero toward Caliban in 1612 projected the future relationship

between the European nations and the colonies, and cultural hegemony can be measured by the extent to which the Prospero/Caliban
paradigm has been and is accepted within the Caribbean.

Colonial Caribbean literature has always been valued according
to its adherence to European letters. The literary tradition in the
Caribbean, from the arrival of the Spaniards in the fifteenth century
until well into the twentieth century, was overtly loyal to the European artistic expression and denied legitimacy to African, Indigenous
or Mestizo influences. Successful Caribbean writers imitated the style,
language, and even the content of the literary models of their Spanish, French, British or Dutch colonizers. And it must be emphasized
that colonial Caribbean literature was regarded as an imitation and
was rarely granted the dignity of a legitimate, first-rate literature.
Insofar as we agree that the measure of good literature is its dynamic
elaboration of the unique historical experiences and aspirations of a
people, we must also agree that any art that is a mere imitation of
another cannot be first-rate. By example, until recent decades it was a
rare reader or critic or university class that evaluated Latin American
literature as equal in quality to Peninsular Spanish literature, or U.S.
literature as equal to British literature. Now, however, these former
colonial literatures are respected for their innovative and culturally
independent art, but it is still a rare critic that generally evaluates
West Indian English literature as equal in quality to British literature
or to U.S. literature, Francophone Caribbean literature as equal in
quality to French literature, or Hispanic Caribbean literature as equal
in quality to Peninsular Spanish or to continental Latin American
literature, or the several Creole/Patois literatures as equal in quality
to any of the above, regardless of the writer's adherence to the models.

To the extent that the Prospero/Caliban analogy applies, we can
know why the colonial literary tradition honored with publication
and international recognition only the writers whose expressions most
successfully imitated the styles and subjects set by European intellectuals. In fact, like the European tradition and most academic critics,
many Caribbean writers themselves still accept the cultural superiority of their colonizers and have sought their literary fame through
imitation, ignoring expressions of unique Caribbean experience and
choosing instead the more universal themes of love, tragedy, nature,
death, and so on. Perhaps intimidated by the same hegemony that
threatened Caliban or perhaps seeking their master's grace like the

defeated Caliban, these writers have bowed to the hegemonic universalization of the European cultural expression. Often they have written about the Caribbean experience from the perspective of the colonizers, romanticizing the relationship between the colonizers and the
primary inhabitants, sometimes projecting the colonizer's cynical
perspective of them as one-dimensional, stereotypical, even comical
characters and subverting their own identity as Caribbeans.

There is, however, a parallel contemporary movement among Caribbean writers which activates the other side of the Prospero/Caliban
paradigm and stands in defiance of the colonial orthodoxy to offer
not an imitation of the European experience but a legitimate art of
the Caribbean people and of their cultural and historical aspirations.
Whereas Prospero saw language as a means of taming and dominat-
ing Caliban, these contemporary writers of the Caribbean have revived Caliban's rebellion, legitimized the voice of the outraged and
defiant citizen and made the language a tool to be used "to curse the
master." They have successfully turned the European literary tradition against itself and transformed the "master's" language into a new
literary expression that is uniquely Caribbean. With conscious irony,
they have chosen Caliban as their speaker— Shakespeare's image of
the uncivilized, inarticulate colonial subject— and transformed him
into the symbol of the new Caribbean, articulate and prepared to
confront world literature on his/her own terms. When Caliban first
confronted his colonial master and declared "This island's mine, by
Sycorax my mother" (1140; I.II.), he was projecting an artistic image
that would resound four centuries later in the voices of writers from
the Caribbean.

Caliban's wisdom and sense of reason, as viewed from our American perspective in the twentieth century, exceeded his master's intelligence. Caliban understood the absurdity of a foreign visitor's un-
founded claim to the island where he was born and ruled, and which,
by the logic of our contemporary laws, was therefore his sovereign
home. Caliban also exhibited a keen sense of observation and deduc-
tion when he accused his master of dishonest motives: "When thou
camest first / Thou strokedst me, and made much of me; wouldst
give me / Water with berries in't; and teach me how / To name the
bigger light, and how the less / That burn by day and night . . ."
(1140; I.II.). Although Caliban's previous experience had never taught
him to be wary of visitors and their intentions, his consciousness was
raised by this relationship with Prospero, and he learned to regret

the innocent trust he had initially placed in the colonizer: ". . . then I loved thee / And show'd thee all the qualities o'the isle / The fresh springs, brine-pits, barren place and fertile / Cursed be I that did so!" (1140; I.II.). His ability to imagine a different historical outcome was demonstrated when, in retrospect, he wished that he had taken Prospero's daughter sexually, as he had been accused of doing, and thereby ". . . had peopled else / This isle with Calibans" (1140; I.II.). Every line of this fictional confrontation between master and slave is a metaphor for the historical relationship between colonizer and colonized and informs us of an outrage which would one day become legitimized as the Caribbean perspective of colonial history.

The first step in Prospero's project, which from the colonizer's perspective was called educating and civilizing Caliban, necessarily began with language training. Prospero dedicated his time and effort to this project, and Caliban successfully learned his master's language. From the dialogue of Shakespeare's play, we can observe that Caliban became eloquent in the use of his master's language, but his outrage against Prospero's dominance was so intense that he refused to speak to his master except to curse him: "As wicked dew as e'er my mother brush'd / With raven's feather from unwholesome fen / Drop on you both! a south-west blow on ye / And blister you all o'er!" (1139; I.II.). In addition to demonstrating Caliban's superior language skills, the education process ironically revealed in Caliban a more subtle and far-reaching wisdom. Caliban's new language skill, turned against his master, would be his weapon against all that his colonizer intended. Caliban understood that the new language contained all the dynamics of the master/slave relationship, and he understood that to assume the master's language as if it were his own could mean submitting to the master's entire perspective as if it were his own. He understood that the process of educating and civilizing, which began with language training, was a subtle form of enslavement that was robbing him of his own culture and independent identity. This is the phenomenon known in the twentieth century as cultural hegemony. Caliban understood that his strength against hegemony would have been to people the island with Calibans, but his innocent dignity had precluded that option. He learned that his failure to do so had diminished his power; and, later alone against the colonizer, he understood that the only weapon he had left was language. He mastered the master's language and turned it against him with dozens of eloquent curses which called upon the sacred spirits of his mother culture to ward off the master's hegemony.

Although the evidence is obvious to us that Caliban was intelligent, more honest and logical than his colonial master, his innocence made him no match for the self-serving and ruthless colonizer whose power seemed unshaken by Caliban's solitary curses. He reasoned that his survival depended on a strategy to patronize Prospero and to act submissive and obedient, but this strategy was motivated by fear and only led to his further enslavement. Caliban's desperate dreams of freedom caused him one day to seize a false opportunity with a drunken colonizer who gave him liquor. Caliban sought his complicity in a scheme to murder Prospero and thereby regain his island and his freedom. The conspiracy failed, and the defeated Caliban was returned to Prospero. Caliban's fate would have been the same regardless of the outcome of the conspiracy because, crazed by the glorious illusions of freedom produced by the liquor, he had unwittingly offered his island and himself as servant to yet another opportunistic colonizer in innocent gratitude for false friendship.

Caliban's confrontations with Prospero have been played many times over throughout Caribbean colonial history and literature, from subversive linguistic maneuvers against hegemony to valiant struggles for sovereignty and innocent alliances formed with false friends offering illusory freedom. Caliban and his island did not experience sovereignty again in his lifetime; and, in fact, the metaphor of Shakespeare's play has continued in the Caribbean throughout the twentieth century.

Women writers of the Caribbean have been doubly colonized, sharing first the limitations imposed on colonial writers as well as the limitations of gender stereotypes. In this context especially, this anthology offers the stage to the sisters of Caliban, the daughters of Sycorax, contemporary women poets speaking in defiance of the colonial orthodoxies. In the past, it was the women who wrote "like men" or women whose literature reinforced the culture's stereotype of the female who were published and sometimes honored and included in literary anthologies. All too often, women's literature submitted to the European colonial hegemony with praises for European culture and with more passive themes of nature and emotion. The classical Western image portrayed women as particularly sensitive to flora, fauna and abstract spiritual and emotional things. Such themes fulfilled the dynamic between reality and literature for many women and reinforced a stereotype consistent with the designs of colonialism and patriarchy. Nineteenth- and early twentieth-century poetry written by women almost suffocated under these expressions. For example, Gertrudis Gómez de Avellaneda (Cuba, 1814-1873) received literary acclaim for her poetry to love, nature, her country and God, and she was praised for "mastering the metric and rhythmic possibilities of Spanish verse" (Chang-Rodríguez 173). Ida Faubert (1883-1968) of Haiti was praised for writing poetry which was "refined, not at all touched by native sentiments" (Herdeck 382). The poetry of Yolanda Corsen (Curaçao, 1918-1969) was described as "tense, enigmatic, gnomic, akin to the verse of Emily Dickinson" (Herdeck 566). The dynamic feminist and anticolonial poems of Julia de Burgos (Puerto Rico, 1914-1953) were dismissed by the canon, yet she became representative of women writers who achieved recognition within the canon for their poems to solitude, lost or unrequited love, anguish, the silenced voice, and death.

No critic would want to deny the historical legitimacy of these expressions for women. They were, after all, artistic elaborations of women's experiences in patriarchal colonial, post- and neocolonial societies. Nor would a good reader fail to read between the lines to find an occasional subversive or ironic twist to the poet's expression. A poem called "Song to the New Maternity" ("Canto a la nueva maternidad") by Amada Nivar de Pittaluga (Dominican Republic, 1898-1984), describes a newborn granddaughter named Rosa América: "Rosa is all woman / and with your name you bear / the seal of your destiny all stamped. / You will have to be beautiful / because beauty is / the burden of every good woman. / You will be perfumed, yes, you will be perfumed / but cruel thorns will make / the triumph of your eternal beauty inaccessible." In a poem ostensibly to motherhood and to her new granddaughter, in a collection *Rosa de América*, dedicated to the beauty of America, the poet satirizes the reality of that beauty for the Dominican Republic under the U.S.-sponsored neocolonialism of the 1950s.

Since World War II, the decades of intense neocolonialism, the anticolonial voice of Caliban has become stronger in Caribbean poetry. Women poets, no longer willing to see the Caribbean experience through European or U.S. eyes, refuse to write passive poems about abstract themes, whether natural or human, as long as the Caribbean reality demands artistic expressions and aspirations of another kind. Their poetry honors Caliban's original confrontation. Whereas

Caliban failed because he was alone, these poets have begun to succeed collectively. Their poetry may be heard throughout the Caribbean, and their voices supersede the traditional, artificial divisions created by colonial identity, language and racial differences. Their outrage summarizes the centuries that passed between Caliban and the present, and their poetic images project sovereign nations united against colonialism in all its forms. The new expressions, forms of "cursing the master," will include, among other things, the use of non-European linguistic traditions; mocking other European-style institutions; historical outrage against colonialism and imperialism, against the oppression of women, against poverty and social corruption; and expressions of hope through revolution and through the awareness of Caribbean unity. The poets of this anthology represent many images of Caliban and the mother culture of Sycorax. Some of the voices are angry, some are militant, some are humorous and some are gentle. They come from several nations of the Caribbean area and from diverse cultural, linguistic, racial and socio-economic backgrounds, but all are, in one way or another, ungrateful and rebellious Calibans. Unlike Shakespeare's Caliban, however, they show no signs of being ultimately submissive. In the words of Dalia Nieves Albert of Puerto Rico, "I want / them not to insist on rhyme from my voice / that they let me write my verses clean / without embellishments / . . . just to say them without doctrine / or ceremony / and later I want them to say / that she was insolent."

The many eloquent voices of Caliban's sisters include Aída Cartagena Portalatín from the Dominican Republic, whose book-length documentary poem *Yania Tierra* traces the centuries of colonialism anticipated in Shakespeare's play. The work is dedicated to all the women who have been killed in the five centuries of political struggles since the arrival of Columbus. The protagonist, Yania, personifies the collective spirit of Dominican history. Through her eyes, the poem describes the conquest and traces the Spanish colonial system of distributing the land among themselves and distributing the citizens to work the land for the new owners, ". . . the Encomenderos / the Repartimientos / The indians / the blacks / The foundation of the Human Tragedy / Called Civilization . . . / From the morning of the 25th / December of 92 of 1400 / When Spanish hidalgos / sons of somebodies and sons of bitches / brought pictures of kings and queens / and of slaves adorned with beads / just enough to make

Yania vomit green," and the centuries of colonization, "Here Sir Francis Drake / Rapes / destroys the Colonial City / Redirects its history / in exchange / for a millionaire's sum / YANIA watches / Factories are erected / her womb is penetrated / Gold is washed / For the kingdoms of Western Europe." Vivid images in the poem elaborate the contributions of women through the decades of struggle toward the independence victory in 1844, through the subsequent struggles against intervention by Haiti, through the landing of U.S. marines upon the shores of the Republic in 1903, 1904, 1907, 1914 and an eight-year occupation from 1916 to 1924, through the years of the U.S.-backed Trujillo dictatorships and further interventions by the U.S. in 1963 and 1965 to secure a U.S.-friendly government and corporate investments in the wake of the Cuban Revolution: "The stories come like births / they all seem deformed / attached to the skin with pins / they come with stains of sour placenta / they keep coming from the North / The pirates plunder / the riches from coffee / sugar / cacao / gold / silver / nickel / bauxite / And the hunger kills . . ." Aída Cartagena was born in 1918 and therefore is one of the oldest of these contemporary writers. Her dedication to her work and her courage to present a historical and feminist perspective clearly mark her as one of the twentieth century's outstanding literary voices. From her first publication in 1944 until her death in July of 1994, she represented the vanguard in Dominican and Caribbean literature—always a contemporary.

Another of the eloquent voices is Merle Collins from Grenada, the author of a collection of poems published in 1985, *Because the Dawn Breaks!* The collection is dedicated to the people of Grenada and is addressed to them in their struggle against the long tradition of colonialism. The poems in the collection begin in 1978 and end in 1985. The collection compiles the experiences of what might seem, in the abstract, a brief seven years; but in the context of Grenada's history, it was a dramatic three eras: from the years immediately preceeding the People's Revolutionary Government headed by Maurice Bishop until after the U.S. invasion in 1983. The poems in the collection correspond to the eras. They begin with moments of historical rage against the desperate poverty of Grenada's people, then rise to moments of revolutionary determination for a better future, and fall again to moments of pain and anger after Grenada falls again under foreign siege. The poems in the collection describe the transformations, both individual and national, brought by the 1979 Revolution. With titles like "Callaloo," the soup, and "The Butterfly Born," the caterpillar becoming butterfly and the young girl becoming woman, the poems conjure images of a new mixture, a new taste, new self-images, and a new reality for Grenada. In "The Butterfly Born," Collins presents Caliban as a female child: "Afraid of she shadow / of de basket shadow / of she dress shadow / of de fig-leaf shadow / But walkin' alone / all kin' o' hour / Hidin' an' cryin' an' hatin'" for the things she couldn't afford, for being a "woman-chile" taking care of her four younger siblings, for being afraid, for being ashamed, for her self-rejection, and for the adults who scolded her for not knowing her place and for not being obedient, quiet and respectful. The poem suddenly changes with the Revolution of 1979, and the new woman Caliban ("the butterfly born") will defy her old fears, step out from "behin' / de blin'. . . / Now / woman-chile / woman / All of a sudden / Not under no table / But out in de open / Demanding equal / recognition / For equal beauty given." These lines project the burst of energy and pride which accompanied the nation's first visions of self-determination. And these poems are courageous in the face of historical change and place Grenada in the international framework of other nations in the hemisphere and in the larger context of what is called the Third World, struggling for historical self-determination. The poems grant that it may be hard to understand the importance of self-determination in the face of changes that sometimes seem chaotic and retrogressive, but there can be no doubt that the results will be richer after the process completes its course.

Merle Collins' poems that follow the tragic events of 1983 are directed to the ethnocentric colonizers who presume to possess the superior culture and proceed, in the name of freedom and democracy, to impose it on the citizens of Grenada. The title poem, "Because the Dawn Breaks," expresses her defiance and outrage, and its language shows that the new Caliban has mastered the master's art form, and the tool has become hers to speak directly to the master on his ground: "We do not speak / to defy your tenets / though we do / or upset your plans / even though we do / or to tumble / your towers of babel / we speak / in spite of the fact / that we do / We speak / because / your plan / is not our plan / we speak because we dream / because / our dreams / are not of living in pig pens / in any other body's / backyard / not of / catching crumbs from tables / not of crawling forever."

The poetry of Merle Collins is not only to confront the master but also to speak to the tamed Caribbean Calibans who "still choose / to skin teet / an' bow head / yes Massa suh / I asks no questions suh" ("The Essence"), to those who welcomed the U.S. intervention in 1983 to reestablish colonialism in her nation (like the original Caliban offering himself as servant to yet another opportunistic colonizer, a false friend who promises to help him regain his independence from Prospero). In her poem "A Song of Pain," she writes, "I sing of pain / even as the anger grows / for you have learnt their evil lesson well". She accuses the submissive Calibans of cultural genocide and of ignoring the devastating results of more than three hundred years of colonialism. She turns her anger upon the Grenadians themselves who were too easily intimidated by the changes and challenges of the new government and by the renewed threats of imperialism, "the ships that came / to scorn my tears / to mock our dreams / to launch the planes / that dropped the bombs / that ripped the walls / that raped the land / that burnt the earth / that crushed the dreams / that we all built."

The Publisher's Note that introduces Merle Collins' book reminds the reader that we are involved in a struggle between two forms of poetry: the one that has dominated our culture and our education since the arrival of the colonizers five centuries ago and the new one that awakens our preference for things real. Merle Collins is one of the new poets, and there are many more who, at the risk of jeopardizing an international literary career, have chosen to defy the colonial tradition which conformed to European artistic guidelines and portrayed Caribbean culture through idealized utopian images, primitive, exotic and false.

The eloquent poetic voice of several Puerto Rican writers in this anthology is dedicated to the ongoing struggle against colonialism in their nation, where official independence was won in 1898 from Spanish domination only to be supplanted by domination by the United States. Poets Lolita Lebrón and Consuelo Lee Tapia were jailed for their participation in the struggle for independence. Puerto Rico's present political status as a "protectorate" is satirized in Olga Nolla's poem "Atmospheric Information" ("Datos atmosféricos") from her 1975 collection, *El ojo de la tormenta*: "We are the only Latin Americans who are citizens / in block / of the United States of North America. / This is notable, they point out to us. / We have won the universal lottery! / Tell me then, you could explain / why do our backs ache, / why do we drag our feet / and why does our bad humor twist our tongue? / why do the young people not know the difference / between the bad weed / and sugar cane? / why does our vegetation / and even the sea / rise up with difficulty moaning from weariness / under layers and layers of trash / and chemical waste?" Her poem points to the "welfare" status of her nation as both the cause and the result of colonialism perpetuated through the twentieth century under a different name.

Louise Bennett of Jamaica attacks every aspect of colonialism as it penetrates the lives, history and culture of her people. In her poems, Miss Lou satirizes the very institutions of colonialism, including the Commonwealth, the government, the law, the economy, religion, education, and, particularly, language. Her poems realize that language is a primary vehicle for conveying the premises of the colonial order; and when she writes her eloquent poems in Jamaican Creole, she does so knowing that Creole, not standard English, contains the rich synthesis that is the Caribbean cultural experience. In her poem "Bans O' Killin," from her 1966 collection *Jamaica Labrish*, she confronts the issue of language versus dialect and the colonizer's desire to standardize English throughout the Commonwealth: "Yuh gwine kill all English dialec / Or jus Jamaica one? / . . . Yuh gwine go feel inferior when / It come to dialec? / . . . Yuh wi haffi kill de Lancashire / De Yorkshire, de Cockney / De broad Scotch and de Irish brogue / Before yuh start kill me! / Yuh wi haffi get de Oxford Book / A English Verse, an tear / Out Chaucer, Burns, Lady Grizelle / An plenty o' Shakespeare! / . . . An mine how yuh dah-read dem English / Book deh pon yuh shelf / For ef yuh drop a 'h' yuh mighta / Haffi kill yuhself." To respect Louise Bennett's poetry is to respect that language is the vehicle of a people's entire cultural and historical experience. The same must be true for all art forms. The colonial tradition that requires that good literature imitate the style and content of the colonizer's literature is a notion that contradicts the dignity of history and must give way.

Cyrene Tomlinson's "Message from the Grave" and Jennifer Brown's "Caviar and Sky Juice" first published in a 1980 anthology, *Jamaica Woman,* present a satire of the vast discrepancy between rich and poor and the institutions that maintain the corrupt social order in contemporary Jamaica. "Caviar and Sky Juice" contrasts the "polished chrome of the Rolls Royce / that glided unseen through customs" with its FM radio playing "We shall overcome" and the dehumanized "bundle of filthy rags / who is compiling a treasury of waste /

paper" as the car drives past. In "Message from the Grave" the poem's voice satirizes the institutions of law and order, false promises of social belonging and society's oppression of the poor. The language of both the poems reinforces the satire. "Caviar and Sky Juice," to emphasize the discrepancy, presents a strobe light effect between standard English and Creole, between the imported culture of the Rolls Royce and the culture of the inhabitants: ". . . sky juice fly in de face of chrome / car door opens, polished shoe tests / the ground / dutty barefoot step offa de rudda!" The young voice in "Message from the Grave" says, "Yes. I go a school / An I pass de sociaty test dem / An I get a job inna de sociaty institution / But wah, I still live inna de ghetto / . . . Dem see I as Savage. Animal. Rapist. Thief. Murderer / Lazy. Wicked. Hooligan. John Crow. Henchman / Gunman . . . " The association between Creole, ghetto, savage, and so on, and standard English, society, police and soldier is fixed. The two voices, one Creole and one standard English, are counterposed in both poems to display the contradictions, and in "Message from the Grave" the voice in Creole reveals human injustice and tragedy while the voice in standard English justifies oppression. This confuses the traditional perspective and satirizes the ruling culture's stereotype of the inarticulate Caliban.

Language was the primary institution used by Prospero to train and control Caliban. The language of the master is associated with classical nobility, wisdom and ideal sentiments like tragedy, love and justice. The training presumed that Caliban's natural disposition had none of these qualities and that his utterances and actions were essentially ignorant and comical. If the use of Creole in these poems produces an image of apparent humor traditionally associated with lower class experience, it is quickly transformed into tragedy, a nobler sentiment, through the linguistic contraposition. By the same means, tragedy for the ruling class is denied. The master's perspective is neither noble, ideal, nor wise, and the perspective of the Creole voice is not, per se, comical. In the context of Caliban cursing his master, the use of Creole to express classical ideal sentiments in a classic art form represents a defiance of the European orthodoxy.

Guyanese poet Mahadai Das, in *A Collection of Poems*, 1977, affirms the important connection between poetry, history and politics: "I want my words scorching pages / Burning tongues / Paging my people's servility." In her poem "Beasts," from her 1989 collection *Bones*, she identifies with the colonized Caliban metaphor and ironically assumes the beastial aura assigned to him/her by Shakespeare as an incarnation of the collective rage and power about to spring forth against the colonizers: "In Gibraltar Straits / pirates in search of El Dorado / masked and machete-bearing / kidnapped me / Holding me to ransom / they took my jewels and my secrets / and dismembered me / The reckoning lasted for years / Limbs and parts eventually grew / a new nose, arms skilful and stronger / sight after the gutted pits could bear a leaf / It took centuries / In the cave where they kept me / a strange beast grew / With his skin of glistening jewels / and his deadly tongue / even I was afraid of him / In the dark Ajanta caves of my breast / ever since he has stayed / with his measure of venom / his exact poison and scintillating glitter / At a certain hour, I almost love him." Mahadai Das' Caliban images recall the historical process from conquest through colonization and reveal a level of sophisticated wisdom nurtured over the centuries. The final line gives life to the metaphorical being, fragmented and dehumanized by centuries of oppression and projects him / her into the future. Das' poems are replete with concrete images which speak to her generation and its children, images which call for education, social, political and economic fulfillment and revolution against the colonial hegemonies.

Mahadai Das understands that her Caliban's voice may offend the literary taste of Prospero's editors and reviewers as she submits her work for publication on the international market. In her poem "The Growing Tip" (*Bones*), she parodies the contemporary U.S./European canon's interest in sampling the poetry of the Caribbean for work which will substantiate and aggrandize the dominant culture's artistic preferences. She assigns her poetry a monstrous Caliban-type image as it reaches the desk of the editor-in-chief: "They assumed a garden: English roses / palms of victory high-raised / on a history of thorns, thick / hedges, neatly-trimmed / They assumed a gardener: / a 'Being There' type seeding / and nurturing and coaxing . . . / What she sent reminded no one of a garden: / pieces of skin, a handful of hair, broken / teeth, bits of glass . . . / horns and tails, arms of different lengths / automatic fangs near bureaucrats, a tail / (a bit of bother when she wore a dress)." But, like Caliban, her poem takes on a dynamic which will overcome the hegemonizing orthodoxies: "Even as they peeled off postage-stamps / horns grew right out of each ear! / When they picked SASE out / from its envelope, a tail uncoiled . . . / As they watched / in high shock / from every tip / it continued to grow."

Grace Nichols of Guyana projects a comprehensive historical image of Caliban in her collection *i is a long memoried woman*, 1983, dedicated to the memory of Nanny the Maroon, "see-far woman / freedom fighter / and rebel queen" and to the memory of Guyanese revolutionary scholar Walter Rodney. Her historical and feminist voice recalls the curses of Caliban and Sycorax: "I coming back Massa" as "mistress of the underworld . . . / dog howling outside / yuh window . . . / ball-a-fire / and skinless higue / I coming back." Her poetic setting is in the romanticized mythic geographical beauty of Guyana's mountains, sunshine, "palm and orange groves," "the sea encircling / all / . . . a spectrum of blue / jewels / shimmering . . ." and the seeming magic of an equatorial jungle and ancient gods, but there is a progression. The poems surreptitiously begin to focus on a different dynamic: of the Guyanese peoples moving toward revolution. The final poems in the collection continue the geography/nature metaphor but introduce the images in ways that echo the curses of the original Caliban: "But Beware / Soft winds can turn / volatile / can merge with rains / can turn hurricane / Mountains can erupt / sulphur springs / bubbling quick / and hot / like bile spilling / from a witches' cauldron / Swamps can send plagues / dysentry, fevers / plantations can perish / lands turn barren . . . / This Kingdom Will Not Reign / Forever."

Cuban poet Nancy Morejón assumes the voice of a female Caliban in "I Love My Master" ("Amo a mi amo") from her 1982 collection *Octubre imprescindible*. The voice historically recalls Caliban's innocent ambivalence toward her master, fear, awe of his power, and outrage. It begins: "I gather wood to start his day's fire / I love his blue eyes / Gentle as a lamb" and proceeds as history to broaden the perspective and pinpoint the identity of the master: "I love his feet that have roamed and pirated / through foreign lands / . . . I love his fine red mouth / that speaks words I can't understand / My language has never been his." And finally Nancy Morejón's Caliban, with increased consciousness, will be victorious: "I curse / this muslin robe he has put on me / these vain laces he has pitilessly made me wear / . . . this language so hopelessly hostile I can't form the words / . . . I love my master but every night / When I go down the flower-lined path toward the canefield / where we secretly make love / I see myself knife in hand / flaying him like an innocent calf." The poem develops three stages of consciousness throughout colonialism and traces the

consciousness of Shakespeare's Caliban. Unlike Shakespeare's Caliban
doomed to merely dream and scheme about his freedom, this contemporary Caliban responds to the metaphorical rhythmic repeti-
tion of her vision in the last lines, which "now drown his cries," and
the vision becomes reality.

The anticolonial perspective of Nancy Morejón's poetry is closely
associated with her feminism. Again, in her poem "Black Woman,"
the voice of historical outrage against the colonizer is the same collective voice of the woman's struggle through history. The memory
of the voice begins before slavery, marks the voyages of the slave
ships and the first generation of African women born in the colonies.
The voice talks of her master for whom she embroidered a coat and
bore a male child, she talks of her work in the fields, her hunger, her
suffering and the deaths of many other slaves. Each tragic stanza of
the poem is broken by a word of defiance: "I rebelled," "I walked," "I
rose up," "I went off to the mountains." And the last stanzas begin:
"Only a century later . . . / I came down from the Sierra." In refer-
ence to the 1959 Cuban Revolution, the guerrilleros in the mountains and the assertion of independence against the long tradition of
colonialism. The poem ends with "Now I exist: only today do we
have and create / Nothing is foreign to us / The land is ours." These
lines recall Caliban's lines of defiance spoken to Prospero.

Nourbese Philip of Tobago, in her 1989 collection called *She Tries
Her Tongue, Her Silence Softly Breaks,* substantiates the connection
between language and history, feminism and colonialism. The poems present myriad images of the word rising from memory, from
history, as it: "breaks the culture of silence / in the ordeal of testimony." The first poems of the collection are the female voice of
historical memory reaching from the past in search of her daughter
"Over Every Land and Sea." The language and the images are superimposed from European and African mythologies to the Caribbean.
The last poems in the collection are a discourse on language and grammar: a poem about the mother/father tongue alongside a formal edict,
rules for slaves, alongside rules of grammar and definitions of English words all connecting to the theme of colonial history; a poem
called "The Question of Language is the Answer to Power" which,
structured like a school lesson, contains vowel sounds with pronun-
ciation examples and a section of "Helpful questions and commentary" all related to slavery; and finally there are the poems where past
meets present, recovering an image from the earlier poems of the

mother's tongue licking the newborn to bring her to life, to awaken the memory of her history: "She was blowing words—her words, her mother's words, those of her mother's mother, and all their mothers before—into her daughter's mouth" and the centuries of silent history become testimony, the title poem. The structure of these poems of vivid historical images ironically interspersed with what seems to be formal proclamations from the colonial institutions of slavery and language activates a powerful dialectical confrontation between opposing versions of colonial history.

Jamaican poet Christine Craig in her poem "The Chain," from her 1984 collection *Quadrille for Tigers,* also envisions the past as a time of patient recovery and planning in anticipation of the historical moment when the collective vision and energy could emerge victorious against the colonizer. "I, me, I am a free black woman / My grandmothers and their mothers / knew this and kept their silence / to compost up their strength / kept it hidden / and played the game with deference / and agreement and pliant will / . . . that silent legacy / nourished and infused such a line / such a close linked chain / to hold us until we could speak / until we could speak out / loud enough to hear ourselves." Her metaphorical Calibans were not defeated but determined to nurture their strength, transfused to subsequent generations, that it might someday successfully banish the oppressive master.

A respect for the history of Caliban and his defiance against the colonizer, as well as a respect for the history of the Caribbean woman and her struggles, characterizes the poetry of many contemporary writers. The respect also contains a certain empathy for their silence, their failures and even for what may seem their weaknesses. Lorna Goodison's (Jamaica) poem "For My Mother" from her 1980 collection *Tamarind Season,* describes her mother as "a child of the petite bourgeoisie" whose "trousseau came by steamer through the snows / of Montreal," but her father, "with the always smile," an orphan raised by his granny, wooed her dressed "as a sunday player in a cricket match / . . . visiting dandy, maroon blazer / cream serge pants, seam like razor / and the beret and the two-tone shoes." Many years later, the poem continues, she knew her mother as the figure who sat at the Singer all day, sewed and taught the children to read as she sewed. "She could work miracles, she would make a garment from a / square of cloth / . . . Or feed twenty people on a / stew made from / fallen-from-the head cabbage leaves and a carrot and a /

cho-cho and a palmful / of meat." The poem's subtitle is "May I Inherit Half Her Strength." The poem forgives the mother's weakness for loving her father in spite of his chauvinism and admires her for her strength, for "that walk, straight-backed, that she gave / to us / . . . and for the pain she bore with the eyes of a queen. . ." The poem suggests, in the midst of historical outrage, that it would be a mistake for late twentieth-century feminism to condemn the silence of women of the past whose choices were not so many. Lorna Goodison's poetic mother represents "the centuries of silent history" (Nourbese Philip) during which women gathered their strength to speak out collectively "loud enough to hear ourselves" (Christine Craig). This strategy would allow their ultimate victory where the strategy of the original solitary Caliban was doomed to failure.

Empathy for the past generations of women is echoed in a 1985 poem by Cuban writer, Cira Andrés. Her poem is called "If I Told My Friends" ("Si les dijera a mis amigos") and understands the differences between her mother's generation in rural, pre-revolutionary Cuba and her own opportunities in post-revolutionary Cuba. The poem's female voice says that her mother is "the most beautiful birth I have given / I have created her like a poem / at night I have put her to bed / telling her about the Evolution of Man / while she laughed like a child / with the stories about apes / After Literacy I taught her / how to make a sentence / and that the world was round . . ." The sense of this poem is not of condescension but rather of compassion for the circumstances of past generations and of excitement and humility before the process of history.

These gentle poems were all born of historical outrage and project a noble role for the earlier Calibans whose struggles were repressed. The poems' gentleness should not be underestimated any more than the original Caliban in his apparent submissiveness or the women in their apparent silence. The responses of these figures, we learn from the poems, must be understood in the context of their historical moment, and their stories must be made part of the dynamics of the present.

The words of defiance found in all these poems against the colonial orthodoxies imposed on artistic expression and against the universalization of the European perspective, find their ultimate challenge in promoting an awareness of Caribbean unity. Surinamese poet, Seketi, addresses this issue to her Caribbean sisters in her "Poem":

"Caribbean woman / From the sunny Guyanas / To the distant waters of the blue sea / How many languages you know how to speak! / How many dances you know how to dance! / How many songs you know how to sing!" and she urges them to turn away from colonial/ neocolonial influences and master their own tongues, dances and songs. The act of defiance will involve reversing the processes of cultural hegemony after centuries of foreign domination, as Merle Collins writes: "tumbling your towers of babel" which have artificially fragmented Caribbean historical consciousness and development. It will involve rewriting the history books and the literary canon from the Caribbean perspective, not the foreign, and reversing the image of Caliban's submissiveness.

The power of language which Caliban understood to be his primary weapon is still very present in the revolutionary dynamics of Caribbean literature. The poetic images contain the strength gathered over centuries of apparent silence. The words contain the evidence of history in all of its perspectives. *No Language is Neutral* is the title of a collection of poems published in 1990 by Dionne Brand from Trinidad-Tobago. The concept of her title and lines from the title poem: "a morphology of rolling chain and copper gong / now shape this twang, falsettos of whip and air / rudiment this grammar," confirm Caliban's premonition of the four centuries of colonial history to come and assert the Caribbean experience as the foundation of its language and literature. Caliban understood that language contained all the elements of reality and that to submit to the master's language was to submit to his reality. But Caliban also understood that language was a tool which he could take from the master, use it and turn it against him to eventual victory. The contemporary poets have served an active part in keeping the metaphorical Caliban's wisdom alive. When other strategies have been illusory, language has served as the constant tool to communicate the vision against the master's hegemony and to project it forward into the next generations. All language is dynamic; and, if colonial language has contained the images of oppression, it has also contained the opposite. The contemporary poets have revived Caliban's curses and are using the master's language with a vision toward deconstructing the power of hegemony; and, in its place, constructing Caribbean history according to their own integral design and inspired by their own experiences.

All Caliban's wisdom prior to the arrival of Prospero—the use of language, logic, knowledge of the land and its laws—had been passed on to him from his mother, Sycorax. The poets in this anthology clearly intend to revive Sycorax' wisdom as it relates contemporarily to the struggle against domination, to revive the importance of the woman's perspective in history, the language and logic of the mother culture. As Merle Collins writes in her poem "Crick Crack," "tales of hunting will always / glorify the hunter / until the lioness / is her own / hiss- / -torian." The list is long of women poets who write to assert a new tradition in Caribbean literature. The list includes women from English-speaking, Spanish-speaking, French-speaking and Dutch-speaking nations of the Caribbean, women of multiple racial and ethnic backgrounds, Amerindian, African, Asian and European, either born in the Caribbean or long-time residents. They are not obscure poets writing what some critics might want to reduce to the realm of the political cliché. They are Caribbean poets with an established reputation, anthologized and with many books of their own. They are the contemporary mainstream. Their poetry is not passive but dynamic, not tragic but energetic and angry. Their poetic images are not abstract but concrete. Their poetic aspiration to defy the colonial tradition is nicely expressed in these lines by Grace Nichols: "O how I long to place my foot / on the head of anthropology / to swing my breasts / in the face of history."

This anthology is testimony that the writers are doing their part to legitimize Caribbean poetry within its own canon, as an expression of the rich cultural heritage alive in the Caribbean. The next challenge is to readers and critics to discard the colonial tradition and find new ways of reading and new ways of discussing Caribbean poetry. Our responsibility as readers and critics is to approach Caribbean poetry not as a branch of British, U.S., French, Spanish or Dutch poetry, not to see where it fits within the dominant canons, but to enter into Caribbean poetry in its own terms as invited by the poets themselves. Haitian poet Marlène Apollon, in her poem "The Month of the Woman" ("Mois de la femme") extends the critical challenge to women "from all the so-called free countries / You who hold the power of words / And who have in principle and by law the right to speak / Who are aware of injustice / And have the courage to reveal it / It's your official month to speak for all the others / For whom the dawn of a cease fire against the daily horror / Is still far away." *Sisters of Caliban* is edited by an Irish-American working class woman, citizen by birth of a "so-called free country" and published by a small press in Washington, D.C., the "cerebral cortex" of a "so-called free country" in support of the poets' challenge. The anthology is not intended to speak for the poets but to offer our resources, our stage, for the poets themselves to speak.

—MJ Fenwick
Memphis, Tennessee
1996

SISTERS OF CALIBAN

OPAL PALMER ADISA
JAMAICA

Market Woman

Me wid
elephant
sappadilla
rear
walk tall
elegant
more poised
than vine-models
of *Vogue*

Fi me life-line
is not de whisper
delicacy of a rose petal
it tells de unyieldin
of de earth at times
of scrubbin
on rock's back
clothes stained with
guineps and aprons
marked with yams
of buffs on
a boy-child's back
growin
wid out a man

See dese breasts
heavin still firm
tauntin men's eyes
dey have nursed
seven pickney
and delighted more men

and is three man
did father me
seven pickney
and me did love all
of dem
no good as dem is
am I not
Granny Nanny
fightin
wid de Maroon
guerrillas
am I not Cudgoe's
woman and Paul Bogle's
too
am I not de
same washer-woman
de one who cut cane
sweep road
and darn de defeat
in men eyes

Me wid
elephant's hide
still glare
stare
still get
photographed
by tourist
but wha
dem know
bout de Market Woman
before rooster crow
and mornin wash its eye
me roll me catta and
bear me fruit pon me head

De truck draw breaks

down Bredda Joe's shop
me mek haste
someone help me wid
me load

As de ride tun-tun
de fritters and fry plantain
pon me chest
me hope de pickney dem
get up fi guh school

Beverly mek dem tea
Keith full-up de drum dem
Jean and Carol sweep out de house
and Trevor and Peter sweep de dust
clean from in front de steps

De market: plenty
ants roastin pon coal,
barterin all around

But wha dem know
bout de Market Woman
whose lips spew froth,
cuss shit den
tun-roun and offer de cheeks
of she hide
Market Day
lady come buy fruits

Goweh yuh
face look like old rag hitch
pon barb-wire

Dem women who squeeze
dem foot inna spike-heels
and powder dem husband

absence, cyaan stan de
contented perspiration
of Market Woman

Goweh
barb-wire face
yuh husband ah sleep
wid me

Market Day, Market Day
lady come buy
fruits, come buy vegs
de Market Woman ah sell
dem cheap, come it's Market

We Are Formed from Volcanoes

jamaica
is not south africa
although a black elite
rules
the poor man
and the rich man
rub shoulders

the boy
who keeps their pool clean
and their garden manicured
must watch their son
while he swims
but he's forbidden
to join him
they are both
black
jamaica
is not south africa

minimum wages
are in effect
blacks   browns
and whites
fraternize
decorum foreign
dress western
speech imitation

she's a live-in
rises at 6 am to
prepare their breakfast
clears the dinner table
at 7 pm
irons a dress
for the misses at 9 pm
for good wages
her mother keeps
her child
worker and employer
are black female mothers
jamaica
is not south africa
down the road
from a million dollar
home equipped with
a satellite dish
three colour tvs vcr
and swimming pool
is a shack with no
indoor plumbing
ten to two rooms
but dem lazy
dem lack ambition

jamaica
is not south africa

independence
is celebrated
every august 6th

A Run-Away

rain
washes out tracks

water
bleaches out smell

night
rest until dawn

sounds travel
conceal deed

sing those songs
that tell us
when to run

eyes to the sun
feet to the moon
run away children
abort fear

trees are beds
that nestle phantoms
trees are food
that direct us
to the river
run children
run
rain falling
run children

run
let your
rope-muscled legs
snake the water
run children
run
let your beating
hearts
propel you forward

you're almost there now
run
you're almost home
remember
the foot
with toes missing
remember
the back
brutalized with scars
remember the arm
that's now a stump
run children
run

water bleaches
scent
night rinses
plans

run
remember your way
back to yourself

JULIA ALVAREZ
DOMINICAN REPUBLIC

Audition

Porfirio drove Mami and me
to Cook's mountain village
to find a new pantry maid.
Cook had given Mami a tip
that her hometown was girl-heavy,
the men lured away to the cities.
We drove to the interior,
climbing a steep, serpentine,
say-your-last-prayers road.
I leaned toward my mother
as if my weight could throw
the car's balance away
from the sheer drop below.
Late morning we entered
a dusty village of huts.
Mami rolled down her window
and queried an old woman,
Did she know of any girls
looking for work as maids?
Soon we were surrounded
by a dozen señoritas.
Under the thatched cantina
Mami conducted interviews—
a mix of personal questions
and Sphinx-like intelligence tests.
Do you have children, a novio?
Would you hit a child who hit you?
If I give you a quarter to buy
guineos at two for a nickel,
how many will you bring back?
As she interviewed I sat by,
looking the girls over;

one of them would soon
be telling me what to do,
reporting my misbehaviors.
Most seemed nice enough,
befriending me with smiles,
exclamations on my good hair,
my being such a darling.
Those were the ones I favored.
I'd fool them with sweet looks,
improve my bad reputation.
As we interviewed we heard
by the creek that flowed nearby
a high, clear voice singing
a plaintive lullaby . . .
as if the sunlight filling
the cups of the allamandas,
the turquoise sky dappled
with angelfeather clouds,
the creek trickling down
the emerald green of the mountain
had found a voice in her voice.
We listened. Mami's hard-line,
employer-to-be face
softened with quiet sweetness.
The voice came closer, louder—
a slender girl with a basket
of wrung rags on her head
passed by the cantina,
oblivious to our presence.
Who is she? my mother asked.
Gladys, the girls replied.
Gladys! my mother called
as she would for months to come.
Gladys, come clear the plates!
Gladys, answer the door!
Gladys! The young girl turned—
Abruptly, her singing stopped.

Bilingual Sestina

Some things I have to say aren't getting said
in this snowy, blond, blue-eyed, gum-chewing English:
dawn's early light sifting through *persianas* closed
the night before by dark-skinned girls whose words
evoke *cama, aposento, sueños* in *nombres*
from that first world I can't translate from Spanish.

Gladys, Rosario, Altagracia—the sounds of Spanish
wash over me like warm island waters as I say
your soothing names: a child again learning the *nombres*
of things you point to in the world before English
turned *sol, tierra, cielo, luna* to vocabulary words—
sun, earth, sky, moon. Language closed

like the touch-sensitive *morivivi* whose leaves closed
when we kids poked them, astonished. Even Spanish
failed us back then when we saw how frail a word is
when faced with the thing it names. How saying
its name won't always summon up in Spanish or English
the full blown genie from the bottled *nombre.*

Gladys, I summon you back by saying your *nombre.*
Open up again the house of slatted windows closed
since childhood, where *palabras* left behind for English
stand dusty and awkward in neglected Spanish.
Rosario, muse of *el patio,* sing in me and through me say
that world again, begin first with those first words

you put in my mouth as you pointed to the world—
not Adam, not God, but a country girl numbering
the stars, the blades of grass, warming the sun by saying,
¡Qué calor! as you opened up the morning closed
inside the night until you sang in Spanish,
Estas son las mañanitas, and listening in bed, no English

yet in my head to confuse me with translations, no English
doubling the world with synonyms, no dizzying array of words
—the world was simple and intact in Spanish—
luna, sol, casa, luz, flor, as if the *nombres*
were the outer skin of things, as if words were so close
one left a mist of breath on things by saying

their names, an intimacy I now yearn for in English—
words so close to what I mean that I almost hear my Spanish
heart beating, beating inside what I say *en inglés.*

CIRA ANDRÉS
CUBA

Si les dijera a mis amigos

Si les dijera a mis amigos
que soy la madre de mi madre
estoy segura que no me lo creerían.
Pero si les explico,
que ella es el parto más bello que he tenido,
que la he ido creando como a un poema,
que por las noches la he dormido
explicándole la evolución del hombre,
mientras ella se reía como una niña
con esas historias de los monos,
que después de la Alfabetización le mostré
cómo enlazar las oraciones
y que el mundo era redondo.
Que le enseñé a amar el Comunismo
cuando me fui a la Habana
y no me vio regresar
con un hijo entre los brazos
sino con muchos en el corazón.
Entonces, estoy segura,
que si les digo a mis amigos:
soy la madre de mi madre,
me creerán.

If I Were To Tell My Friends

If I were to tell my friends
that I am my mother's mother
I know for sure they would never believe me.
But if I explain to them,
that she is the most beautiful birth that I have ever given,
that I have been nurturing her like a poem,
that at night I have laid her to sleep
explaining to her about the evolution of humankind
while she laughed like a child
at those stories about monkeys,
that after the Literacy Campaign I showed her
how to weave sentences together
and that the world was round.
That I taught her to love Communism
when I went away to Havana
and she did not see me return
with a child in my arms
but with many in my heart.
Then, I am sure,
that if I say to my friends:
I am my mother's mother,
they will believe me.

MARLÈNE RIGAUD APOLLON
HAITI

Tiers Monde

Tiers est mon monde
Où les enfants vont nus
Panse en avant.

Un tiers ne vaut pas mieux
Mais deux tu n'auras pas.

Tiers est mon monde
Où les femmes se traînent
Mains en avant
Nourrissons aux tétons.

Meurs, enfant, meurs
Dans les bras impuissants de ta mère.

Tiers est mon monde
Où les hommes se retrouvent
Mors aux dents
Gros Jean comme devant.

Crevez, crevez, bonnes gens
Bêtes de somme de mon monde.

Tiers est mon monde
Où les élus déambulent
Nez en avant.

Tête altière, bouche en coeur
Pour mieux ignorer la misère, mes amis.

Tiers est mon monde
Tiers est ma vie.

Third World

Third is my world
Where the children go naked
Bellies swollen

A third is not worth more
But two you will not get

Third is my world
Where the women drag along
Hands in front
Babies at their teats

Die, child, die
In the powerless arms of your mother.

Third is my world
Where the men slave all their lives
And end up with nothing

Die, die, good people
Beasts of burden of my world

Third is my world
Where the chosen stroll about
Noses in the air

Heads held high, mouths puckered
To better ignore the poverty, my friends

Third is my world
Third is my life.

Comptines

Une Mercedes
Deux BMW
Trois Pajeros
À la barbe du peuple.

Deux ranchs floridiens
Quatre chalets suisses
Six châteaux en Espagne
Sur la tête sur peuple.

Trois millions
Trente millions
Trois cent millions
Sur le dos du peuple.

Un crime
Cent crimes
Mille crimes
Sur les enfants du peuple.

Une fête
Deux fêtes
Trois fêtes
Et pouf !

Counting

One Mercedes
Two BMW's
Three Pajeros*
In the face of the people.

Two Florida ranches
Four Swiss chalets
Six castles in Spain
On the head of the people.

Three million
Thirty million
Three hundred million
On the back of the people.

One crime
One hundred crimes
One thousand crimes
On the children of the people.

One party
Two parties
Three parties
And poof!

---

*Pajeros are expensive 4-wheel drive vehicles used primarily as status symbols.

Mois de la femme

C'est ton mois, femme,
Toi là-bas à Sarajevo,
Musulmane ou chrétienne, serbe ou bosnienne.
Toi la grand'mère tuée alors que tu portes en terre ton petit-fils.
Toi qu'on viole et qu'on engrosse avec méthode et maléfice
Pour que la souillure et la dégradation demeurent indélébiles.
C'est ton mois, femme de Sarajevo.

C'est ton mois, femme,
Chilienne, Salvadorienne ou autre sud-américaine, hélas.
Toi des pays aux généraux amnistiés.
Toi qui jour après jour,
—Mois de la femme ou non—
Portes sur le coeur et dans le coeur l'image de ton "disparu".
C'est ton mois, femme d'Amérique du Sud.

C'est ton mois, femme d'Irlande,
Catholique ou protestante.
Toi la veuve, l'orpheline, la manchotte d'une soeur, d'un frère,
La procréatrice dont le fruit des entrailles est transformé chaque
jour en chair à canon.
Toi, victime de la tuitième guerre de religion
Don l'être humain, inventeur de religions, a la passion.
C'est ton mois, femme d'Irlande.

C'est ton mois, femme d'Hébron,
Palestinienne aujourd'hui, juive demain.
Toi qui as vu massacrer l'un des tiens
Par un de ces fanatiques religieux
Qui croient en un Dieu haineux, raciste et intolérant à leur image.
C'est ton mois, femme d'Hébron.

C'est ton mois, femme des barrios et des bateys
Et de leurs équivalents de par le monde.
Toi, vendue pour une bouchée de riz ou une verge de canne.
Toi, condamnée à vie à la "générosité" des industrialistes des
grands pays,

The Month of the Woman

It's your month, woman,
You over there in Sarajevo,
Moslem or Christian, Serbian or Bosnian.
You the grandmother killed as you were burying your grandson.
You, raped and impregnated systematically and maliciously
So that the stain and the degradation remain indelible.
It's your month, woman of Sarajevo.

It's your month, woman,
Chilean, Salvadoran or other South American, alas.
You from countries where generals are granted amnesty.
You who day after day,
—whether it's the month of the woman or not—
Wear over your heart and in your heart the image of your "missing."
It's your month, woman of South America.

It's your month, woman of Ireland,
Catholic or Protestant.
You the widow, the orphan, the amputee of a sister, of a brother,
The procreator whose fruit is transformed every day into
cannon fodder.
You, victim of the nth war of religion
For which the human being, inventor of religions, has a passion.
It is your month, woman of Ireland.

It is your month, woman of Hebron,
Palestinian today, Jewish tomorrow.
You who saw one of your kin slaughtered
By one of those religious fanatics
Who believe in a hateful God, racist and intolerant in their image.
It's your month, woman of Hebron.

It's your month, woman of the barrios and the bateys*
And of their equivalent everywhere in the world.
You, sold for a handful of rice or a stick of cane.
You, condemned for life to the "generosity" of the industrialists of
the great powers,

Attelée pour toujours à une machine à rendre plus douce leur vie et
celle de leurs constituents,
Chanceuse, parce que tu n'as plus à te chercher une subsistance dans
les déchets des riches.
C'est ton mois, femme des barrios et bateys.

C'est ton mois, femme haïtienne
Où que tu sois:
Dans l'Haïti des durs et des coriaces,
Violée et violencée chaque jour.
Toi, maintenue en esclavage et en ignorance par tes propres soeurs.
Toi qui dois dire "Oui, monsieur, oui madame" pour une assiette de
restes.
Toi, la grand-mère dont on ne respecte plus les cheveux blancs
Et qui assistes, impuissante à l'assassinat de ton petit-fils sur son lit
d'hôpital.
C'est ton mois, femme haïtienne
Où que tu aies abouti dans les milles recoins de la terre.
Toi, empêchée de te faire une existence dans un pays hostile à ta
nationalité
Et esquivant sans cesse les patrouilles mises à tes trousses pour te
rapatrier.
C'est ton mois, femme haïtienne
Où que tu dérives:
Dans un kantè, ta seule définition "d'Espoir"
L'âme en qui vive contre les coups de vents d'une mer imprévisible
Ou les coups de filets d'une marine étrangère qui râte rarement sa proie.
Toi, naufragée, dans l'océan au large des Bahamas,
Disputant éperdument aux requins n'importe lequel de tes
quatre enfants.
C'est ton mois, femme sans pays.

C'est ton mois, femme, fille
De partout.
Toi, dupée et abandonnée par l'homme qui t'a mis un enfant dans
le ventre.
Toi qui portes seule le blâme et la responsabilité de votre "péché"
commun.
Toi, sans cesse bafouée

Bound forever to a machine to make their life sweeter and that of
their constituents,
Lucky, because you no longer have to scrounge for food in the
garbage of the rich.
It's your month, woman of the barrios and the bateys.

It's your month, Haitian woman
Wherever you are:
In the Haiti of the hard and tough,
Raped and abused everyday.
You, kept in slavery and ignorance by your own sisters.
You who much say, "Yes, Sir, Oui, Madame" for a plate of leftovers.
You, the grandmother whose white hair is no longer respected
and who witnesses, powerless, the murder of your grandson on a
hospital bed.
It is your month, Haitian woman
Wherever you have landed in the thousand corners of the world.
You, kept from making a decent life in a country hostile to your
nationality
Constantly avoiding the patrols looking for you to repatriate you.
It's your month, Haitian woman
Wherever you happen to be:
In a boat, your only definition of "Hope"
Your soul vigilant against the blows of the fathomless sea
Where the nets of a foreign navy rarely miss their prey.
You, shipwrecked, in the ocean off the Bahamas,
Hopelessly fighting to keep the sharks from getting any of your
four children.
It's your month, woman without a country.

It's your month, woman, girl
From everywhere.
You, duped and abandoned by the man who put a child in your
belly.
You who alone bear the blame and the responsibility for your
common "sin."
You, beaten constantly
And who dream treacherously or desperately to brandish a vengeful
knife.

Et qui rêves parfois perfidement ou désespérément de brandir toi
aussi un couteau vengeur.
C'est ton mois, femme, fille de partout.

C'est ton mois, femme, fille
De tous les pays du monde.
Toi, la riche et toi, la pauvre.
La grasse, la maigre,
La belle, la laide,
La vieille, la jeune.
Femme à hommes.
Femme sans homme.
Femme-fille-mère, grand-mère, ou arrière-grand-mère.
Femme sans enfants par choix ou par perte brutale.
Qui que tu sois sur la terre partout en tumulte,
C'est ton mois, femme, fille de tous les pays du monde.

C'est ton mois, femme,
Même si tu n'es pas au courant ou n'y crois pas
Parce que, pour toi, ça ne change rien à rien
Et qu'en mars, tu souffres et pleures autant que pendant les onze
autres mois.
C'est ton mois, femme.

C'est spécialement ton mois, femme des pays dits libres.
Toi qui détiens la force des mots
Et qui as en principe et de par la loi le droit de parler.
Toi qui as la conscience des choses pas justes
Et le courage de les pointer du doigt.
C'est ton mois officiel pour parler pour toutes les autres
Pour qui l'aube d'un cessez-le-feu contre l'horreur quotidienne
Est encore bien loin.
C'est ton mois, femme des pays dits libres.

C'est ton mois, femme,
Le mois du printemps,
Le mois de la Vie.
C'est ton mois, femme-vie.

It's your month, woman, girl from everywhere.
It's your month, woman, girl
From all the countries of the world.
You, the rich one, you, the poor one.
The fat one, the skinny one,
The beautiful one, the ugly one,
The old one, the young one.
The woman of men.
The woman without a man.
Woman-girl-mother, grandmother, or great-grandmother.
Woman childless by choice or because of a brutal loss.
Whoever you are on this earth in tumult,
It's your month, woman, girl of all the countries in the world.

It's our month, woman,
Even if you don't know it or don't believe in it
Because, for you, it doesn't change anything
And in March, you suffer and cry as much as in the other
eleven months.
It's your month, woman.

It's especially your month, woman from all the so-called free
countries.
You who hold the power of words
And who have in principle and by law the right to speak.
Who are aware of injustice
And have the courage to expose it.
It's your official month to speak for all the others
For whom the dawn of a cease fire against the daily horror
Is still far away.
It's your month, woman of all the so-called free countries.

It's your month, woman,
The month of Spring,
The month of Life.
It's your month, woman-life.

---

*Barrios and bateys are slums in Spanish and Haitian Creole, respectively.

MARÍA ARRILLAGA
PUERTO RICO

A las poetas de mi generación

Me moriré con mis sueños
Es un desierto
Las luces se ven a lo lejos
Me crece el cabello
Lo suelto, lo peino, lo aprieto
Me aprieto, me suelto
Me escapo corriendo
Regreso despacio
Camino
Me pienso camino de todos los míos
incluyendo aquellos que son
enemigos
Qué mucho y qué poco sabemos
Qué poco decimos, qué mucho pensamos
Me duele tu frío contigo, conmigo
¡Qué pena que nos falte amor!
Hablarte, tocarte; tocarme y hablarme
Escucharte, escucharme
Saber tu belleza, que sepas la mía
la pienses, la digas; la piense, la diga
La nieve que cae construye silencios
creando el vacío
No es tuya ni mía, no es nuestra
No hay forma que sepa, querida mujer,
sino hincar tu cuerpo, que hinques el mío
con tus trinitarias, con mis trinitarias
para hacer el mundo que nos corresponde
mientras revivimos el mito del fuego que
mata el dragón, para liberarnos e ir en
busca de eso que yace incompleto mientras
no se cumpla en solidaridad valiente

To the Poets of My Generation

I shall die with my dreams
It's a desert
The lights can be seen at a distance
My hair grows
I let it loose, I comb it, I pull it back
I pull myself back, I let myself loose
I run away
I come back slowly
I walk
I think of myself as the road for all my people
including those who are
enemies
How much and how little we know
How little we say, how much we think
I suffer your coldness with you, with me
What a shame that we lack love!
To talk to you, touch you; to touch me and talk to me
To listen to you, to listen to me
To know your beauty, that you may know mine
that you may think it, say it; that I may think it, say it
The snow that falls builds silences
creating the emptiness
It isn't yours nor mine, it isn't ours
There is no way that I know, dear woman
but to prick your body, that you may prick mine
with your trinitarians, with my trinitarians*
to build the world that belongs to us
while we revive the myth of the fire that
kills the dragon, to liberate us and go in
search of what lies unfinished as long as
it isn't done in valiant solidarity

desafiante el mundo de nuestra poesía
que hinca y que cura, que cura y encanta
que encanta y asciende seguro —intercepta
a Icaro—para establecer el vuelo feliz
donde somos:
chiringas del pueblo, valquirias del trópico,
mujer maravillas de símbolo autóctono
desde nuestra tierra que clitoriaremos
con la construcción de nuestra verdad.

Sinfonía del todo y de la nada

Bella es la noche
cuando en la soledad escribo
con pedazos de espejo roto,
la amargura de sillas desencoladas,

        de pianos que no suenan
        de poesía que no tiene ritmo
        de bailes que no se bailan
        de comida que envenena
        de aviones que no se vuelan
        de agua que no moja
        de fuego que no quema
        de niños que no lloran
        de flores que no florecen
        de gatos que no maúllan
        de perros que no ladran
        de agujas que no se ensartan
        de caminos que nos llevan a la nada
        de viajes que no merecen la pena
        de plantas muertas
        del desierto
        de un beso en el vacío
        de una mano sola que aplaude

the world challenges our poetry
that holds steady and cures, that cures and charms
that charms and rises secure—it will intercept
Icarus—to establish the happy flight
where we are:
the kites of the people, the kites of the tropics,
woman wonders of an indigenous symbol
from our land that we will clitoricize
with the construction of our truth.

---

*Trinitarians are flowers with strong, thorny stems like the bougainvillea.

Symphony of Everything and of Nothing

Beautiful is the night
when in solitude I write
with pieces of a broken mirror,
the bitterness of unfastened seats,
   of pianos that don't sound
   of poetry that has no rhyme
   of dances that aren't danced
   of food that poisons
   of planes that don't fly
   of water that doesn't wet
   of fire that doesn't burn
   of children that don't cry
   of flowers that don't bloom
   of cats that don't meow
   of dogs that don't bark
   of needles that don't thread
   of roads that take us to nothing
   of trips that aren't worth the trouble
   of dead plants
   of the desert
   of a kiss in the emptiness
   of a single hand that applauds

de los muertos
de los vivos
de la sangre
de una pintura al revés
de un libro que no se lee
de un rompecabezas que le faltan piezas
de un carro que no corre
de un barco que se hunde
de las bombas en Vietnam
de los pobres de la tierra
de mi pueblo esclavizado
del monstruo engordando
de tentáculos que nos agarran
    y nos sueltan en el vacío
de peces que no procrean
de poetas destruyéndose
de bombillas que no alumbran
de velas que no se prenden
de sillones que no mecen
de animales enjaulados
de brujas sin escobas
de la cuerda rota
de una flor sin pétalos
de peces sin escamas
de gatos sin pelo
de árboles sin hojas en el verano
de oraciones que no llegan
    ni al cielo ni a los infiernos
de una pluma sin tinta
de un niño mudo
de un viejo sin zapatos
y deste bolso de trucos
y del amor todo tristeza.

II

Y es que hay que creer en la alegría
y en las visiones de esta energía loca de la tierra,

of the dead
of the living
of blood
of a painting turned backwards
of a book that isn't read
of a puzzle with missing pieces
of a car that doesn't run
of a ship that's sinking
of bombs in Vietnam
of the poor people of the land
of my people enslaved
of the monster getting fatter
of tentacles that grab us
    and cast us into the void
of fish that don't spawn
of poets destroying themselves
of lightbulbs that don't shine
of candles that don't light
of chairs that don't rock
of caged animals
of witches without brooms
of a broken cord
of a flower without petals
of fish without scales
of cats without fur
of trees without leaves in the summer
of prayers that don't reach
    either heaven or hell
of a pen without ink
of a mute child
of an old man without shoes
and this bag of tricks
and of love all sadness.

II

And the fact is that you have to believe in happiness
and in the visions of this crazy energy of the land

loca de mi yo,
loca de locura,
a pesar de la política del amor,
de la inocencia
del odio
del sexo
de la cobardía
de la malicia
de la ropa
y la comida
de gustos y manerismos
de los amigos
de los enemigos
de los confundidos y definidos
de la familia y del empleo
de las calles
de los cafés
de los que recogen basura
de los que guían taxis
de los idealistas oportunistas
y de los oportunistas idealistas
de los intelectuales
de las organizaciones
de los artistas
de los burgueses
de los capitalistas
de los que creen tanto que no creen en nada
de los mártires y de los déspotas
de la revolución y la reacción
del dormir y el despertar
del caminar,
evacuar,
prender luces y apagarlas
de música bien escogida
de poesías de buen gusto
de vidas justificadas
de lo controversial y de lo aceptado
de lo que vale y lo que no vale

           crazy about myself,
           crazy from craziness,
in spite of the politics of love,
       of innocence
       of hate
       of sex
       of cowardice
       of malice
       of clothing
           and food
       of tastes and mannerisms
       of friends
       of enemies
       of the confused and the defined
       of the family and the job
       of the streets
       of the cafes
       of those who pick up trash
       of those who drive taxis
       of the opportunistic idealists
           and of the idealistic opportunists
       of the intellectuals
       of the organizations
       of the artists
       of the bourgeois
       of the capitalists
       of those who believe so much that they believe in
           nothing
       of the martyrs and the despots
       of the revolution and the reaction
       of sleeping and waking
       of walking,
           of emptying ourselves
       of turning on lights and turning them off
       of music well chosen
       of poetry of good taste
       of justified lives
       of the controversial and the accepted

de la arbitrariedad de los tiempos
de reglas de segundo que no sirven al minuto
de minutos encapsulados
de la obsesión del tiempo
de la fama
del saber
de la ignorancia
de la lucha de los pueblos
de la lucha de mi patria
de la lucha de mi yo
de la lucha-lucha de la lucha
del todo y de la nada
Hacia el infinito de la paz del universo recreándose
sólo él en mi alma sola mía,
porque hay obreros y hay patria
y en un pedazo de tierra, revolución.

of that which is valuable and that which is not
of the arbitrariness of the times
of rules of the second that don't serve the minute
of encapsulated minutes
of obsession with time
of fame
of knowledge
of ignorance
of the struggle of the people
of the struggle of my country
of the struggle of my self
of the struggle-struggle of the struggle
of everything and of nothing
Toward the infinity of peace in the universe recreating itself
only this in my soul alone,
because there are workers and there is a homeland
and on one piece of land, revolution.

VERA BELL
JAMAICA

Ancestor on the Auction Block

Ancestor on the auction block
Across the years your eyes seek mine
Compelling me to look.

I see your shackled feet
Your primitive black face
I see your humiliation
And turn away
Ashamed.

Across the years your eyes seek mine
Compelling me to look
Is this mean creature that I see
Myself?
Ashamed to look
Because of myself ashamed
Shackled by my own ignorance
I stand
A slave.

Humiliated
I cry to the eternal abyss
For understanding
Ancestor on the auction block
Across the years your eyes meet mine
Electric
I am transformed
My freedom is within myself.

I look you in the eyes and see
The spirit of God eternal

Of this only need I be ashamed
Of blindness to the God within me
The same God who dwelt within you
The same eternal God
Who shall dwell
In generations yet unborn.

Ancestor on the auction block
Across the years
I look

I see you sweating, toiling, suffering
Within your loins I see the seed
Of multitudes
From your labour
Grow roads, aqueducts, cultivation
A new country is born
Yours was the task to clear the ground
Mine be the task to build.

LOUISE BENNETT
JAMAICA

Bans O' Killing

So yuh a de man, me hear bout!
Ah yuh dem sey dah-teck
Whole heap o' English oat sey dat
Yuh gwine kill dialect!

Meck me get it straight Mass Charlie
For me noh quite undastan,
Yuh gwine kill all English dialect
Or jus Jamaica one?

Ef yuh dah-equal up wid English
Language, den wha meck
Yuh gwine go feel inferior, wen
It come to dialect?

Ef yuh kean sing "Linstead Market"
An "Wata come a me y'eye",
Yuh wi haffi tap sing "Auld lang syne"
An "Comin thru de rye".

Dah language weh yuh proud o',
Weh yuh honour and respeck,
Po' Mass Charlie! Yuh noh know sey
Dat it spring from dialect!

Dat dem start fe try tun language,
From de fourteen century,
Five hundred years gawn an dem got
More dialect dan we!

Yuh wi haffe kill de Lancashire
De Yorkshire, de Cockney
De broad Scotch and de Irish brogue
Before yuh start kill me!

Yuh wi haffe get de Oxford book
O' English verse, an tear
Out Chaucer, Burns, Lady Grizelle
An plenty o' Shakespeare!

Wen yuh done kill "wit" an "humour"
Wen yuh kill "Variety"
Yuh wi haffe fine a way fe kill
Originality!

An mine how yuh dah-read dem English
Book deh pon yuh shelf

For ef yuh drop a "h" yuh mighta
Haffe kill yuhself.

Colonisation in Reverse

Wat a joyful news, Miss Mattie,
I feel like me heart gwine burs'
Jamaica people colonizin
Englan in reverse.

By de hundred, by de t'ousan
From country and from town,
By de ship-load, by de plane-load
Jamaica is Englan boun.

Dem a-pour out o' Jamaica,
Everybody future plan
Is fe get a big-time job
An settle in de mother lan.

What a islan! What a people!
Man an woman, old an young
Jusa pack dem bag an baggage
An tun history upside dung!

Some people don't like travel,
But fe show dem loyalty
Dem all a-open up cheap-fare-
To-Englan agency.

An week by week dem shippin off
Dem countryman like fire,
Fe immigrate an populate
De seat o' de Empire.

Oonoo see how life is funny,

Oonoo see de tunabout,
Jamaica live fe box bread
Outa English people mout'.

For wen dem catch a Englan,
An start play dem different role,
Some will settle down to work
An some will settle fe de dole.

Jane say de dole is not too bad
Because dey payin' she
Two pounds a week fe seek a job
Dat suit her dignity.

Me say Jane will never find work
At the rate how she dah-look,
For all day she stay pon Aunt Fan couch
An read love-story book.

Wat a devilment a Englan!
Dem face war an brave de worse,
But I'm wonderin' how dem gwine stan'
Colonizin' in reverse.

MARION BETHEL
BAHAMAS

Sons of Adam

Your profane litany of gold was wholly perverse
in a catholic rite of possessing and naming
you feigned Adam's dominion, man of the universe
in Guanihani, hallowed traditions you were claiming

They have no iron; you chimed across the seas

branding them livestock with tools of slavery
an abscessed spirit seared their native legacies
thirst for silver and silk exposed your knavery

They have no religion; you prayed a holy conquest
haunted by spirits of birds canoes winds corals
burning Hatuey like a witch in your savage inquest
his soul boarded a winged boat resting on his laurels

They have no clothes; you sang a lusty Solomon song
taunting the eleventh commandment, "Thou shall not rape
exploit", you possessed 'the other' with a naked tongue
fearing your own dreamed fantasy of wild man and ape

They are not black; you pealed bells throughout Spain
but in sleight of hand you created man-eating slaves
and Caliban, 'a thing of darkness', for the sugarcane
mirrored a lost vision of sacred rites in your caves.

Remember Grenada

Remember Grenada and remember
we tried to alter the tides
the way we touch one another

Beware of our present stilted dance
of imitation, a sweaty half-digested
waltz of our cloned statemongers

liveried in their new mask and cloak.
Know that our supple limbs have their
own survival rhythms creating global

movements. Remember Grenada and know
all our ankles, wrists, necks remain
roped together. The chain-gang managers

try to gild our eyes from Brazil to
Barbados to the Bahamas. The whip,
the noose, hangmen and functionaries

are undisguised in their costume of
death. Remember Grenada, the Caribbean
sea is our home. Each island must

shore up each other's coral reefs. One
hundred, ninety-four years ago Toussaint
fed Bonaparte's army to the jaws of the

sea. A twelve year struggle against local
masters, successive invaders trooping flags
It is here the British learned to 'beat

the retreat' perfectly. Today our own overseers cram their bellies, Spanish galleons
careening loading nonstop cotton sugar rice

tobacco gold spices. Remember the Isle of
Spice. Remember San Domingo. Remember our
capacity for resistance. Each one must help

to solder all the manacles of gold, silver
and iron while still holding tight pushing
forward together under the heat of the sun.

Incubation

From the guts of the earth
I come
your darkskinned woman
of ochre
incubating for
five millennia
four centuries

three decades
two years
one day
I am ready.

VALERIE BLOOM
JAMAICA

Life in Uncle Sam's Backyard

Livin in Uncle Sam's backyard ain't easy
Livin in dat backyard's no fun
For Uncle Sam have a dang'rous hobby
Him love collect bomb, grenade an gun.

An when mi Uncle get eena temper
When him wan tell de world him hard
De fus place Uncle Sam cas him yeye dem
Is roun my way eena him backyard.

An mi cyaan do a ting bout Uncle
Him have de biggest weapons bout de place
For him always love fe know seh
Him come fus in every race.

Mi woulda like fi tek a stand
An exert mi own authority
Mi come of age, but when him throw dat grenade
A wha a go happen to mi?

An a so him interfering
Him wan fe pick an choose mi fren
An ef mi chat to those him don like
Him mek sure mi no do it again

Him tek some o him collection
An tes dem out by him backdoor
Or else him henchmen dem come visit
An gently advise mi nuffe see mi fren no more.

Any rubbish Uncle wan dump
Yuh noh haffe ask whey im a go
Only de bes fe Uncle fambly
Wid fe mi fambly anything wi do.
Den Uncle Sam jus love fi dabble
Him have a finger in every pie
An when him decide fi try out commerce
Guess a who him tell fi buy!

Mi fine some ore eena mi garden
Was tinking bout sending it fi process abroad
Uncle Sam jump een tek ova
Say, 'It was found in my backyard.'

Him tell mi, mi shoulda happy
Him teckin such good care o mi
An mi haffi count mi blessing
When mi memba cousin Nicky

Since mi little, mi noh frighten Uncle
Jus as long as mi keep in step.
But Nicky bigger, an wus dan dat
Him living pon Uncle Sam doorstep.

An dat man act like him a God
In everything but name
Mi jus a wait fi de hallelujah
When God get tired o de game.

JANET BOHAC
BONAIRE

Candiru

If you had been
on that South American trip
with me,
you'd have no trouble understanding
what I mean when I say—
I wish I were a candiru.
I would swim up the smallest orifice,
tucking myself away,
out of sight,
then fan out my fins,
lodging myself in your unsuspecting skin.
You would be made to notice me
and I would sit trapped inside you,
giggling like a naughty child
while you screamed like a lunatic
to get me out of your body.

People would look on
with sad, knowing eyes that say—
That one's fallen in love again.
Made crazy by love.

Meanwhile, I'd continue to swim
your great tributaries,
attacking your heart a while.
Next, I'd be in your ear,
coursing the whispering canals,
deafening you with a rush of fluid cries.
When I reach your fingertips,
everyone you touch will have the pain
of me upon their skin.

Once in your eye,
you will see only me
superimposed upon those pretty,
meaningless faces.
In the blood of your lips
you will speak only of me
to ears expecting their own names.
At last, at home in your brain,
I will pierce all those neurons,
jolting them out of their scientific patterns
and all you are
will be reduced
to a solitary obsession.

I want to cripple you
with this body
so small, so seemingly sleek.
I want to puff up my spines
in that tiny hole.
I want you to feel where I am.
I want you to know I am here.

JEAN BINTA BREEZE
JAMAICA

we speak through the silence of our stares

we who dare
shake a shoutin pharisee
from the ego tree
and bigotry
of telling we
what to be
or not to be
we

of weary waiting
holding hands with humour
watching
hatching
seeds of struggle
mapping ideas
for the crossing
of our dreams
to reality

we speak through the silence
of our stares

looking through your
looking glass reflection
noting the curl
of index finger
signal your desire

we, the figures
graphed
on the abnormal curve
of your five year plans
pierce
your long range missile
eyes
silently
for words
even true words
can betray

Red Rebel Song

is lang time
i waan sing dis song
        sing it loud
        sing it long

no apology
no pun
jus a raw fire madness
a clinging to de green
a sargasso sea

is years
of ungluing Iself
from de fabric of lust
dat have I
in a pin-up glare

years
of trying to buil
de trust

lang time I waan
free Iself
from de white black question
from de constant hairpulling
breadfruit baiting
coconut shaking
hypocrisies
            of I skin
                    having nutten to do
but lie dung
pon Massa bed
outside
            field slave sing loud
                        to open sky
hear dem own ancestral echo
                        in de wind
I een de house
tie up wid apron
between bedroom
where white mammy
practising piano

an kyan quite
reach de blues
an de kitchen
where black mammy
reign supreme
where mi soul
                steam out
smell like fresh clothes

                                wash wid roses soap

lang time
my song lock up tight
eena mi troat
like if a ever open mi mout
                                jus to breathe
de roar would shake dis eart
an matterkine

                                split
an microchip   cho   jus fly

yes!
I feel like I
sitting on a timb bomb
an I kyan get angry
fah yuh would see
mountain quake
an certain bway
weh ah entertain
delegation after delegation
an still kyan solve
a likkle irrigation
shoulda jus get lick
an stamp pon a envelope
wid no return address

                nuff sista an bredda like I
red wid anger

kyan explode
            is I an I leg split
            open
cross dis sea
of hatred an indifference
            tekkin injection after injection
fi cure di madness an pull we foot togedda
            is I an I
   did climb mountain
   an try carry a cloudful
   a tears
   pon we head
   so Noah wouln't haffi
   buil a nex ark
   fi save we fram de waters

            I is de red rebel
woman
            holding eart
north pole to
south
            tropical
            wet
heating whole continents wid a
            rain forest intensity
let go eida side
            is to lose part of I
                  bridge
            over troubled water lay
some loving on I now
            watch I
      painted halfbreed
        centrespread
            I nah
                tek no abuse fram eida direction
            I is
      red ribba

foot shape outa country clay
Madda
of white children red children an black
who!

lang time
I waan sing dis song
sing it loud
sing in long
no apology
no pun
jus a rawfire madness
a clinging to de green
a sargasso sea

I release Iself
from de promise
of eternal compromise
from de bed of rapists
black or white
from page 3
from
cho
if I waan gi yuh piece
is mine
free
no apology

lang time I reaping

byblows
peepshows
whoknows
wat amount of dose

I live it
I feel it
I sing it

it don't mek life no easier

                          but it sure don't mek it wrong
          I is de free christian
          who know Jah
          de one who roam
          an come home
          I is de red rebel
          woman
          accepting I madness
          declaring I song
          nah siddung eena attic
          tek no fire bun
          I singing it loud
          i singing it long
          think seh I done
          well
          I jus a come
                    I I I own rainbow
                    I I I own song

JENNIFER BROWN
JAMAICA

Caviar and Sky Juice or C & S

Lances of light strike
the polished chrome of the Rolls Royce
that glided unseen through customs.
Power steered downhill
with effortless ease
by a manicured pinky
it glides past the bundle of filthy rags
who is compiling a treasury of waste
paper.

It lik a pot 'ole

one 'polish tin' wheel fly
offa de hand' cart
dat did mek outa
ole boawd
'trow-wey' tin
and Foreshore Road rubba
de sky-juice dat sell
nasty it up like
an 'im did tief de steerin' wheel.

The pinky curves the chrome round
a corner han' and bady strain to tun
de steerin' wheel chrome and cart
lik up!
sky juice fly in de face of chrome
car door opens, polished shoe tests
the ground
dutty barefoot step offa de rudda!
pure palava
FM plays "We shall overcome."

Africa and the Caribbean

I came to you
fresh
dew wet
child of these islands
jewel of the Caribbean Sea
and you loved
my skin
like black sand beaches;
my hair
like coconut fibres
my lips
large and generous
tasting of sun and fruit.
You took me home

and together we dug
until we found
my long lost navel string;
we recalled the ceremonies
that had subsided in my skin;
I sang for you
my new songs
and we slept together at dawn.

BARBARA BURFORD
JAMAICA

Daughters of Eve

Out of the flame-tipped
whisper-shadows beneath
The Tree of Life, I step.
Never to return.
Coiling, drifting down,
I stroke sister earth.
Ship to my life-raft,
both stretched and scarred
by birth wounds.

Swirling, shouting up,
a jewel dance in the air
at the corner of your vision,
I breathe your clouds,
cry you rain.
My grey lightning mane
lashes the blue scoured noon,
a diamond scatter of hail
flung from one hand,
a fine sugar-sift largesse

of snow, from the other.

Out of the flame-tipped
whisper-shadows beneath
The Tree of Life,
I have stepped.
I will never go back.
Mysterious keeper of the deep magics,
or heedless dragonfly
skim-dancing with time's river.
Out. Aware. Woman.

JULIA DE BURGOS
PUERTO RICO

A Julia de Burgos

Ya las gentes murmuran que yo soy tu enemiga
       porque dicen que en verso doy al mundo tu yo

       Mienten, Julia de Burgos. Mienten, Julia de Burgos.
La que se alza en mis versos no es tu voz: es mi voz;
porque tú eres el ropaje y la esencia soy yo;
y el más profundo abismo se tiende entre las dos.

       Tú eres fría muñeca de mentira social,
y yo, viril destello de la humana verdad.

       Tú, miel de cortesanas hipocresías; yo no;
que en todos mis poemas desnudo el corazón.

       Tú eres como tu mundo, egoísta; yo no;
que todo me lo juego a ser lo que soy yo.

       Tú eres sólo la grave señora señorona;
yo no; yo soy la vida, la fuerza, la mujer.

       Tú eres de tu marido, de tu amo; yo no;
yo de nadie, o de todos, porque a todos, a todos,
en mi limpio sentir y en mi pensar me doy.

       Tú te rizas el pelo y te pintas; yo no;
a mí me riza el viento; a mí me pinta el sol.

       Tú eres dama casera, resignada, sumisa,
atada a los prejuicios de los hombres; yo no;
que yo soy Rocinante corriendo desbocado
olfateando horizontes de justicia de Dios.

To Julia de Burgos

People are saying now that I am your enemy
          because they say that in verse I am giving your "I" to the world

          They are lying, Julia de Burgos. They are lying, Julia de Burgos.
It's not your voice that rises in my poems: it's my voice;
because you are the trappings and I am the essence;
and the deepest abyss stretches between the two.

          You are the frigid doll of social falsehood,
and I, the viril sparkle of human truth.

          You, the darling of polite hypocrisies; not I;
for in all my poems I bare my heart.

          You are like your world, selfish; not I;
I risk everything to be what I am.

          You are only the serious proper lady;
not I; I am life, strength, woman.

          You belong to your husband, your master; not I;
I belong to no one, or to everyone, because to everyone, to everyone,
in my pure feelings and in my thinking I give myself.

          You curl your hair and paint yourself up; not I;
I am curled by the wind; painted by the sun.

          You are the lady of the house, resigned, submissive,
tied to the prejudices of men; not I;
for I am Rocinante running free
smelling the horizons of God's justice.

Tú en ti misma no mandas; a ti todos te mandan;
en ti mandan tu esposo, tus padres, tus parientes,
el cura, la modista, el teatro, el casino,
el auto, las alhajas, el banquete, el champán,
el cielo y el infierno, y el qué dirán social.

En mí no, que en mí manda mi solo corazón,
mi solo pensamiento; quien manda en mí soy yo.

Tú, flor de aristocracia; y yo, la flor del pueblo.
Tú en ti lo tienes todo y a todos se lo debes,
mientras que yo, mi nada a nadie se la debo.

Tú, clavada al estático dividendo ancestral,
y yo, un uno en la cifra del divisor social,
somos el duelo a muerte que se acerca fatal.

Cuando las multitudes corran alborotadas
dejando atrás cenizas de injusticias quemadas,
y cuando con la tea de las siete virtudes,
tras los siete pecados, corran las multitudes,
contra ti, y contra todo lo injusto y lo inhumano,
yo iré en medio de ellas con la tea en la mano.

Romance de la perla

El sol se sale muriendo
        en sombras del caserío,
y el mar se lame la vida
sobre horizontes de niños.

Duerme el hombre su ancha pena
del llanto de pan del hijo,
y toma forma de piedra
por la escalera del risco.

You aren't your own boss; everyone bosses you;
your husband bosses you, your parents, your relatives,
the priest, the designer, the theatre, the casino,
the car, the jewels, the banquet, the champagne,
heaven and hell, and what society will say.

Not I, for my heart alone bosses me,
my thoughts alone; I am my own boss.

You, flower of the aristocracy; and I, flower of the people.
You yourself have everything and you owe it to everyone,
while I, I owe my nothing to no one.

You, stuck to the static ancestral dividend,
and I, a one in the sum total of the social denominator,
we are the duel to the death that verges on fatal.

When the multitudes run riotous
leaving behind the ashes of burned injustices,
and when with the torch of the seven virtues,
after the seven sins, the multitudes run
against you, and against everything unjust and inhumane,
I will go in the midst of them with the torch in my hand.

Ballad of the Pearl

The sun comes up dying
        in the shadows of the housing project
and the sea laps up life
on the horizons of children.

The man sleeps off his broad grief
from the child's cry for bread,
and takes the form of a stone
along the path of the cliff.

¿A dónde se irán sus pasos
hinchados de ahuecar bríos
en la antesala del sordo
capitalista edificio?

Ni la mañana le esconde
la mueca de su suplicio,
ni echa de ver que en sus ojos
hay ausencia de rocío . . .

¡Una mirada vacía
lo tira de nuevo al nido!
¡Perla! La perla encrespada
como un hotel colectivo
en una mancha que el mar
se sacudió en raro ímpetu:

¡Perla! La perla dejada
en un fantástico olvido
para ilusión de los hombres
heridos de hambre y de frío,

¡Perla! La perla tirada
desde el tejado del risco,
que bajo tu blanca pena
exprime dolor de siglos.
¡Piedra que miras al cielo
como arrabal desteñido!

¿Quién dice noche estrellada
ante los ojos caídos
de esa frontera del hambre
que va apretándose en gritos?

¿Quién dice marco de espumas
ante el puntal de martirio
que se reseca en las almas
huéspedes del precipicio?

Where will his steps go
swollen from wasting his energy
in the front office of the deaf
capitalist building?

Not even the morning hides
the grimace of his anguish,
or notices that in his eyes
there is an absence of dew . . .

One empty look
sends him back home!
Pearl! The pearl brought forth
like from a collective hotel
in a spot that the sea
shook loose with a rare force:

Pearl! The pearl left
in a fantasy oblivion
for the illusion of men
wounded by hunger and cold,

Pearl! The pearl thrown
from the top of the cliff,
under your white grief
wrings out the sorrow of the centuries.
Gem that looks to the sky
like a discolored slum!

Who can talk of a starry night
before the fallen eyes
of that frontier of hunger
that is suppressed into cries?

Who can talk of rings of seafoam
before the martyrdom
that dries up in the souls
guests of the precipice.

La vida rueda temblando
sobre el jirón extendido
en un juego con la muerte
que quiere atrapar el risco.

El mar se lame la vida,
y el sol se arropa de frío . . .
en cada lecho de muerte
vigila el sueño de un niño . . .

¡Perla! La perla más blanca
de la gran mina del rico.
¡Perla! Que ya te desgastas,
de balancearte en suspiros.

¡Perla! Que ya te derrumbas
bajo tu pecho sombrío
mientras se elevan cuarteles
y el mar se infecta de tiros.
¡Piedra que miras al cielo
como arrabal desteñido . . . !

El color rojo se tiende
en tinte de último aviso
sobre el puñal de tus noches
y tus puntales caídos.

Al otro lado del mar
nos duele tu sed de siglos.
Tu voz resuena más lejos
que los cañones temidos.

En la antesala del mundo
ya anuncia el sol colectivo.
¡Perla! ¡Levanta tus manos
y alza tu dolor en bríos . . . !

Life goes trembling
along the extended strip
in a game with death
that wants to trap the cliff.

The sea laps up life,
and the sun becomes cold . . .
on each deathbed
the dream of a child watches . . .

Pearl! The whitest pearl
from the great mine of the rich man.
Pearl! You are already wasting away,
from swaying among sighs.

Pearl! You are collapsing
under your somber chest
while tenements rise up
and the sea becomes infected by gunfire.
Gem that looks to the sky
like a discolored slum . . . !

The red color spreads out
in the hue of the last warning
over the dagger of your nights
and your fallen foundations.

On the other side of the sea
your thirst of the centuries hurts us.
Your voice resounds farther
than the feared cannons.

In the front office of the world
the collective sun now declares.
Pearl! Raise your hands
and lift your sorrow in determination . . . !

AÍDA CARTAGENA PORTALATÍN
DOMINICAN REPUBLIC

de *Yania Tierra*

YANIA vomita oro
                    sangre
                            azúcar
Sabe que la historia comienza en
Marién
Con un cacique / luego dos / después
todos /
Que los Encomenderos / Los
Repartimientos
Los indios / los negros
Base de la Tragedia Humana /
Llamada Civilización
Desde un día 25 todas las golondrinas
Durante cinco siglos
Continuamente trazan círculos
Sobre los mástiles de los navíos
Con cargazones de lanceros en busca
de tesoros
Con toneles de vino para alentar la
abulia

Bloques de piedras del Alcázar
Torre del Homenaje / La Catedral y
                            otros
monumentos
Donde albergan / claro /
depredadores de
Aragón y Castilla
En resumen / de toda la Ibérica
Península

*   *   *

From *Yania Tierra*

YANIA vomits gold
            blood
                      sugar
She knows that history begins in
Marién
With one cacique / then two / finally
all of them /
That the Encomenderos / the
Repartimientos
The indians / the blacks
The foundation of the Human
Tragedy / Called Civilization
Since day 25 all the swallows
For five centuries
Continually trace circles
Above the ships' masts
Carrying huge cargos of soldiers in
search of treasures
With kegs of wine to ward off
boredom

Blocks of stone from Alcázar
Tower of Homage / The Cathedral
                      and other
monuments
Where they / naturally / shelter
pillagers from
Aragón and Castilla
In fact / from the whole Iberian
Peninsula

            *   *   *

En el 63 del 1500
Hawkins sale de Inglaterra
Con corsarios, piratas, bucaneros
                              y otros
elementos fatales

Llega desde Sierra Leona a Puerto
Plata
En la Vieja Isabela impone el
cambalache
                              de
cueros
                              de
azúcar
Por la triste mercancía de los esclavos
                              negros
Humilla al Monopolio del Imperio
Español

86 del 1500
Desde Londres Isabel la reina virgen
Mujer que lee a Maquiavelo
Usa a sus súbditos piratas
Saquean los tesoros del mundo
Aquí Sir Francis Drake
Despoja / daña la Ciudad Colonial
Condiciona su marcha
                              a
cambio
                              de
millonaria suma

YANIA observa
Se levantan ingenios / se penetra su
vientre
Se lava oro
Para los reinos de Europa Occidental
El negro explotado como bestia

In the year 63 of 1500
Hawkins leaves England
With plunderers, pirates, buccaneers
                        and other
murderous types

He comes from Sierra Leon to Puerto
Plata
In Old Isabela he directs
the exchange
                        of
hides
                        of
sugar
For the miserable merchandise of black
                                    slaves
He humiliates the Monopoly of the Spanish
Empire

The year 86 of 1500
From London Elizabeth the Virgin Queen
A woman who reads Machiavelli
Uses her pirate subjects
To loot the treasures of the world
Here Sir Francis Drake
Rapes / destroys the Colonial City
Redirects its history
                        in
exchange
                        for
a millionaire's sum

YANIA watches
Sugar mills are erected / her womb is
penetrated
Gold is washed
For the kingdoms of Western Europe
The black man exploited like a beast

Los extraños / padres / padrastros del
saqueo
Yania como una rosa verde o una rosa
de fuego
Las Montañas baten agua
truenos
      relámpagos
           rayos y
               centellas
El hambre llena el transcurso del
tiempo

*   *   *

SALEN / salen historias que parecen
mancas
Prendidas a la piel con alfileres
Sonido
Olfato
Lágrima
Y la degustación a plomo puro
Salen historias como partos / Salen
Con aureola de placenta agria
Llegan aún del Norte / Los piratas
saquean
La riqueza del café / azúcar / cacao
oro / plata / níquel / la bauxita

Y el hambre mata al hombre
Caen y se levantan muertos
Sin el toque personal de algún delito

YANIA se desconcierta del juego y
las apuestas
Con el cordón umbilical atado
El macho que rechaza
Es devuelto con retrato de esqueleto
Sin derroche / tan cierto

The foreigners / fathers / step-fathers
of the looting
Yania like a green rose or a flaming
rose
The mountains stir up water
thunder
      lightning
            thunderbolts and
                  flashes
Hunger fills the course of
time

          *   *   *

THEY COME / stories come that
look deformed
Attached to the skin with pins
Sounds
Smells
Tears
The taste of pure lead
Stories come like births / They come
With an aroma of sour placenta
They keep coming from the North /
The pirates loot
Riches from coffee / sugar / cacao
gold / silver / nickel / bauxite

Hunger kills man
The dead fall and rise up
Not because of some petty crime

YANIA is disconcerted by the game
and the stakes
With his umbilical cord attached
The man who fights back
Is returned a skeleton
No waste / so certain

Que su estirpe respetan las Manuela
Las Olaya las Josefa
Es la Historia / Luto negro

GRITA EL COJITO CON ALEGRIA Y PENA
INDIAS / NEGRAS / BLANCAS / MESTIZAS /
MULATAS / LAS AMAN LA JUSTICIA Y EL
AMOR CON RESPETO   ¡VENID!

¡Ea! ¡Mujeres!
¡Ea! ¡Mujeres!

¡Soltad los pájaros de la esperanza!
¡Ea! ¡Mujeres!
¡Soltad Palomas!

That his offspring will respect the Manuelas
The Olayas the Josefas
It is History / A black mourning

THE CRIPPLE CRIES WITH JOY AND SORROW /
INDIAN WOMEN / BLACK WOMEN / WHITE
WOMEN / MESTIZA WOMEN / MULATTA
WOMEN / JUSTICE AND LOVE
LOVE THEM WITH RESPECT   COME!

                    Come on! Women!
                    Come on! Women!

            Release the birds of hope!
                    Come on! Women!
                         Release the Doves!

LOURDES CASAL
CUBA

Yemayá

De nuevo,
Yemayá,
voy recorriendo tu reino.
Recuerdo que a mis ojos infantiles
el oscuro fragor de tus ropajes
meciéndose con el viento en la bahía,
arremolinándose en la noche contra el flanco
de la pequeña lancha
me imponía temor.

Y sin embargo,
al mismo tiempo,
me excitaban,
el olor a salitre mezclado con petróleo,
los golpetazos de aire contra el rostro,
las luciérnagas
que prendían sobre tu manto
las minúsculas embarcaciones;
la espuma fina
que como encaje íbamos bordando
mientras la gente
te lanzaba monedas de cobre desde las ventanillas.
Porque eras
el terror de la máscara de Olokun
pero también,
la madre,
también los brazos siempre abiertos
y el vientre cálido.

Ahora son enormes trasatlánticos
los que llenan de luces la bahía

Yemayá

Again,
Yemayá,
I am running around in your kingdom,
I remember how to my infant eyes
the dark din of your trappings
rocking with the wind in the bay,
swirling around in the night against the side
of the small boat
instilled terror in me.

And nevertheless,
at the same time,
they excited me,
the smell of potassium nitrate mixed with oil,
the blows of air against the face,
the fireflies
that lit up over your cloak
the tiny boats;
the fine seafoam
like lace that we were embroidering
while the people
threw copper coins to you from the windows.
Because you were
the terror of the mask of Olokun
but also,
the mother,
also the arms always open
and the warm belly.

Now there are enormous transatlantic ships
filling the bay with lights

mientras la refinería con su fuego eterno
hace estallar la noche en rojo.
El Morro iluminado
parece un espectral castillo;
o una vieja fortaleza cubierta por la nieve.
El puerto
es ahora otra ciudad.
Quedan
los viejos bares,
las iglesias,
y hasta algunas de las viejas casonas señoriales
que bordearon
tus predios
cuando La Habana
se desperezaba de Muralla a la Alameda
y el muelle vivía coronado de coches y calesas.
Pero ha crecido
una nueva ciudad
y para colmo,
es fin de semana de carnaval
y un verdadero
mar humano
se extiende desde el antiguo convento de San Francisco
hasta la Fuente de la Juventud
que ahora lanza retos de luz y agua
contra la noche
allá en Paseo y Malecón:
en lo que fue el Vedado
y ahora es
el Municipio Plaza.
Repito con Obbatalá el viejo patakin:
"La tierra.
La cosa está en la tierra".

while the refinery with its eternal fire
makes the night explode in red.
El Morro illuminated
looks like a ghostly castle;
or an old fortress covered by snow.
The port
is now another city.
Remaining are
the old bars,
the churches,
and even some of the old manor houses
that bordered
your property
when Havana
stretched from Muralla to Alameda
and the wharf lived crowned with carts and buggies.
But a new city
has arisen
and to top it all off,
it's carnival weekend
and a true
human sea
extends from the old convent of San Francisco
to the Fountain of Youth
that now shoots out threats of light and water
against the night
there on the Paseo and the Malecón;
in what was the Vedado
and now is the Municipal Plaza
I repeat with Obbatalá the old refrain:
"The land.
The thing is in the land."

MERLE COLLINS
GRENADA

The Butterfly Born

Something old
Something new
Something borrowed
Something blue

The caterpillar dead
The butterfly
born

Alé asiz anba tab-la!
Zòt fouten twop.
Go an siddown under de table!
You too fas.
You tink it easy?
Even wid all o dat
Wid de mudder shoutin
In days long ago
Dat little girl
Used to walk two, three days a week
From St David's town
By the police station
Where she Mammie use to work
Right up to Sauteurs town
By de ball-pitch groun
Afraid of she shadow
of de basket shadow
of she dress shadow
of de fig-leaf shadow
But walkin alone
all kin o hour
Hidin an cryin an hatin

Becus she Mammie
couldn't afford it
An to besides
Was really a waste
o good money
To pay de bus a whole
eight pence ha'penny

De biggest girl of five
Walkin to bring
de little piece o bread
de two grain o bluggoe
for Iona an Joycelyn an Jude
an Stephen
To keep body an soul togedder
Woman-chile
A giant of nine
Strong since den
Strong even when bathed
in tears
Strong when blisters formed
from walking
A strong
premature
nine-year-old mother

Part of the history
Part of de life
De strength inherited
De weakness taught
Something old
Something true

I
must remember dat day
when Auntie Iona come from
England

I
Hold on to de blin
An watch Mammie
in de sittin room
An Auntie Iona
nice nice nice
Wid earring
an stocking
an lipstick
an ting

Auntie
Auntie
Iona
Oh hello!
Isn't that
Antoinette?

An Mammie
So vex she could bus
She face
tellin de story
Of dogs among doctors
Of little girl who
don know dey place
An I
squeezin back
behin
de blin
Not darin to answer
One Ionic question
Lookin straight
At Mammie face
An slinkin back

Behin
de blin

Den come
de eruption
De whispered
benediction
Clear out
Kadammit fout
Children
must know dey place
An especially
little girl
Somebody
talkin to you?
Outside!
All you always dey
To make people shame

Something borrowed
Something
blue

Mother
Teaching
As she was taught
Little girls
Must learn
To be seen not heard
Or is certain
destruction
Is pillar of saltness
Oh God!
Look how Lot
smart
An he wife
so fas
A pillar of salt!

De lesson

passed on
Alé asiz anba tab-la!
Zòt fouten twop
Dammit fout
Chile
Nuttin good
Could come out o you
Little girl like you
Only rompin an runnin
An climbin tree
Like dose little boy
Oh Jesus
De Lord
Give me a trial
An is me
people go blame
Yuh know

Woman-chile
Crying for the world
Crying for me
Crying because
I couldn't find their Eve
Who
In times past
Had shouted
When told to whisper
And lived
To expose
De deadly truth
Dat de wages of sin
Is life
before death

Sa ki fè'w?
Sa ou ka pléwé pou?
What wrong wid you?

What you cryin for?
Vini tifi
vini
vini
mwen kay hélé ba'w
I go bawl for you

Something
blue

Wid a lesson
like dat
1979 revolution talk
not no easy ting
But de strength was dey
De weakness imposed
De adventure was dey
De spirit just hushed
Now
woman-chile
woman
All of a sudden
Not under no table
But out in de open

Demanding equal
recognition
For equal beauty given

Something new
Something true

From
Zòt fouten twòp
You too fas
To Woman step forward
To Woman

Equal in defense
Huh
You tink it easy?

Something new
Something true

What that mean?
You tink is a puzzle?
Something dead
Something born

But
De caterpillar's death
De butterfly's birth
Is only a miracle
If you doh know
de story
Is only a mystery
if you doh know the history
Is only truly
a puzzle
If you can't find
the pieces
If you can't explain
de changes

Is de beauty of science
If you follow
the history
Is the poetry of science
If you watch
de movement
Famn
Alé douvan
Woman
Step forward

Something new
Something true

The caterpillar dead
The butterfly born!

Because The Dawn Breaks

We speak because when the rain falls in the mountains
the river slowly swells

It comes rushing down over boulders, across roads
crumbling bridges that would hold their power
against its force

We speak
for the same reason that the thunder frightens the child
that the lightning startles the tree

We do not speak
to defy your tenets, though we do
or upset your plans, even if we do
or to tumble your towers of babel
but in spite of the fact that we do

We speak
because your plan is not necessarily our plan
We speak because we dream

because our dreams
are not of living in pigpens
in any other body's backyard

not of catching crumbs from tables
not of crawling forever along the everlasting ant-line
to veer away in quick detour when the elephant's foot

crashes down. Not of having to turn back
when the smell of death assails our senses
not of striving forever to catch the image of
other people's Gods within our creation

We speak
for the same reason that the flowers bloom
that the sun sets
that the fruit ripens

We speak
not to agitate you
but in spite of your agitation

we speak, really
because we know
we were not born to be your vassals.

Chant Me a Tune

When you see me weak and wondering
as you sometimes will
chant me a tune

move with me across the weeping atlantic
through the blood tears death pain and hurt
through the thundering angry sighing sobbing fury
of the startled atlantic
throbbing with the pulsing pages of a story
written as footnotes to an eager quest for land

chant me a tune
move with me beyond the rattle of the chains
and watch me rise with Nanny in Jamaica
where they pulled the cup drained the sorrow
rooted out the pain

and are still seeking beneath the hope

when you see me weak and wondering
as you sometimes will
don't try to dust my story
into the crevices of time
chant me a tune

speak to me of Mary Seacole
who washed their tears
and calmed their fears
and got lost behind white nightingales
somewhere in the telling of their story

when you see me weak and wondering
as you sometimes will
remind me how much
i am a part of your surviving
just as you are a part of my believing

Remind me
that though i am a part of those who died
because they simply could not bear to live
i am also of those who lived
because they refused to die

chant me a tune
speak to me of what we have been
of what we are
of what we are creating

when you see me weak and wondering
as you sometimes will
i need you
to remind me
that, like you,
i am the oceanic roar

of angry strength
that never dies
that never dies
that never will die

AFUA COOPER
JAMAICA

Atabeyra

Atabeyra
Great Mother of the Arawaks
mistress of all moving waters
moon woman
lady of childbirth,
Night and day you drift on the foam
of the Caribbean sea
drifting from Florida to the Guianas
tearing your long hair
in grief for your lost children
Atabeyra
you stand on the tallest peak of Seville mountains
straining your eyes over the vast expanse of
the Carib sea
looking for your lost children
Isis searching the world over for Osiris
Demeter mourning her loss of Persephone
Ishtar weeping for Tammuz
Yemaya lamenting for shango
Atabeyra
in your mind's eye you can see your children
making canoes
pounding dried cassava to make bread
playing ballgames

swimming
and shamans making sacred ceremonies
calling on your name
and the names of Yocahu and Opiyel-Guaobiran
and we know that when women want children,
a safe pregnancy and delivery they
invoke only your aid
Atabeyra
draw near
come, let me plait your hair
listen, though your children may be gone gone gone
to the overworld, to Coyaba
if you sit still and listen carefully
you will hear their voices in the wind and the waves
of the ocean
if you look intently you will see them walking swiftly
among the cassava patches
You should know Atabeyra that they are not dead
so please my lady weep no more

Breakin Chains

So no
                I
breakin chains
breakin chains
        until
nothin remains but my freewon
breakin chains of
racism
sexism
and neocolonialism
        free
my hands tied no more
        free
time to settle the score

FREE
FREE
FREE
FREE
FREE

i breakin chains
throwin dem in da flame
chantin in da rain
lookin to da East
lookin to da West
i look to da North and South
i see people
oppressed humanity
claiming their liberty
claimin their dignity
regainin their freewon
            yeah!
fightin and makin revolution

Woman

breakin chains
            of
ISOLATION
MIND AND BODYCOLONISATION
MALE IDENTIFICATION
            AND PATRIARCHAL INSTITUTIONS
WE BREAKIN CHAINS

freein my mind
from fears and snares
learnin to see myself as i am
learnin to accept myself as i am
learnin to love . . .

and breakin chains

               of
racism
sexism
neocolonialism
          sing
shout
SCREAMMMMMMMM!
we breakin chains
freewon screamin in my brain
victory runnin thru my veins
FREE!

CHRISTINE CRAIG
JAMAICA

The Chain

I no longer care, keeping close my silence
has been a weight,
a lever pressing out my mind.
I want it told and said and printed down
the dry gullies,
circled through the muddy pools
outside my door.
I want it sung out high by thin-voiced elders,
front rowing murky churches.
I want it known by grey faces queuing under
greyer skies in countries waking
and sleeping with sleet and fog.
I want it known by hot faces pressed against
dust streaked windows of country buses.

                    And you must know this now
                    I, me, I am a free black woman.

My grandmothers and their mothers
knew this and kept their silence
to compost up their strength,
kept it hidden
and played the game of deference
and agreement and pliant will.

It must be known now how that silent legacy
nourished and infused such a line,
such a close linked chain
to hold us until we could speak
until we could speak out
loud enough to hear ourselves
loud enough to hear ourselves
and believe our own words.

Elsa's Version

Lawd God
I tired fe hear it
I tired fe hear it
so till.
All dem big talk:
"Women are the backbone
of this country"
Me no bone inna
no body back
nor rib outa
no body side.
Is who dem tink
dey a go fool
while dem still a
treat we to no-count wages.
An we shouldn' mind
dat we riding fine
in nuff dutty song

a boom shaka boom
pon every street corner.

You rass man
stop put we down
in dutty song or
high-up editorial.
You can confuse, abuse
an mess wid you own self
till you good an ready
to deal wid I as
a real somebody.

Till dat day come

>   Lef me alone
>   an me modda
>   an me sista
>   an me gal-pickney.

MELANIA DANIEL
ST. LUCIA / BARBADOS

No Man's Land

An aged man
A late learner
Drives down the middle of the road
Angry drivers honk abuse at him,
'This ain't no man's land,' he yells back
And continues his cruise of indifference
On that part of the highway where he can stake
No legal claim to be.

Unknowing,

He has a following. The decrepit shacks
That squat defiantly on the edge of the road
Echo his challenge to all that allots humanity
To a left side, a right side of living.
'We ain't got nothing to hide,'
Shreds of linen flapping urine odours in the faces
Of passing motorists seem to scream. For those who
Dare articulate offence by homes that stoop on stones
And void their bowels right there in the middle
Of the road, they claim this no man's land as theirs.

Standing at the roadside with a permanence, like
Monuments to their own penury, these houses are
A lesson in resilience. New roads are built which
Wind their way through lives and send the hovels
Scampering into bushes, yet they come back. Always
To deface the landscape of roadbuilders' conscience.
On their roads politicians erect platforms on promises;
They bait votes but fail to catch the remoteness
That flickers in the hut-dwellers' eyes—even while
Their hands applaud. For the unaspiring masses, it seems that
The focus of their aimlessness is to spare themselves
The battle of directions by pressing closer to the center
Of a no man's land.

Early Birds

Fluttering wings of straw-brooms
Swoop down on dirty sidewalks,
Early birds scavenge
On the nocturnal follies of a city,
While more creatures of the dawn
Are moulded in the clouds,
They catch glimpses of the rising sun
And leap to life.

A grandmother, wrapping a thinning cloak of darkness about her
Feeds the sea a pailful of leftovers from an alimentary feast.
On her way home she stops to worship, her quivering charges
Forced along. They pray to gods distant as the echo of an echo
In the hollow church. The blessed madonna cuddled demurely
Unto herself watches over them. The children's searching eyes
Implore the saints to hasten grandma through their ordeal of
epistles.

A bus, trudging uphill from insufficient sleep
And the broad-hip loads of market ladies
Turns a bend past a town; a misty mountain village
Slumbering in a hammock of clouds sways into view.
Off in the distance, a crouching figure puffs commands
At tepid ashes to recreate last evening's fire. They disobey.

A man sets off to the uncertain gains of forest farming,
The waking sun-god shakes his quilt, gold dust glides down
The sunbeams like children playing on a chute. A speck glints
Off the peasant's helmet and falls into the bush.
Searching for the treasure, his swinging cutlass clears
A track across his day, he slashes through a clump of blackbirds
And from a hundred startled throats come inspiring songs of
greetings.

Further on, a canoe struggles to avoid the chilly morning plunge,
Resistance dragged along behind its owner, the silhouette
Of a fisherman painted against the easel of a sunrise,
A priceless effort, yet no bidders at this auction. On the horizon
Where sea and sky lie in ceaseless copulation, his boat balances
A dancer on a tightrope etched across the waves. Returning home
When the rays of dimming sunlight paint a path of gold
Bobbing on the swells, this early bird's too late to sell his catch.

For the unweary birdwatcher
Early birds are all arresting subjects,
Eternal images captured by a flicking camera

Of awareness. Early birds, foraging at the spot
Where the first sunbeam falls to earth
Waiting to gulp the treasure,
The birdwatcher laments,
They've only been catching the worms.

MAHADAI DAS
GUYANA

Beast

In Gibraltar Straits,
pirates in search of El Dorado
masked and machete-bearing
kidnapped me.
Holding me to ransom,
they took my jewels and my secrets
and dismembered me.

The reckoning lasted for years.
Limbs and parts eventually grew:
a new nose, arms skilful and stronger,
sight after the gutted pits could bear a leaf.
It took centuries.

In the cave where they kept me,
a strange beast grew.
With his skin of glistening jewels
and his deadly tongue,
even I was afraid of him.

In the dark Ajanta caves of my breast
ever since he has stayed,

with his measure of venom,
his exact poison and scintillating glitter.
At a certain hour, I almost love him.

The Growing Tip

They sought the 'growing tip of poetry,'
its first frail-green shoots
on which to 'ooh' and 'aah.'

They assumed a garden: English roses,
palms of victory high-raised
on a history of thorns, thick
hedges, neatly-trimmed.

They assumed a gardener:
a 'Being There' type seeding
and nurturing and coaxing gardening's
lengthy process from seed to flower;
finally, beaming with his gloating,
false pride of parenthood.

They assumed a house
to which the garden attached,
a black leech of thirst upon
an oasis of blood; a benevolent master,
gentle mistress, mischievous, annoying
harmless children.

Perhaps they assumed a car or two,
a dog, a cat, a singing canary
hanging by its wiry prison on the porch;
a jolly postman, a friendly milkman,
an ever-so-often handyman.

What she sent reminded no one of a garden:

pieces of skin, a handful of hair, broken
teeth, bits of glass—an iron chest, rusty, grim . . .

She told of jungles, of suppers of snakes
and monkeys; of bills evaded by a change-of-address;
of late payments as a matter of principle;
of forgetting genres of old people, babies
and children; of a living-for-oneself philosophy
which led one, like a modern-day Christ
to bear his cross to the Lonely Hill of the Gallows.

Oh she had things that grew—
horns and tails, arms of different lengths,
automatic fangs near bureaucrats, a tail,
(a bit of bother when she wore a dress);
aunts whose heads she preserved in bottles
of pickles on a shelf, a father stones
by a proliferation of Oedipal daughters—

'Aiee!' they cried, 'What a monster!'
'This is not a plant!' said the editor-in-chief.
'It's not a tree!' cried another.

'It's not a rosebush!' (they) cried in unison,
'Not a weed!' a shy one piped at last.

A plant from another planet?

Not a plant?

Even as they peeled off postage-stamps,
horns grew right out of each ear!

When they picked SASE out
from its envelope, a tail uncoiled,
(it caused quite a shriek!)

'My God! It grows,   it grows,   it grows!'

As they watched,

    in high shock,

From every tip,

    it continued to grow.

My Final Gift to Life

Death would be my final gift to life.
Then: if I must die, I must.
Let the progeny of stars light my path to heaven.
'Me' will be one more star to fiercely light
the darkness of this land.
This body will bear the final calamity.
I will not be the fish caught
in his wily net.
I will not touch his rotting sceptre beaded
with murder
nor eat my bread in a crumbling house overrun
with rats.
All over the land is heard the sound of women
weeping; the muffled voice
of children starving in the drought.
Who can inhale the stench of wickedness
or dwell whole in this leprous air?
In their sad coat of mange, dogs
hang their hungry heads.
The night is pierced by strange cries of woe.
But he who stirs their tears
in the cauldron on his vanity,
preparing for a feast and a night of loud song;
little knows he of we who
sharpen our spears in night's
naked hours.
Death be my final gift to life.

TANIA DÍAZ CASTRO
CUBA

Todos me van a tener que oir

un día me voy a transformar
en un pomo recto de boca ancha pero sin tapa
un día de éstos confundo a las mariposas
con los murciélagos
un día venzo al sol y te lo pongo
sobre la mesa con el pan a ver cuál es su sabor
a ver si el amarillo es candela o qué carajo
y te indigestas
un día de éstos me voy a vietnam y allí me quedo
un día de éstos me miraré al espejo
para hablarme muy en serio como nunca
un día de éstos escribo un poema sobre la inteligencia
y me pongo a decir que es necesario estudiar
sexología en todos los niveles
un día de éstos me convierto en piedras
y digo a romper los cristales de todas las farmacias
y desaparezco porque no estoy de acuerdo
con muchas cosas
un día tú verás que comienzo a escribir poesía
y todos me van a tener que oir

Everybody's Going to Have to Listen To Me

one day i'm going to change myself
into a tall wide-mouthed bottle without a lid
one of these days i'll confuse the butterflies
with the bats
one day i'll conquer the sun and i'll put it
on the table with the bread to see what its flavor is
to see if the yellow is a candle or what the hell
and it'll give you indigestion
one of these days i'll go to vietnam and i'll stay
one of these days i'll look at myself in the mirror
to talk to myself very seriously like never before
one of these days i'll write a poem about intelligence
and i'll say that it's necessary to study
sexology at all levels
one of these days i'll change myself into stones
and i'll say break the windows in all the pharmacies
and i'll disappear because i don't agree
with many things
one day you'll see that i've begun to write poetry
and everybody's going to have to listen to me

¿cobardía del siglo veinte?

sin dar un grito me tendí en la cama
abro los ojos
cuento lluvias y cuento serpentinas
cayendo de lo azul gigante
sin dar un grito me tendí en la cama
¿para qué un grito si duermen los espejos?
a leguas está el mar casi lo escucho
la vida se concentra a veces en un grito
pero suspiro
y callo como callan los niños cuando piensan
como callan los viejos cuando se les detiene
el corazón lleno de líneas
ahora me reviento de esperanzas y de esperar
                    una trama
                    una trampa
                    el trance
una gota y otra que se empolve con el polvo y con el agua
una gota de amor amor aquí tan sola
yo la indócil la insumisa
sin dar un grito me tenderé también mañana en la cama
un grito de águila de halcón
la vida se concentra a veces en un grito
y pienso algo terrible: ¿podré mañana tolerar
el desayuno con este grito adentro que no doy
por pena a los vecinos?

cowardice of the twentieth century?

without a scream i stretched out on the bed
i open my eyes
i count the rain and i count the ripples
falling from the giant blue
without a scream i stretched out on the bed
why scream if the mirrors are sleeping?
i almost hear the sea far away
life is concentrated sometimes in a scream
but i sigh
and i become quiet the way children become quiet when they think
the way old people become quiet when their heart
stops full of lines
now i am bursting with hope and with waiting for
                    a plot
                    a trap
                    the trance
a drop and another that is dusty with dust and with water
a drop of love love here so alone
i the unruly one the defiant one
without a scream i will stretch out also tomorrow on the bed
a scream of an eagle of a hawk
life is concentrated sometimes in a scream
and i think something terrible: tomorrow will i be able to tolerate
breakfast with this scream inside me that i won't let out
out of concern for the neighbors

MARIA DIWAN
CURAÇAO

Yunan di solo

Yunan di tera, solo
bientu i laman
ku dia den dia'fo
ta karisiá nos isla
koba su kustía
skuma alegria i pena
bai kun'e.

Bientu ku ta karga nobo
trese pa chuchubi plama.
Notisia di yunan
bon kriá i mal fadá.
Flornan ta kologá kabes,
datu ta lèn di banda
warawara ta gjèrta na shelu.

Den Laman Caribe
un muhé drumí ku tur
su larg'i kurpa.
Solo ta sker su kueru
Bientu ta fria su doló
su kurason ta bati hanshá

Ku brasa hanchu habrí
e ta yama yunan di tera,
solo bientu i laman
bin kome maske ta kolokolo
di su wea
na lugá di pan ku djabel
a mansa hòrna den fòrnu friu.

Sunchildren

Children of land, sun
wind and sea
that day after day
caresses our island,
digs in her hips
enrolls joy and sorrow
in foam and takes them away.

Wind that brings the news
for the mockingbird to spread.
News from well raised and
fed up children.

Flowers hang their head
Cactus bends forward
Vultures scream to the skies.

In the Caribbean Sea
a woman sleeps stretched out.
The sun tears her skin
the wind soothens her pain
Her heart beats wildly.

With arms wide spread she calls
the children of land, sun, wind
and sea,
to come eat the leftovers
instead of devil's bread
made and baked in cold ovens.

ADELINE DORLIPO
GUADELOUPE

Femme

Femme !
Femme noire !
Femme des champs !
Femme de la ville !
Que t'arrive t-il ?
Que se passe t-il dans ta vie ?

Aurais-tu honte de toi
Pour te cacher sous un masque étranger ?
Aurais-tu honte de toi
Pour ensevelir ton créole sous une langue imposée ?
Que t'arrive t-il ?
Que se passe t-il dans ta vie ?

Pourquoi fuir ta terre natale
Pour aller vivre à tout jamais chez l'autre ?
Pourquoi fuir tes coutumes
Pour ramasser celles de l'autre ?
Que t'arrive t-il ?
Que se passe t-il dans ta vie ?

Pourquoi revenant de là-bas
Trouves-tu que ta terre natale
N'est plus un endroit pour vivre ?
Pourquoi revenant de là-bas
N'essaies-tu pas de comprendre tes soeurs,
Celles que ne sont jamais parties

Femme !
Femme noire !
Femme des champs !

Woman

Woman!
Black woman!
Woman of the fields!
Woman of the city!
What is happening to you?
What is going on in your life?

Could you be ashamed of yourself
For hiding under a foreign mask?
Could you be ashamed of yourself
For burying your own creole under an imposed tongue?
What is happening to you?
What is going on in your life?

Why flee your native land
To reside forever among the other?
Why flee your customs
To pick up those of the other?
What is happening to you?
What is going on in your life?

Why returning from there
Do you find that your native land
Is no longer a place to live?
Why returning from there
Don't you try to understand your sisters,
Those who never left

Woman!
Black woman!
Woman of the fields!

Femme de la ville !
Pourquoi souffles-tu la flamme de vérité
Quand elle vient t'éclairer dans ton ignorance ?
Femme !
Femme noire !
Femme des champs !
Femme de la ville !
Reviens vers tes toeurs
Reviens vers elles
Reviens avant qu'elles n'aillent connaître
Les tribulations que tu as connues
Reviens pour qu'ensemble nous apprenons à vivre chez nous
Reviens car il se fait tard
REVIENS

Woman of the city!
Why do you put out the flame of truth
When it comes to enlighten you in your ignorance?

Woman!
Black woman!
Woman of the fields!
Woman of the city!
Come back to your sisters
Come back to them
Come back before they know
The trials you have known
Come back so that together we can learn to live at home
                    Come back because it is getting late
                        COME BACK

MARCIA DOUGLAS
JAMAICA

Voice Lesson From The Unleashed Woman's Unabridged Dictionary

Cimarrón.
Cimarrón.
Remember to roll the r's.
(Think of the sound of galloping mustangs on a Nevada plain)
Cimarrón
(or the pound of buffalo hoofs)
Cimarrón
(or your grandma's mules broken loose last year.)

Maroon.
Maroon.
Breathe in deep,
say it like a warrior hurling her spear through the air.
Maroon
(Now think of bloodhounds, armed men at your heels)
Maroon
(or Nanny's boiling cauldron set to catch them)
Maroon
(or women wearing the teeth of white soldiers around their
ankles.)

Maroon.
Pronounce the "a" soft like the "a" in "alone."
That's right,
marooned.
(Imagine dangling from an orange tree, blindfolded—
stockings from someone's clothesline noosed around your neck)
Marooned.
(or the one dollar to your name,
the eviction notice taped to the door)

Marooned.
(think of a cold, soundproof room.)

Maroon.
Say it slow like a rich, full thing to the mouth—
Maroon
(Remember yourself, six years old, talking sassy in your mother's
dark lipstick)
Maroon
(or Zora's lips mouthing *just watch me,* her felt hat tilted to the
side of her head)
Maroon
(or all those women's mouths in Ebenezer choir, *Free at Last,*
singing for the fire locked up in their bones.)

Here's your chance now,
follow the instinct of your tongue
and say it your way,
Maroon.
Put on that hat you wear when you're all stirred up and need to
have a word or two.
Hurl your spear if you like,
or change the accent on the "a"—
perhaps something wide, free like the "a" in gallop—
Maroon!
(Hear the call of an old abeng?)

Maroon!
Say it
Say it rich
Say it full
(The twitch near your ear is only the remembrance of thunder.)
But listen.
Listen for the feet of summer rain behind you.
Say it strong
Say it *now*
Break loose speckled horse,
and take yourself back.

Electricity Comes to Cocoa Bottom

Then all the children of Cocoa Bottom
went to see Mr. Samuel's electric lights.
They camped on the grass bank outside his house,
their lamps filled with oil,
waiting for sunset,
watching the sky turn yellow, orange.
Grannie Patterson across the road
peeped through the crack in her porch door.
The black cable wire was drawn like a pencil line across the sun.
The fireflies waited in the shadows,
their lanterns off.
The kling-klings swooped in from the hills,
congregating in the orange trees.
A breeze coming home from sea held its breath;
bamboo lining the dirt road stopped its swaying,
and evening came as soft as chiffon curtains:
Closing. Closing.

Light!
Mr. Samuel smiling on the verandah—
a dark silhouette against the yellow shimmer behind him—
and there arising such a gasp,
such a fluttering of wings,
tweet-a-whit,
such a swaying, swaying.
Light! Marvellous light!
And then the breeze rose up from above the trees,
swelling and swelling into a wind
such that the long grass bent forward
stretching across the bank like so many bowed heads.
And a voice in the wind whispered:
Is there one among us to record this moment?
But there was none—
no one (except for a few warm rocks
hidden among mongoose ferns) even heard a sound.

Already the children of Cocoa Bottom
had lit their lamps for the dark journey home,
and it was too late—
the moment had passed.

Murline

Six years old.
Me and my best friend Murline
play dandy-shandy at Marse Lloyd's storefront.
We sit on the steps.
Her hands clap over mine,
the prints on our palms match—
five, ten.
We clap our knees, clap five.
Clap our knees, clap five.
Clap our knees, clap ten. Clap ten.
Cut off
Nanny tail.
Hang
Nanny tail
from the
man-
go
tree.

Me and my best friend Murline.
The pot holes in the road deepen,
and I go to college.
She stays at Marse Lloyd's storefront
selling peeled oranges, tamarind and jew plums soaked in salt
water.
The men at the rum shop across the street
watch her body from the corners of their eyes.
From miles away I hear her voice
high and sweet like ripe bombay:

Cut off
Nanny tail.
Hang
Nanny tail
from the
man-
go
tree.

Holidays, I come home searching the streets for childhood songs.
Murline round and puffy as a spoiled potato, remembers.
Remembers.
Holding up her hands before me,
the palms dark and criss-crossed like dirt tracks,
we clap our knees. Clap ten.
Clap our hands. Clap ten.
Clap ten. Ten. Ten. Ten. Ten.
Cut off
Nanny tail.
Hang
Nanny tail
from the
man-
go
tree.

Now a baby sucks the hem of Murline's skirt.
She has rotting teeth and a missing finger.
Her oranges turn soft in the hot sun.
A white film over her eyes,
the school children drop pennies in her basket.
Through her one good ear,
she hears their songs pure as fresh milk:
Cut off
Nanny tail.
Hang
Nanny tail

from the
man-
go
tree.

EUGENIE EERSEL
SURINAME

The Plantation

what's haunting me is not a shadow
i wish it was . . .
it's a story told to me
when we passed a sugar plantation
in equatorial Suriname
on our usual Sunday-family-ride.

in this place they still use
the same cane crushers
as in slavery days
mama said
the Dutch would mark
she said
the installation of a new machine
by picking out and crushing
the most beautiful young Negress
as offer to the God of Profit.

it's her scream
resounding from times long past
that's curdling my blood
and keeps sleep away from me
at times when i think
of our Sunday-family-ride.

RAMABAI ESPINET
TRINIDAD—TOBAGO

Spirit Lash

You cannot provoke the ghosts of the collective ancestors of all our dark races forever, and receive no comeback. A lash is coming from beyond, and the spirits riding that lash (all the swarthy spirits) will show no mercy as you, the real spooks: colour of bone-ash and driftwood bleached for centuries in an aging sun, fall before their wrath. We call such force a spirit lash.

When a hawk beats
His dying wings into a vermilion
Sun—once gold and flaming
And carries rainless eyes
Yellow with rage
Into his final uncaring
And cats' eyes weep
Dogs' days burn hollow . . .

Dread the hillsides
Dreadful too the scorched
Sea-lashed earth
Holding no grace but salt

In such dread times
Of sallow sea-fever curses
Yellow rime and quicksand
An eagle—bald and riven
With curses of a thousand
Griefs,
With old contradictions
Choked upon but swallowed
whole,

Random, uneven calculations
Of destiny
Now becoming manifest

A bald eagle
Forever distanced
From breaking into BEING,
And no righteous man
No grace
No song unsung . . .
His haunted visions
Sweetening the breathing cadences
Of the winds of war, volleys
From the battle for love
Of a precious familiar clay
(and now being fought at a cellular
level,
with germs, sickle-cell splicing,
mosquitoes,
napalm, pesticides, ddt, micro-
chips,
food chains, gene pools, eco-
systems,
plain and simple misfortune,
and other unimaginable evils)
A clay almost gone sour,
No grace
Not even salt

Only a schoolboy's coarse and
Lecherous fancies for the moon
and sun
And all eternal desire
Crammed into his puff-fished face,
While the whole staggering world
Creeps on—
Myopic, unbelieving, grasping at

Every stray tendril of sunlight,
Blinded by fakelights
Christmas tree blinkers
Neon fanlights
And such . . .

But our dead are with us still.
They do not sleep, unstilled
Like yours whom you fear.
They are not white-coated spooks
Striding through the dark
Haunting the undead
Railing at the unrighteous
Usurping your terrors
And killing your children.

They remain, unaffright,
Sturdy as immortelles
Searching with us for
A world alight with being.
And your still waters,
Now disturbed,
Will die too:
Not so much by eternal
Fire-rage
At Sodom, Gomorrah
Or the Pillar of Salt,
But by slow, blind
Uncaring.

The hawk lashes,
The bald eagle frets,
The seas run together
The dying sun wears down.

Crebo

I erased my black skin
My rimless eyes
And purple seaweed hair
And joined the lake

I erased my backward steps
And lived on top
The grey-glassed lake
One summer long

—All these erasures happened
A long time ago—
Then I gathered up my hair
And eased into my skin

My hands had wrinkles
But rims grew around my eyes
My skin became ebony and rose
And my tongue grew long beyond
words

An Ageable Woman

This Caribbean is mine
Not because I've bought it
Or bartered it
Or because I sell
Trade or use it
Or find it to be
"A lovely piece of real estate"

This Caribbean is mine
Because when sun burn my back
And cane cut my legs

And jiggers bore holes
Through my rice-planting feet
I wait for evening
And the sun goes down
And the night is full
Of crickets, frogsong
And a man of Carib soil

And when the blue-winged
Marauders come
I see how we can't wait
Destiny lies covered
In the turquoise sea
And how long, how long
My son and daughter
Can we wait
To part the waves
To weld the bonds
To fish for the jewels
Waiting in the sea

I do what I can
Old now, weak and strong,
I wait for the young
To recover from sleeping
And too much purple dreaming
I wait for the warriors
Of a new mind—the small girls
And boys—
To bear the banners
We made them for
From our blood and bone

And I, an ageable woman now,
Think of times to come
When cowards will fall
And blue waves cover them

As the cycle moves on
When the young now
Sailing in coconut boats
Through calm lagoons of memory
Will breathe with fiery breath
Our aging swansongs
Our visions
Our people's truth

Take the leavings of cities
And let me return
Home: buried in green mountains
Without caskets or gilt
Running through the eternal silver
Of rock rivers
And breathing the freedom
Of an earth not caught
Under a whitened sepulchral
Heel, not subdued
Not stripped bare and pillaged

Won by new warriors
And old gods, black and brown
Green and fearless,
Learning the discourse
Of a new war
As, ageable but strong,
I sing a song for our own
For healing and the earth
Delivered from falsehood
And laden with new colours
For all.

SANDRA MARIA ESTEVES
PUERTO RICO / DOMINICAN REPUBLIC

1st poem for Cuba

We are the silent poets of the night

We breathe in whirling tropic oceans

We are the dancing black campesinos de Oriente
holding drums within our bodies

With your eyes
We feel the spaces around us

With your hands
We touch a dreamer's place
hiding just beyond the walls of this world

With your voices
We catch the sun
as it rises to the east
holding in our wombs
the hammers of proud and righteous people

Flowing in the currents of many rivers
We slowly wear away great mountains
returning to the sea
where life is born
to find you and ourselves again.

Puerto Rican Discovery #5, Here Like There

Chaos spills over from another era
they had no part in the making.

Weeds appear from remote corners
only the sun notices. A world evolves
busily ignoring its own blinded sight.
Songs from Managua hit in counterbalance,
geometrically perpendicular to stone forests,
petrified like soldiers fearing the unknown.

An infant gun creates a canyon of history
exploding paths into oblivion,
searching split-seconds of focus into its birth,
a hurricane gnarled and twisted,
sheltering a brooded following,
demanding attention on a world stage.
Insisting space, a voice in its own house.

Like there in Puerto Rico,
mountains and sea wage vain attempts
to purify the plastic layer
breathless and tight over its victim,
a flag stuffed luscious,
laying to rot in ambivalent warehouses
of aborted children
from an indifferent

> . . . mother.

Anonymous Apartheid

There is a stranger in our house
who looks half blind at us,
does not know our name,
assumes our earth is flat,

wraps a ball and chain around our tired legs,
barricades our windows with formless visions,
illusions of no consequence.

This stranger thinks we are alley cats, purring
in heat for violent attentions,
feeds us our day-old fish and dead meat,
leaves our fruit basket empty,
does not speak our language, wear our colors,
nor understand the soul of these tender thoughts.

The stranger upsets our garden,
turning over seeds of potential into desert soil,
laying waste the promise of life's harvest,
denied, for no better reason than greed,
chopping down innocent buds to feed
their wealth of scavengers, and thieves,
growing fat from the treasures we are.

This stranger steals us from our mother,
separates us from our brothers and sisters,
does not listen to our million crying petitions,
cuts off our rebellious tongues,
laughs when our tears fall on stone,
orders us to kneel, though we refuse.

Each day the stranger drinks a nectar of blood at high noon,
wears clothing spun from blood,
worships a heathen blood god made of gold,
destroys the covenant of humanity
for the sake of a synthetic blood mirror, cracked,
tarnished quicksilver, ungrounded and formless,
traveling a broken spiral of blood.

This stranger lives here uninvited,
an unwelcomed alien ravaging us in gluttonous consummation,
throwing a soiled shroud over our altar,

expecting us to accept a life of disgrace.
Yet, we refuse.

There is a ruthless stranger in our house
who has no voice of its own,
mimics our words in crude scorn,
suggests we are low, worthless, incompetent,
grinning at itself
while we are held hostage in a doomed drama
where act one lasts more than five hundred years,
in plots of bigoted abuse,
dialogues of racial condescension, poverty,
transitions of rapes, muggings, lynchings,
scenes of jailhouse tortures and hangings,
life sentences to minimum security housing projects.

There is a stranger in our house
plundering our womb,
stealing our newborn with a dry knife,
drug-thirsty for their blood,
bargains in exchange for their lives,
tells us to throw away our weapons, love one another,
rejecting our religion,
forcing us to sell our worth,
poisoning the rich center of our spiritual essence,
speaking the lecherous tongue of split truth.

Yet we refuse, and will continue to refuse,
along with our planetary relatives who also refuse
this stranger in our house
who has no face.

PATRICIA M. FAGAN
VIRGIN ISLANDS

Charcoal

I

black man bent under
tropic sun
burning lignum vitae
for charcoal
to boil morning tea.

black woman's hands
carry coal
for **Rotterdam**'s steam
a cent a bucket buys
little sugar
her cracked yellow feet
mark the earth
step by step
under Danish flag.

Millions of years ago
in another tropical forest
trees, flowers, plants
absorbed sun
day after day
then sank into earth's bosom
metamorphosed to coal.

The **Dannebrog** lowers a past
"We must progress" captions
the coal carrier's dreams of
golden roads and electric light.

Blackbeard's pieces of eight
pay for Old Glory.

II

But those were old photographs
viewed in a wrinkled olive book
The Danish Isles of the West.
Now kodak snaps the Red
White and Blue cooly
waving over tin shacks
sweltering in blistering sun
for bargain hunter's
trade magazine.

While in the dark
a specter's scream
of freedom's flight
Queen Mary, the one-legged
slave jumped to her death
on the jagged rocks of the sea

The stories chant,
"Look to the water!"
reminding us of her yearly
apparition and a bloody sea

And we weep to the drums
that beat somewhere else
to marching rats and fighting roaches
while old man tends his coal pot
and Lennox Avenue screams identity.

HONOR FORD-SMITH
JAMAICA

Aux Leon . . . Women

Before the sunlight
splits the dry rock
their eyes open
on coarse board walls and
guttered
government
land

mind set begins
with stumbling over
a sleeping child
an animal immobile

"catch up the fire / scrape and grate the cassava / carry the water
(uphill) / boil the tea / the toloma / beat the castor oil seeds /
wash clothes / nurse baby / soothe old lady / weed garden / chop
banana / load banana / carry it down the stony road /
Un cadeau pour Monsieur Guise"
la lin coowee, coowee
la solei joo baway
(the moon runs
it runs
till the sun
catches it)
"how much are the bananas today / the housewife said
unbuttoning her coat / laying down her string bag in the
Islington shop / hurry up there / don't have all day / she added
himself will be home soon and the tea not ready / nothing
changes / only the prices rise / Gimme a dozen a them / bruised
lot you got here today /"
la lin coowee, coowee

la solei joo baway
(the moon runs
it runs
till the sun
catches it)
scrape / boil / beat
"sleep baby sleep
father working far away
he give me something   i take it
he give me nothing   i take it"

Aux Leon women
This morning
when the sunlight strikes
the rock
Let us sweep that old yard clean.
Let us beat our quarrels into one voice
with the rhythm of the hardwood pestle.
Let us light our fires on this hillside
so all the islands will see
this labour is not free.
Let us burn the sweet wood
for its scent will fill the nostrils
of the blind and deaf.

listen
(la solei coowee coowee
la lin joo baway)
The stroke of a cutlass in water has no meaning
(la solei coowee coowee
la lin joo baway)
Listen, a song—
a song is beginning
right here
among us

Aux Leon is a small community in Saint Lucia created by squatters on
the high and rocky backlands of an old estate.

JOAN FRENCH
JAMAICA

Camera Ready

I ain' worrin' wid you;
I jus' here goin' about my business
Doin' what I mus' do. An I ain' business
If yu tink a jus' too silent
An' a doan skin up wid certain creature
An' me jeans wash out
An' di hole on di leg want patch up
An' me hair look to you untidy
An' me shirt want changin';
Look how yu want,
I don't care a damn,
I jus' here marchin'
In di ranks of di trying-to-make-it-out-of-oppression
On di road dat will one day lead to liberation
Even if a catch me dead along di way.

I ain' worryin' wid you;
Who matter is dem woman I wid in di jail
Who sing "Abide wid me" to pass di night
An' when di jailer come to charge disorderly conduct
Tell him to charge dem so dey could go to court
An' tell di judge di officer did charge dem
For worshippin' dey God.

I ain' worryin' wid you;
You ain' see a silent?
A ca'an even bother to waste me breath on you;
I jus' here goin' about my business
I jus' here marchin
Slim, cool, me an me camera . . .
But di camera not for you . . .

Is Rookmin I takin',
Rookmin who plant on di back-dam
An wade thru canal an' clear cane
Till her back ben'
For 30c a day.

I ain' business wid you;
Is plenty lick I takin'
When I march in dem march
An' go pon dem demonstration
An' when I go I doan see you
So I doan business wid you;
Is a new Guyana I makin
Wid di family up by Essequibo
No doctor for miles and miles
And mosquitoes and flies
An' disease all roun' dem
An' still fightin';
An' Marlene wid her children belly full o' rice, two peas
An' nutten;
Who still fin' time for organisin'
An' di sister who say she ain' hidin' nutten
Nutten—Burnham was a pig
An' Hoyte ain' no better; is people he foolin'
(People like you);
Is dem I studyin'
So I ain' business wid you;
Step aside;
I passin'.

CORNELIA FRETTLÖH
BARBADOS

The Speech of the Sisserou

I Sisserou, colourful feathered chronicler of the rain-forest,
I greet you, Waitukubuli, Tall-is-her-body, land of the Caribs,
proud defiant island, fire spitting risen out of the turquoise blue
sea. Still you can hear me, little graceful humming-bird, fou-
fou, you who brought Hiali, He-has-become-bright, he, the
founder of the Carib nation, to his father right up in the moon, a
man with a dirty face. As a reward you got your splendid
feathers and your cap and yet today you see his sons and
daughters defeated and dying.

There, look at them, these men and women, once a proud
feared people, that defied and resisted and today plait baskets
and put them up for sale. Listen to me, all you pronged and
dotted snails, small and big, look out, all you lizards and
iguanas. Still the sound of their names can be heard, Colihaut,
Calibishie and Salibia, but nevertheless it is a dying people.
Columbus didn't conquer them, he, who saw land on a Spanish
sunday: domingo.

Many they saw coming and going until they stayed and
engraved their names in their land: Pointe Michel, Soufriere
and Marigot, Portsmouth, Scotts Head and Hillsborough. They,
the colonists, became many until no more space was left for
those who once had set off from the Orinoco and came to settle
from island to island. Doubtless they banished the Arawaks,
killed the men thus founding their fierce reputation, and yet
took their women as wives, the strange language in their
mouths, became a people of masculine and feminine words, but
nevertheless you see them beaten today, thrown aside, expelled
to a reserve. Take an example from them, agoutis and
manicous, make sure that you don't end up like those, a dying
people.

Hasn't this island got 366 rivers, streams and brooks, one for
every day and one more? The sweetest fruits and rarest berries,
don't they grow here? Mountains, valleys and lakes, don't they
gleam daily under the coloured brightness of the rainbow?
I, Sisserou, ancestor of primitive times, admonisher of the
future, watchman over peaks and gullies, I call you, palms,
ferns and mosses, trees, bushes and grass. Doubtless hurricanes
brought devastation and misery, and yet tins, plastic and too
much concrete confuse the mind. Today many eyes are looking
northward deceived by a glittering shine. Shall we go and live
in the sea like the fish? once asked a distressed and despoiled
people. Today you see them dying, their own language already
dead. Barely our forgetfulness remembers, recollects old wisdom and lost art.

I Sisserou, heraldic animal of this island, of an impassable
hidden dream, I call you, animals and plants:
Apres Bondie Cest La Ter! After God The Earth!

PHILLIS GERSHATOR
VIRGIN ISLANDS

Concretely Celebrating the Quincentennial

I

On the islands they're mixing concrete
for monuments and markers
to celebrate fourteen ninety two
when Columbus, sailing off the face of the map,
touched these shores and gave them new names
and proved at last—in the year of heresies,

recantations, lies and burnings at the stake—
the world is round, not flat

II

We appreciate
the science of it all
the accidents
the hand of fate
We celebrate Discovery
not the loose ends
unfurling in its wake
not greed
not power lust
not the flag with a cross
With mixed feelings
we approach the date

III

Progress is a mixed blessing
so let the concrete mixing begin!

A blind man's concrete lighthouse
rises on the shores of Hispaniola
A concrete K-mart in the Virgins
buries an Arawak village
Another concrete hotel
blocks the beach

Here, there, and everywhere
concrete for Columbus
for capitalists
for consumers
for caudillos
Concrete for the sake of concrete

JOYA GOMEZ
TRINIDAD—TOBAGO

New Woman

She whose fickle face once launched
A thousand Spartan ships, and troth
To Trojan Paris a love debauched,
Still lives—and still by l-awful oath
A thousand years of Time we span,
Unmummified, she lives again.
Not in fairest face but wan
And rather in the minds of men.

See her fairless prowhead stand
Against the sea of Egypt, Troy
And now my peaceful Caribbean.
Sly, she skirts this sentinel buoy
Then breasts the surge of salty slime
In seeming triumph, for the thousandth time.

On Receiving An 'Ostrichian' Egg From Him

That easter ovum birthed today
intact
on the third day of its hatching from
the spring of your temperate arms:
delicately I balance its crimson cowl
in the noonday fires of my palm
anxious-ambivalent, lifting the flap
prolonging the Joy . . . perusing instead
your familiar weave of feathered tracings, noting
its power to set my centre cheep-chirping
involuntary, like a newborn chick:
later, in this nest of my room

excited and reluctant, I unveil
rare hybird—ostri-phoenix blend:
with expert ease and skill of centuries old
Masai-imprinting on my soul, I
extract the saffron yolk—food for broken
body, salve parched lips, then . . . taste
the ashen sub-text of its sustenance, but
eat, nimble; assimilating stones; savouring
each syll-a-ble with each sense;
how with tribal thrift that hollow still-life shell
transformed
to water-carrier now, offers
drink new life
against this desert heat of separated lives:
one consolatory drop, we sip,
enough
only to bridge the gape of memory, but
will not slake that unfathomed/able chasm thirst
which
flames a phoenix-love,
but cracks
the myth that will not
live,
again.

LORNA GOODISON
JAMAICA

The Road of the Dread

That dey road no pave
like any other black-face road
it no have no definite colour
and it fence two side
with live barbwire.

And no look fi no milepost
fi measure you walking
and no tek no stone as
dead or familiar

for sometime you pass a ting
you know as . . . call it stone again
and is a snake ready fi squeeze yu
kill yu
or is a dead man tek him
possessions tease yu
Then the place dem yu feel
is resting place because time
before that yu welcome like rain,
go dey again?
bad dawg, bad face tun fi drive yu underground
wey yu no have no light fi walk
and yu find sey that many yu meet who sey
them understand
is only from dem mout dem talk.
One good ting though, that same treatment
mek yu walk untold distance
for to continue yu have fe walk far
away from the wicked.

Pan dis same road ya sista
sometime yu drink yu salt sweat fi water
for yu sure sey at least dat no pisen,
and bread? yu picture it and chew it accordingly
and some time yu surprise fi know how dat full
man belly.

Some day no have no definite colour
no beginning and no ending, it just name day
or night as how you feel fi call it.

Den why I tread it brother?
well mek I tell yu bout the day dem
when the father send some little bird
that swallow flute fi trill me
And when him instruct the sun fi smile pan me first.

and the sky calm like sea when it sleep
and a breeze like a laugh follow mi.
or the man find a stream that pure like baby mind
and the water ease down yu throat
and quiet yu inside.

and better still when yu meet another traveller
who have flour and yu have water and man and man
make bread together.
And dem time dey the road run straight and sure
like a young horse that cant tire
and yu catch a glimpse of the end
through the water in yu eye
I wont tell yu what I spy
but is fi dat alone I treat this road.

For My Mother (May I Inherit Half Her Strength)

My mother loved my father
I write this as an absolute
in this my thirtieth year
the year to discard absolutes

he appeared, her fate disguised,
as a sunday player in a cricket match,
he had ridden from a country
one hundred miles south of hers.

She tells me he dressed the part,
visiting dandy, maroon blazer
cream serge pants, seam like razor,
and the beret and the two-tone shoes.

My father stopped to speak to her sister,
till he looked and saw her by the oleander,
sure in the kingdom of my blue-eyed grandmother.
He never played the cricket match that day.

He wooed her with words and he won her.
He had nothing but words to woo her,
On a visit to distant Kingston he wrote,

"I stood on the corner of King Street and looked,
and not one woman in that town was lovely as you".

My mother was a child of the petite bourgeoisie
studying to be a teacher, she oiled her hands
to hold pens.
My father barely knew his father, his mother died young,
he was a boy who grew with his granny.

My mother's trousseau came by steamer through the snows
of Montreal

where her sisters Albertha of the cheekbones and the
perennial Rose, combed Jewlit backstreets with French-
turned names for Doris' wedding things.

Such a wedding Harvey River, Hanover, had never seen
Who anywhere had seen a veil fifteen chantilly yards long?
and a crepe de chine dress with inlets of silk godettes
and a neck-line clasped with jewelled pins!

And on her wedding day she wept. For it was a brazen bride in
those days who smiled.
and her bouquet looked for the world like a sheaf of wheat
against the unknown of her belly,
a sheaf of wheat backed by maidenhair fern, representing Harvey River
her face washed by something other than river water.

My father made one assertive move, he took the imported cherub
down from the heights of the cake and dropped it in the soft territory
between her breasts . . . and she cried.

When I came to know my mother many years later, I knew her as
the figure who sat at the first thing I learned to read: 'SINGER', and
she breast-fed my brother while she sewed; and she taught us to read
while she sewed and
she sat in judgement over all our disputes as she sewed.

She could work miracles, she would make a garment from a square
of cloth in a span that defied time. Or feed twenty people on a stew
made from fallen-from-the-head cabbage leaves and a carrot and a
cho-cho and a palmful
of meat.

And she rose early and sent us clean into the world and she went to
bed in the dark, for my father came in always last.

There is a place somewhere where my mother never took the
                                                younger ones
a country where my father with the always smile

my father whom all women loved, who had the perpetual quality of
wonder given only to a child . . . hurt his bride.

Even at his death there was this 'Friend' who stood by her side,
but my mother is adamant that that has no place in the memory of
my father.

When he died, she sewed dark dresses for the women amongst us
and she summoned that walk, straight-backed, that she gave to us
and buried him dry-eyed.

Just that morning, weeks after
she stood delivering bananas from their skin
singing in that flat hill country voice

she fell down a note to the realization that she did
not have to be brave, just this once
and she cried.

For her hands grown coarse with raising nine children
for her body for twenty years permanently fat
for the time she pawned her machine for my sister's
Senior Cambridge fees
and for the pain she bore with the eyes of a queen

and she cried also because she loved him.

Guinea Woman

Great grandmother
was a guinea woman
wide eyes turning
the corners of her face
could see behind her
her cheeks dusted with
a fine rash of jet-bead warts

that itched when the rain set up.

Great grandmother's waistline
the span of a headman's hand
slender and tall like a cane stalk
with a guinea woman's antelope-quick walk
and when she paused
her gaze would look to sea
her profile fine like some obverse impression
on a guinea coin from royal memory.

It seems her fate was anchored
in the unfathomable sea
for great grandmother caught the eye of a sailor
whose ship sailed without him from Lucea harbour.
Great grandmother's royal scent of
cinnamon and escallions
drew the sailor up the straits of Africa,
the evidence my blue-eyed grandmother
the first Mulatta
taken into backra's household
and covered with his name.
They forbade great grandmother's
guinea woman presence
they washed away her scent of
cinnamon and escallions
controlled the child's antelope walk
and called her uprisings rebellions.

But, great grandmother
I see your features blood dark
appearing
in the children of each new
breeding
the high yellow brown
is darkening down.
Listen, children
it's great grandmother's turn.

Nanny

My womb was sealed
with molten wax
of killer bees
for nothing should enter
nothing should leave
the state of perpetual siege
the condition of the warrior.

From then my whole body would quicken
at the birth of everyone of my people's children.
I was schooled in the green-giving ways
of the roots and vines
made accomplice to the healing acts
of Chainey root, fever grass & vervain.

My breasts flattened
settled unmoving against my chest
my movements ran equal
to the rhythms of the forest.

I could sense and sift
the footfall of men
from the animals
and smell danger
death's odour
in the wind's shift.

When my eyes rendered
light from the dark
my battle song opened
into a solitaire's moan
I became most knowing
and forever alone.

And when my training was over

they circled my waist with pumpkin seeds
and dried okra, a traveller's jigida
and sold me to the traders
all my weapons within me.
I was sent, tell that to history.

When your sorrow obscures the skies
other women like me will rise.

Mother, the Great Stones Got to Move

Mother, one stone is wedged across the hole in our history
and sealed with blood wax.
In this hole is our side of the story, exact figures,
headcounts, burial artifacts, documents, lists, maps
showing our way up through the stars; lockets of brass
containing all textures of hair clippings.
It is the half that has never been told,
and some of us must tell it.

Mother, there is the stone on the hearts of some women and men
something like an onyx, cabochon-cut,
which hung on the wearer seeds bad dreams. Speaking for the small
dreamers of this earth, plagued with nightmares, yearning
for healing dreams
we want the stone to move.

Upon an evening like this, mother, when one year is making way
for another, in a ceremony attended by a show of silver stars,
mothers see the moon, milk-fed, herself a nursing mother
and we think of our children and the stones upon their future
and we want these stones to move.

For the year going out came in fat at first
but toward the harvest it grew lean,
and many mouth corners gathered white

and another kind of poison, powdered white
was brought in to replace what was green.
And death sells it with one hand
and with the other death palms a gun
then death gets death's picture
in the papers asking

"where does all this death come from?"
Mother, stones are pillows
for the homeless sleep on concrete sheets.
Stone flavors soup, stone is now meat,
the hard-hearted giving our children
stones to eat.

Mother, the great stones over mankind got to move.
It's been ten thousand years we've been watching them now
from various points in the universe.
From the time of our birth as points of light
in the eternal coiled workings of the cosmos.
Roll away stone of poisoned powders come
to blot out the hope of our young.
Move stone of sacrificial lives we breed
to feed to suicide god of tribalism.
From across the pathway to mount morning
site of the rose quartz fountain
brimming anise and star water
bright fragrant for our children's future
Mother these great stones got to move.

LUCILE GOTTIN
GUADELOUPE

Guadeloupe, Mon Ile

O Mon ile, oserais-je un jour à nouveau dire de toi.
O Femme courageuse, ò Femme libre.

Les premiers sont venus, ils t'ont violée, its t'ont atteinte dans ta
    chair.
Désemparée, honteuse, meurtrie, tu t'es dit:
A quoi bon te garder pour des lendemains meilleurs qui sans doute
ne viendront jamais.
Aujourd'hui, courtisane, tu reçois des amants des quatre coins de la
    terre.
Ils viennent te souiller, se repaitre de toi.
Guadeloupe mon île qu'a-t-on fait de toi?
Où est ta beauté d'antan? Ton charme insouciant? Ton rire
    ensorcelant? . . .
Tes enfants tu les as oubliés.
Ils s'en vont ça et là à la recherche d'une paternité.
N'es tu rien d'autre qu'une île perdu dans l'immensité?
Avec Amour et nostalgie tes poètes exilés ont chanté ta beauté!
Au nom d'une civilisation qui n'est peut-être qu'un mirage, tu es
    piétinée, salie.
Tes enfants angoissés voient disparaitre chaque jour ces merveilleuses
    cannaies,
et avec elles ces parfumes enivrants qui enchantaient leur coeur.
Sans cesse à leurs oreilles meurtries raisonnent avec fracas ces portes
d'usines que se ferment.
Mais . . . vivre n'est-ce pas espérer?
Et ils vivent tes enfants?
Oui ils vivent en espérant qu'un jour viendra le libérateur.
Oui ils vivent en espérant qu'un jour viendra ce "Manuel" tant
    attendu.
Oui ils vivent! . . .

Guadeloupe, My Island

Oh my island, would I dare to say of you one day.
Oh courageous Woman, oh free Woman.

The first came, they raped you, they wounded your flesh.
Bewildered, shamed, bruised, you thought:
What's the use of saving yourself for better days that will never come.
Today, courtesan, you entertain lovers from the four corners of the
    world.
They come to sully you, to gorge themselves on you.
Guadeloupe, my island, what have they done to you?
Where is your beauty of long ago? Your carefree charm? Your
    bewitching laughter? . . .
You have forgotten your children.
They go here and there looking for their birthright.
Are you nothing more than an island lost in the immensity?
With Love and nostalgia your exiled poets sang your beauty!
In the name of a civilization which is perhaps only a mirage, you
    were trampled, soiled.
Your anguished children see these wonderful canefields disappearing
    each day,
and with them these heavy perfumes which enchanted their heart.
Their bruised ears argue constantly against the noise of these closing
    factory doors.
But . . . isn't living hoping?
Aren't your children alive?
Yes they are alive, hoping that one day the liberator will come.
Yes they are alive, hoping that one day this long awaited "Manuel"
    will come.
Yes they are alive! . . .

JEAN GOULBOURNE
JAMAICA

Jamaica: January 16, 1980

The shadows
of the night
descend
upon a city
with no moon
and moves
like a wave
across the moulds
of drifting sands
and shifting debris.
the dog hounds
its protest
and the cat
stalks its cool walk
across the dark.
Clouds are dimmer
curses move across the city
and like a fog
hangs heavy
upon the wind.

the nation waits
the cold calm descends,
and the armies
of ragged children
puny, with no food
follow the piper
whose tune is hunger.
Life hangs heavy
with sparse flesh
and the skin

of the nation
rots
and folds
with the growth
of an anger
like unto cold murder.

Magnificent Sun
has slithered
into the deep well
of the ocean
and the city
with no moon
drools saliva
at garbage
waiting
for the ultimate
explosion.

Shadow

So they called him
Shadow.
So he wept
when the shores of his land
disappeared
in an orgy
of dim horizon mist.
So he felt the pain
of parting
deeper
than the whip.

And so he came
deprived
unrelenting in his hope

to return
to his shores,
certain in his death
so he toiled.

And as he toiled
The sun burnt his back
deeper than the pain
of the whip
So his lot
burnt his soul
deep
within the recesses
of his mind.

The multi summers
came and went
and he aged.
The lines of his face
stood dirty
with the soil
of experience.
So he waited.

Now he is an old man—
my noble slave.
He is not dead.
The youth of his grey hairs
call him
'Warrior'
He fought
and he won.
His history
is the story
of a beautiful people.

Like a Bridge

The forever
nine month
swollen belly
pushes another
in front
and the woman
recipient of many men
deep with hanging carcasses
of breasts
that bled milk
A dozen years
to a dozen
half fed
off spring

Face of youth
As hard
As the sidewalk
that support
her varicosed
legs

walks
down the street
On Spanish Town
road
Hangs
the fumes
of people
in its breath.

Cigarette smoke
of the half smoked
finished butts
of the tied

jacketed
personnel
who seek work
in offices

Slugging
at paper
on carpet supported
desks

These butts
half smoked
feed the tobacco hungry
of the street.

The big benz
crawls slowly
out of dock

The coconut man
with his
tough coated
subservient mule
bawls his life out
in one word
As his own Benz
ghetto erected
moved slowly
down the rotting sidewalked
street

Star
and
star
upon the fuming
night
echoes

of hate
echoes of
poverty
echoes of murder
echoes of money
echoes of wealth
echoes of the uptown
downtown difference

The man
on Rum Lane
and the high-heeled
debutante of Seventh Avenue
and Manor Park

Tons of skin
that scream
in loud tones
Tons of hands
outstretched

Woman
with the persistent
nine month belly
walks
her varicosed grief

Down Spanish Town
road.

CYNTHIA JAMES
TRINIDAD—TOBAGO

New World Soldier

I heard your name
go for the sake of all the children
go because the world needs the new soldier
to civilize the mind

and when you lean upon those slight podia
rock them heavily
the gift is yours
of all the chairs yours the arrow enters

this is the chance
the only chance, the children's only only chance
guns are inadequate: see the evidence of the millennia
the battle is now for the highground of the mind

and there is much too much blood
we do not want to shed blood even of brothers
so when they call you
(and as you have found out)

they mean come alone and leave the tribe behind
go, for by your success
in time it will not matter
where and when or who and what the tribe

word them rockets
blaze bomb rain starwars
from the highground of your cranium
on the uncivilized

span concrete bridges, glasshouses

interlocking ropes hanging from the sky
infect the statues
and don't forget the false lady with the blind torch

gift-wrapt in the mist across the river
warm her breath
the frozen freedom lady curdled in coldblood
facing the shoreline

fix the radar within black crosses
lock in
and when the target, all of it is centre
not before

BULLSEYE!
blow glaciers
see rivers flow: hearts soften
heal

my new ambassador
I disfranchise those decoys at Geneva
(but this our secret
leave the chess game
with its rooks and pawns
its bishops and its sitting ducks)

the future burns brightly
in the filament of your mind, go,
because the way the world goes
groundsoldiers squash like treebugs
missiles scudd across the sky
not even comets now meet eye to eye

since the cows will never be returned
go bring the milk as Cia sermons
Polyphemus has but one eye, a greedy eye
hand on to the belly of the ram

let him pass his hand
over the humps on the outer hide

a new world waits, my brave one
Caliban's italics suffice
to circumvent all wiles
the one who calls does not know
you learnt to solder
with the blowtorch of your mind

Amerindia

sleep no sleep
trembling all over
in a half-snatch of reverie
where the zigzag of lightning
courses straight up the belly
a teenaged surrender
in the throes of a hunger
for the poetry of love

but I am wedded to a stale plot
on unploughable land
the topsoil swept over
by twenty dry seasons
only a ghost of a dream
where tears no longer fall

so I lay out my palm
and beg unashamed
since I can
not have that hand
that the spirit of the world
lift me an imprint
bring me a stamp

hand on hand
lower it
first the quick
then the tip
and with my palms
so open
I sleep

for I no longer want
fragmented poems
exercises in lament
dry sticks of verses
disjoints of memory
blotting the page
I want to trade widowed poems
for whole songs strummed
from the frets of my hand

comes a messenger
of alarming composure
reassuring and tender
balded and battered
reflecting her storms
on a stone axe-head face
just the hint of a grin
harbouring her ghosts
but whose dreams
none can touch

and takes down her fingers
from their pyramid sculpture
unsteeples the indexes
lowers her imprint
with the scorch of contact
I wake with a shout
and look for the stamp
no sign of the messenger

with the stone axen head

but with tingling desire
my fingers afresh
begin to uncurl

A Street Vendor Goes Home

Who are you, lone woman?
coppered bracelets shackle wrists
a weight in either hand,
the case upon your head is wide
and bare remains inside,
who are you, lone woman,
your shoulders square
support twin breasts of justice
worn low on either side,
hard corned jewels
adorn the scales
on both your flattened feet
and straight and strong
you balance on
above the barren street.

Who are you, lone woman, brown?
painted bright, my tinsel
threatens to reveal me
I follow far behind,
your solid mantle
shames the neons
who are you, lone woman, brown,
man, child, everybody gone?
do I know you?
that dog, he knows you
mooning as he waits your tread
to guard your ulcered feet

until some bitch's scent
distracts him careening off
sniffing beyond the drooping udder
already taken down

Might I know you, lone woman, down
were not the stripes pressing round
dampened to your coppered crown
shadowing in your sunken face
haloed out by empty greasy case?
might I know you, lone woman, down,
if you dragged no weight
were unparceled by remains,
is that why my eyeballs burn
to feel the chastening of your gaze
to see my face in your face
why I linger every night behind
yet long to reach you, touch, turn you round
and wipe my defiling spittle
caked now your cheek down,
why can't I say I love you?

Wait . . .
I know you, you know me, lone woman strong,
do you still love me?
the early hours chime so far away
it were as though you were never young,
I am the still-born child you grieved
the ghosted douen with backward feet
you lost to easy el-doradoed streets
why will you not turn around
Wait . . .
give me your mantle brown
so like Elisha, lone woman, strong,
tomorrow I may go a-balancing down,
the case is always heavy,
empty, full, going up or down,

leave me, grant me not lose,
Chaconia, Ibis, Sister Hills
by which your name shall never be sung . . .

Port-of-Spain by Night

my city is a bitch
an old strayway bitch
ten drooping teats that can't go down
ten to celebrate each and every time she get raze
watch her, fleas like bush
mange eat away the skin across her ribcage

but don't mind
everybody have to survive
when daylight slash her with his ripe knife
he whet red hot on the edge of the concrete
the blade of light silverthin like a nailfile
that old jealous son-of-a-bitch
is then she get brazen
holding her head high and walking like a beauty queen
and the things he call her in the middle of the street
no respecter of persons
'mother cattle boil' is the only one I can repeat
that worthless man in front of everybody
and you know Bank Clerk, The Mayor, The Archbishop
anybody who is anybody must use Frederick Street

whole day today he mumbling like Bull Boy
he say he have to drop a piece of pipe on her
because she moving out of her class
he catch her inside Woodford Square with the preacherman
the vagrant elect if you please!
so he wait till evening drop the metal mask
like a soldering iron firing sparks behind dark shades
he cut her off above Cipriani Statue

so she run down past South Quay
and slip into the room underneath the dark light house
where she still waiting for the moonshine
I just pass her on what used to be the rotten jetty
soaking in the Gulf of Paria
night turn into a bottle of iodine

but with all that the man love her
go down to The Drag
he making her a pair of sandals and a slaveband
she will go back to him
take that from a woman who know man
because my city like a sousou: she pass from hand to hand
Spanish man: English man: not all of them pay back but all
of them dip they hand: now she with the catchass craftsman
go down to The Drag go and watch him
he not making things for her alone
by tomorrow morning he finish your and my handbag
he there pounding out tomorrow's souvenir and talisman
watch him under the faint glow of the streetlight
all for love trying to go blind

so I not worried
all man does play the fool sometimes
she will survive
my city: she too sweet
she is one old dog: she is a bitch
more man than he can't kill that concubine

MARGARET ALIX JAMES
JAMAICA

Sidewalk Prophet

Jamaica,
of spreading green forest
running down the north and south
until the land's spray edge gives way to the sea;
emerald mango dropping island
pushing back the Caribbean sea
and striving up towards the day-long sun—
land of hills
convulsions of tropical growth
marking the sky's end—
I know you
for I have followed your twisting roads
to the centre
and have found a question poised
by shoddy houses
perched sideways on steep slopes;
have seen it repeated
in the broad-faced vendor
selling bunches of full-bodied oranges
from his heaped up booth
marking the highway's shoulder—
the question is echoing down Spanish Town Road
by the stick and zinc houses
tossed up
along the people littered streets—
with swollen eyes
dogs,
left on street corners by careening cars
are asking—
the look the children have,
sitting dustward, torn and skinny

query to despair what I am seeking
down the swept cane acres—
let us go and find an answer:—

the glow that is dawn
is rising from the night's floor—
behind palm trees
fisherfolk are dragging nets into the bay—
swollen arms of strength
swinging into the surf
and hear the voices of my people
singing—
knowing
fishing today is better on the morrow—
sun-clean
they are pushing back the tide;
songs are calling me
but eyes,
that are the children's,
beg me forth—
I have come to the set along coast towns
of shacks and white beaches
that are dropping hibiscus into the streets—
with plump water nuts
people tempting me out of the sun
into coconut shade
where faces are showing
it is not so urgent here
what I am seeking—
tasting sweet juice I see
where unpaved trails still lead into the bush
to find blocked-up houses—
the children are in falling away clothing
but they are laughing
and on the beach swimming
and selling the wound-up conch—
villagers pulling together

up the beach bringing in the boat
and playing,
they are running full out
along the strand—
and the one that was blind among them
is led to resting on a citadel of driftwood—
sightless eyes young with gravity;
(I have seen these blindmen before
knocking with sticks down pavements in Kingston
weary bundles seeking a lifetime of alms)—
seasoul messages
whispering down vegetation spilled ways—
I am seeing papaw coming golden
beside ackee
splitting black-seed tongues into showing—
and the breadfruit-coconut swells
banking up the yellow figged banana acres—
and the bent
falling fruit mango
drip sweet rounds into passages
we are following
back
to that we would answer—
Garden Eden land of cornucopia colour—
fruit lush and left lying
while empty-bellied children
in fourless button shirts
yell newspapers
on crush-people streets—
Kingston—
town of Mercedes Benz and Donkey Carts—
of mansions and run-down slums—
of big Diesel buses
dragging fumes
down the overflowing
orange peeled pig peopled
jammed car streets—

Curbside voice that is mine
telling of wound-rag headed women
with collapsed age men
on street-ends
shadow voiced, tambourine beating
for the circling crowd—
of rib-showing hunger boys
shoeless in doorways begging—
of multi-children girls
worked seven bob a day
(three milk worth and a bus fare)—
and we—
that out of many would be one
in self-led ways dividing—
deaf to sea-soul echoings
and Church loud "Doing unto others"—
and they—
poverty hungered
in the brimmed garden land
await, thick-swelled and massing
sprung-storm rage impending.

MEILING JIN
GUYANA

Strangers in a Hostile Landscape

When people ask me where I come from
I tell them this story.

I was born in the Southern Hemisphere
in the early hours of the morning
when night exchanges with day
and the light gains ascendancy.
What I have to say is brief,

so listen,
and make of it what you will.

When my grandmother was a girl,
paddle-boats crossed the river
from the town.
They brought all sorts of people
looking for
God only knows what.
Unspeakable riches, I suppose.
Instead, they found sugar-cane;
sugar-cane and mosquitoes.
They worked hard on large plots of land
dem call plantation.
Slaves worked the plantations originally
and when slavery was abolished,
freed slaves worked the plantations.
And when they were decimated,
we worked the plantations.
We were called,
indentured labourers.

My grandfather sailed on the ship
Red-riding Hood:
part of a straggly band
of yellow humanity.
They severed the string
that tied them to the dragon,
and we grew up never knowing
we belonged
to a quarter of the world's people.

A damn plot you might think.
Yes indeed, it was called,
colonial-ization,
spelt with a z.
The prince of the plot was called Brit Ain

but actually, he had many brothers,
Holl And, France and so on.
They fought each other occasionally,
but essentially, they were intent
on making themselves rich
thro' robbery and by brain-washing us.
They stole from us.
And at the same time,
sung psalms,
Such sweet psalms
and sung so well
wash the sweat and tears away.

After much time
and many millions of £s later,
they leased us back our land
through a deed called In-Dee-pendence.
This meant the land was ours,
but everything we produced,
was theirs.
We even got our own leaders:
men of great worth
to them.

Meanwhile,
another plot called Imperial-Ization
had worked its way through the world
and the earth was carved up
and re-aligned

Back on the Plantation,
we all fought each other
(with a little help from out side).
We squabbled over what would remain
when the In-Dee-pendence deed was passed
and the prince departed for home.

And so,
in the midst of the troubles,
my parents packed their bags.
They followed the general recruitment drive
to the imperial palace itself.

We arrived in the Northern Hemisphere
when Summer was set in its way
running from the flames that lit the sky
over the Plantation.
We were a straggly bunch of immigrants
in a lily white landscape.
We made our home among strangers,
knowing no one but ourselves.

When I was a girl
I lived in a box
that is why, my head is square.
I lived on jam
and played on the streets
I survived in this hostile landscape.

And when one day
I was chased from school
I turned and punched their teeth out.
Too harsh, you say,
I don't agree,
they would have smashed
my head in.

One day I learnt
a secret art,
Invisible-Ness, it was called.
I think it worked
as even now, you look
but never see me.

I was born in the Southern Hemisphere
in the early hours of the dawn
and when I die
I shall return
to a place I call my own.
Only my eyes will remain
to watch and to haunt,
and to turn your dreams
to chaos.

Judgement

My poems are all jagged at the edges
because I am a woman
who is jagged at the edges
I speak only of what I know.

Our memories are like broken glass
rubbing over smooth skin
the glass pierces the skin
and splinters there
blood oozes out and gives birth
to a cry: long and silent,
a cry for justice.
It shatters the universe.

Our memories are like jagged glass
they betray you
they speak of racism,
torture, deliberate genocide and rape.

This is our hell
but yours is the next.

The white leopard shall stalk the streets
devouring everything in its path
even the hand that spawned it.

People will run before it falling
amid the stench of rotting flesh.
We shall fall and disappear
but the earth shall refuse
to accept your carcass.

This is *your* nightmare.

Shame Shame
everybody knows
your name
and your crime

I am a woman
jagged at the edges
no longer able to forgive
I speak only of what I know
I know the universe
moves in a circle
so that your deeds
will find you.

AMRYL JOHNSON
TRINIDAD—TOBAGO

Watchers and Seekers

Squared
within the vast
and smaller angles
which line the walls
a gallery of eyes
which do not sleep
follow the range of sounds

which rise and fall
direct against their vision

Unchecked
the seekers come forward
stop
move on
come back to stand
in trance
before the scenes from
other people's lives
held in trust

Committed
to defence which stands
at a tangent to the
main field of interest
guards hold ground
seemingly oblivious
to the strength
of their shadow role as
surrogates for interaction

This is balance
of an intricate kind

Far Cry

Loud voices in the market place
barter with wily vendors in head ties
The ample hips sway to an awareness
of their sensuality
The touch and feel of their own
uniqueness
The memory plays tricks
and I saw them

coming out of the frightened jungle
still coming
coming

in chains of bewilderment
Lost insufficient souls
chained to the yoke which
would be their hallmark for centuries
erasing from the memory of future generations
the boundaries of a continent
beyond which
existence and death
had not seemed conceivable
and where they would be

coming with the impetus of the whip
still coming
coming

to fields where sweat never dries
and the question mark of selection
burns a charred and bitter trail
in your heart and understanding
Stranded in a horror where the spirit is trained
to cower and servility rewarded with a bone
Fear is the hunter which traps you
in your skin
They found themselves

coming to feel they were less than human
still coming
coming

to terms with the alien tongue
plunged into an alternative culture
The shut lips are a slash of silence
where anger is just one more sip
of the bile which foams ferments then
rises like a volcano you then swallow

The lava flows down to the stream of degradation
until one day you find yourself
                              coming with the first unsteady step
                    still coming
                         coming

through that tunnel of darkness
drawn to a light burning pale
Where it strikes with a faint glow
it hits the twisted gnarled labour
of your body distorted gestures of
freedom discredited by shapes which
still follow shadows of shackles on the wall
New found courage to turn from the power of
its glare habit of obedience and look at
yourself without feeling shame you start
                              coming to face the mirror
                    still coming
                         coming

to shake the dust from your elbows and knees
learn to stand straight before reaching down
to pick up the pieces with the will
to fit them together again trying hard to
accept there are sounds which time can
never fade
Moving with caution on the road to dignity
until your footsteps are firm and sure
You walk now with the lust to survive
and begin
                              coming to build your own foundations
                    still coming
                         coming

to lay the first willing stone of walls built
with nails which split wood
and knots which bend nails

Your house stands on unsheltered ground
where you scratch the soil which the
fowls search both looking for the same grain
of corn provisions of little
And the hills you are climbing are the same
hills you climbed but the timber on your back
makes your burden much less so you are
                    coming in search of more fertile land
            still coming
               coming

to find your children's hunger for knowledge
is the tool which is needed to chisel the future
The features of your destiny were carved in
reply to their search for a solution
Now the landscape of time has become your
dream of tomorrow and the violence which
erupted your vast solid earth to a clump
of small islands in the reshaping of
decades met you
                  coming through the line of coconut palms
            still coming
               coming

to where the cars speed on the new highway
The concrete houses with electric kitchens
leave small space for doubt
and much room for indulgence
in swimming pools and hot and cold showers
but the uneven pace left so many behind
that a few with a particular brand
of awareness came to show their people
another road which found them
                  coming towards the fire
            still coming
               coming

from the charred macabre chasms of consciousness
a sound like the scraping of dead bones
Too many lives too many fears
Too many years of too much suffering
Too much anger too much pain
blood and mutilated flesh
The strain and tension
wear of the centuries still tear
the islands can never lie still

                coming with hurricanes and earthquakes
          still coming
            coming

to bind the last few strands of a rope
bargaining hard for the clean break
and the laughter in the market place
ringing mocking and hollow is hushed
All heads turn to listen once again
to the sound which had them swaying their
hips but only one may feel the filaments
which tease the comprehension when she
finds herself

                coming when the drum mutation calls
          still coming
            coming

to gyrate on the streets
on Monday and
Shrove Tuesday

and be silenced
on Ash Wednesday

MARIE-ANGE JOLICOEUR
HAITI

Mon Ile

Avec des mots qui chantent
Avec des mots qui pleurent
Avec ce long cri sombre
A la limite des jours
Et toutes ces pénombres
A la taille des collines
Avec le tam-tam sourd
de nos plaines à matines
Avec des mots d'espoir
et d'autres d'agonie
Je te revois, mon île.

Avec des mots qui rient
Et le sang répandu
Avec le vent inquiet
psalmodiant les secrets
Avec la vague morte
Et un deuil de la lune
Avec le vaste champ
d'un coumbite d'étoiles
balayant l'infortune
des autrefois perdus
Je te revois, mon île.

Avec ton sable chaud
Et les rumeurs du soir
Avec les heures veuves
du tic-tac des pendules
Avec ton nom plus beau
qu'une perle de soleil
couchée dans l'archipel
Là sous le bleu du ciel

My Island

With words that sing
With words that weep
With that long somber cry
At the days' end
And all those dark shadows
At the foot of the hills
With the muffled drums
of our plains at dawn

With some words of hope
and some of anguish
I see you once again, my island.

With words that laugh
And blood spilled
With the restless wind
murmuring its secrets
With the stillness of the wave
And the grief of the moon
With the vast field
of toiling stars

sweeping out the misfortune

of lost yesterdays
I see you once again, my island.

With your warm sand
And the murmurs of the night
With the bereaved hours
of the clocks' tick-tock

Je te revois, mon île
Avec ton sable chaud
Avec la vague morte
Avec les heures veuves
du tic-tac des pendules.

LUCIE JULIA
GUADELOUPE

Fleurs de sacrifices

J'ai ouvert le livre d'un passé trop amer
Aux pages sanglantes des souvenirs vivants.
J'ai vu la nudité, la honte de nos pères
Leurs interdits profonds, triste et sombre néant.

J'ai capté le bruit sec du cliquetis des fers
Bouclés aux chevilles portant encore les traces.
J'ai frémi dans ma chair aux claquements dans l'air
De ces fouets cinglants marqueurs de tant de faces.

J'ai senti la douleur aux yeux de SOLITUD
Jalouse de Liberté, ce bien à conquérir.
J'ai vu bien de femmes, jetant la servitude,
Fleurs de sacrifices, à Baimbridge, mourir.

Fleurs-âmes des aieules que ne doivent faner
Qu'au ciel les étoiles arrosent de leur sang
Par les nuits de larmes tout au fil des années
Pour qu'elles repercent rouges à travers champs.

With your name more beautiful
than a pearl of the sun
nestled in the archipelago
There, under the blue of the sky,
I see you again, my island
With your warm sand,
With your lifeless wave
With the bereaved hours
of the clocks' tick-tock.

Sacrificial Flowers

I opened the book of a too bitter past
To the bloody pages of living memories.
I saw the nakedness, the shame of our forefathers
Their deep deprivations, the sad and dark void.

I heard the harsh clanking sound of irons
Chained to ankles still bearing their traces.
I shivered in my flesh at the crack in the air
Of the sharp whips which marked so many faces.

I felt the pain in the eyes of SOLITUDE
Jealous of Freedom, still to be won.
I saw all those women, casting off servitude,
Sacrificial flowers, dying, in Baimbridge.

Flowers—souls of our foremothers which must never fade
Let the stars in the sky water them with their blood
On nights of tears all through the years
So that they might spring again red across the fields.

Chancelante amère, j'ai choisi le chemin
Qu'à travers la forêt, Delgrès nous a tracé.
J'ai vu les balisiers qui fleuriront demain
Etendards vifs et fiers du haut des monts dressés.

Je me suis arrêtée à la source de vie
Où SOLITUD sentit ses entrailles bouger
Son fils, fruit qui jamais au soleil ne mûrit
Nous a laissé l'espoir, qu'un jour tout peut changer.

Faltering, bitter, I chose the path
That Delgrès traced for us through the forest.
I saw the balisers which will bloom again tomorrow
Proud, bright standards flying up on mountain tops.

I paused at the source of life, the spring
Where SOLITUDE felt her womb stir.
Her son, fruit that never ripened in the sun,
Left us hope, hope that one day everything can change.

Solitude is a legendary heroine in Guadeloupean history. Although
about to give birth, she took part in a famous Maroon struggle to resist
the French. Louis Delgrès was a Martinique military leader who died in
1802 in Guadeloupe fighting against (Napoleon's) troops seeking to
reimpose slavery which had been abolished after 1789.

BARBARA ALTHEA JONES
TRINIDAD—TOBAGO

West India

what can i say
of my people
ebony on ivory
walls of clime
hang green
upon the
lizards of
the sun and
shines the
cinnamon
zephyr from
the coral
knives of seas.
cantonese
from the punjab
yoruba
of the thames
benin bronze
gleaming in
a matadors
prized ear
to the champs elysee
of caribs
and arawaks.
christopher
you betrayed
my ancestors
and the foetuses
of their
civilization.
weep weep

into the
mediterranean
sighing limp
over the niger
where the blue
nile sees no
apparitions
and hears
not the white.
path winding
on the razors
blunt edge
of a moving
history
forbids me
to hate
your castanetted
pleas for
forgiveness.
fleur de lis
drenched in
blood
plantations
of suspended
souls fly
and leap
into
armadas.
teutonic
lions roar
devouring the
droppings
of the niger
and the
matador
swings
on the

fleur de lis
christopher
you betrayed
my ancestors
what then
can i say
for my people.
i can say
distilled
in a
conquistadors
thimble from
black blood
in the mango
wisdom of
confucius
cauldroned
with the
fires of
krishna
the palm trees
now view
venus and jupiter
under the
chimneys
which float
across the
bay into
sticks of
sugarcane
and the drums
beat out the
witches brew
of my
people.

JANE KING
ST. LUCIA

Sad Mother Ballad

There's a woman outside singing
of the wrongs that she endures
how a man has made her captive,
fettered, childed, kept, indoors.

One day she cries I'm young, I'm lovely
I'm on fire like girls must be
but the man of my desire
quenched it in a freezing sea.

And my thoughts are like sea serpents
snaking up to sink below
sometimes I still feel the beauty
then I rage because I know

that another alien creature
soul-thing wandering through space
has invaded my torn body
to suck its life from my embrace.

These space monsters have me shackled
bounded by these walls, their home.
He brings bread, and I must feed it
but I want to give them stone.

Want to savage them, to tear them
want to cram their throats with stone
maddened with these buzzing voices
wanting just to be alone.

Now my singing voice is shattered,
now my throat is raw and hoarse,
mermaid songs it once had uttered,
now it curses, harsh and coarse.

CHRISTINE LARA
GUADELOUPE

Vaudou

J'aurais damné mon âme
Aux puits de la découverte . . . .
J'aurais maudis mon âme
A tout savoir . . . Demain.

La vérité sa bat sur le tam-tam du temps.

Sombres murmures . . . d'outre-tombe
Sourdes rumeurs . . . d'outre-noir

Le tambour malsain résonne
De loin en loin

Par delà le noir
Et par delà l'espoir
De loin . . . en loin . . .

Ma conscience malade
Se révolte en douceur
Révolte d'une âme réincarnée . . .

Zombi des souvenirs . . .
Des âmes revenant du passé
Qui hurlent dans mon présent
Vaudou . . . Vaudou . . .
Vaudou noir . . .
Vaudou rythmé . . . Vaudou cruel
Vaudou du nègre qui s'enflamme
Nègre à tête . . . Tête de nègre

J'aurais damné mon âme
Pour oublier ces chants

Vodun

I would have damned my soul
at the wells of discovery . . . .
I would have cursed my soul
Just to know everything . . . Tomorrow.

Truth beats on the drum of time.

Somber murmurs . . . from beyond the grave
Muffled rumors . . . from beyond the blackness

The unhealthy drum resounds
From far far away

Beyond the darkness
And beyond hope
From far . . . and far . . .

My sick conscience
Softly revolts
The revolt of a reincarnated soul . . .

Zombie of memories . . .
Of souls returning from the past
Which screams into my present
Vodun . . . Vodun . . .
Black Vodun . . .
Rhythmic Vodun . . . Cruel Vodun
Vodun of the Negro who burns
Negro with a head . . . The head of a Negro

I would have damned my soul
To forget these chants

J'aurais damné mon coeur
Pour à jamais, tout ignorer.

L'histoire d'un peuple
Ne s'efface qu'avec le présent
De l'histoire du méme peuple.

O Vaudou . . . Mambo . . .
Ufasimba . . . Amawonbé
Indounas . . . Kwabulawayo

LOLITA LEBRÓN
PUERTO RICO

Poema del tiempo

Subsionando la vida del obrero
viven los opresores y usureros.
Con la sangre y sudor de los humildes
se erigen las pirámides al cielo . . .

Aquí los faraones tienen celo
del infinito Ser Alto y Supremo:
Los ladrillos por verdes ricos frenos
son puestos en los hombros pordioseros.

Es para hacer las torres de Babeles
de las corporaciones; es la traición
al ser humano noble y sin reveses.

. . . Hablan los tiempos de una gran fermentación
en donde el árbol de las casas crece . . .
y la Tierra en secreto se florece.

Un nuevo pan en día de primicia

I would have damned my heart
To forget all this forever.

The history of a people
Can only be erased with the present
The history of the same people.

Oh Vodun . . . Mambo . . .
Ufasimba . . . Amawonbe . . .
Indounas . . . Kwabulawayo

Poem of the Time

The oppressors and the money lenders live
by sucking out the life of the worker.
With the blood and sweat of the humble
they erect their pyramids to the sky . . .

Here the pharaohs are envious
of the infinite High and Supreme Being:
Bricks are put on the shoulders
of beggers by rich green obstacles.

It's to make the towers of Babel
for the corporations; it's the betrayal
of the noble human being and is irreversible.

. . . The times speak of a great unrest
where the tree of the houses will grow . . .
and the Land will secretly flourish.

On the day of the first fruit the worker's hand

está forjando la mano del obrero:
Es el capullo de su sol que abre
un alba nueva para el pobre pueblo.
Es el sol de redención que ya amanece
tras los verdes ladrillos del imperio.

Oye

Oye
me estoy comiendo un dulce
me sabe a medicina,
tiene química de Alderson.
Hay que curar, curar,
curar la herida
que han hecho a mamá.
La herida
que han hecho los yanquis
a nuestra HERMOSA TIERRA.
¡Ay, bendito! ¡no te rías
de mi lenguaje!
¿Tu has oido hablar
los matorrales?
Yo sé que las hojas de malangas
sirven de copas.
Oye
yo sé del lodo.
Con el lodo escribo
en estos capullos
florecidos en mi copa.
De lodo tengo los pies:
y como lodo florecido
en alimento delicioso.
Tiene raíces de hueso,
carne y alma,
tiene sol,
y está coronado

is forging a new bread.
It is the bud of their sun that will open
a new dawn for the poor people.
It's the sun of redemption that is now dawning
behind the green bricks of the empire.

Listen

Listen
I am eating a piece of candy
it tastes like medicine,
it has the chemistry of Alderson.
We have to cure, to cure,
to cure the injury
that they have done to Mama.
The wound
that the yanquis have made
on our BEAUTIFUL LAND.
Oh, blessed one! don't laugh
at my language!
Have you heard
the thickets talking?
I know that the malanga leaves
serve as cups.
Listen
I know of the mud.
With mud I write
on these buds
flowering in my cup.
I have feet of mud:
and like mud flowered
into delicious food.
It has roots of bone,
flesh and soul,
it has a sun
and is crowned

en todo su ser
del gran caracol.
Tiene un arroyuelo
de los océanos
todos pariendo frutos
para los senos.
El lodo es leche.
y en él crecen blancos lirios.
También florecen
espadas afiladas
para cortar los yugos
y hacer que salgan
cadenas y clavos.

CONSUELO LEE TAPIA
PUERTO RICO

Libre empresa

La explotación se ha supermecanizado.
Mordizco a mordizco tritura la patria.
La deforma
la veja
mutila su belleza
para que todo vestigio de riqueza
pase por sus mecánicas entrañas
al tonél de sangre humana
que extrae gota a gota
a niños, mujeres y hombres.
La explotación última moda es "transnacional".
Creen que el cambio del término, "internacional"
o "ultramar" duele menos.
No es que a ellos les preocupe
este dolor nuestro de cada día.
Es que nuestros sentidos (como el de las palabras)

in all its being
by the great seashell.
It has a stream
from the oceans
all bearing fruit
for our breasts.
The mud is milk
and in it white irises are growing.
Also sharpened swords
are flowering
to cut the yokes
and to break
the chains and the nails.

Free Enterprise

Exploitation has been super-mechanized.
Bit by bit it destroys our homeland.
Deforms it
disturbs it
mutilates its beauty
so that all traces of wealth
pass through its mechanical entrails
to the cask of human blood
which it extracts drop by drop
from children, women and men.
The latest style of exploitation is "transnational."
They think that changing the term, "international"
or "overseas" will hurt less.
It's not that they are worried about
this daily pain of ours.
It's that they think they can silence

creen acallar
durante una generación más
    (cada generación de explotadores vive para sí sola)
    cada generación explotadora, sí.
Los hijos que engendran, contados como "ganancias" o "pérdidas"
en sus computadoras
serán aprovechados para
que no muera la avaricia.
Todo tiene su uso "explotativo".
El amor se compra o se vende.
La pornografía se compra o se vende.
La policía, la Guardia Nacional,
la prostitución
la marihuana,
los cerebros
los talentos
se compran o se venden.
El amor maternal
con su día inmenso de ganancias
y el amor paternal
por si algo queda
tiene un día en el calendario.
Papeles que certifican
si uno es apto para el trabajo,
y todo género de actividad humana.
—abogado, juez, comerciante, dueño de cuchifritos,
médico, educador
—¡usted escoja!—es libre la empresa.
La pobreza se compra y se vende.
Hasta el bocado
que te han robado
se compra y se vende.
La humillación y el cinismo,
las máquinas y sus inventores,
se compran y se venden.
El agua, el sol, el aire
y como dice Juán (el mío)

our senses (like the sense of words)
during one more generation
        (each generation of exploiters lives only for itself)
        each exploitative generation, yes.
The children that they produce, counted as "earnings" or "losses"
on their computers
they will make good use of them so
that greed doesn't die.
Everything has its "exploitative" use.
Love is bought or sold.
Pornography is bought or sold.
The police, the National Guard,
prostitution
marijuana,
brains
talents
are bought or sold.
Maternal love
with its immense day of earnings
and paternal love
so if something is left
it will have a day on the calendar.
Papers that certify
if one is suitable for work,
and any kind of human activity.
—lawyer, judge, merchant, owner of fried snacks,
doctor, educator
—you choose!—the enterprise is free.
Poverty is bought and sold.
Even the morsel
that they stole from you
is bought and sold.
Humiliation and cynicism,
machines and their inventors,
are bought and sold.
The water, the sun, the air
and they show their

la simpatía con
"la sonrisa de caja registradora".
Si los hijos se quejan
los desheredan
Pero hay substitutos
que los ayudan
en su libre empresa
de recojerlo todo
sin dejar perder
ni suspiros,
ni sonrisas
ni sentimientos
ni cosas que antes se les daba
a la tierra gratuitamente.
De cuando en cuando
uno de ellos se vuela
la tapa de los sesos, o se la vuelan,
ante tan estúpidos conceptos de la vida.
Y la tumba, las flores,
el hueco en el cementerio
el servicio religioso
y las lágrimas de algunos cocodrilos
se compran y se venden.
Pero—pues siempre hay uno, es decir un "pero"—
lo que es incomprable e invendible
es la eterna potencialidad
de la humana felicidad
que cada nuevo ser
trae al nacer.
El futuro feliz
de la humanidad.
Los que llegan a desbaratar
los sinsentidos,
que son legión,
esos se enterarán
a través de libros
que pueden ser

sympathy with
"the smile of the cash register."
If their children complain
they disinherit them
But there are substitutes
that help them
in their free enterprise
to recover everything
without letting anything be lost
not sighs,
nor smiles
nor feelings
nor things that used to be given
to the land freely.
From time to time
one of them blows
his top, or someone blows it for him,
over such a stupid concept of life.
And the tomb, the flowers,
the hole in the cemetery
the religious service
and the crocodile tears
are bought and sold.
But—well there is always one, one "but"—
what is unbuyable and unsellable
is the eternal potential
of human happiness
that each new being
brings at birth.
The happy future
of humanity.
Those who come to destroy
those without feelings,
that are legion,
they will be found out
through books
that can be

de arqueología
ecología
antropología
antigüedades
enfermedades
calamidades
y hasta posiblemente historia.
Y esas máquinas que en sus manos
destruyen y son temibles
como dinosauros modernos,
como gigantescas girafas alimentadas por rayos gamma
recojerán el pensamiento noble
del humilde inventor
el que pensó en aliviar la faena
a que el explotador
sometía al trabajador
siendo ellas las futuras madres
que servirían a todos con recato y libremente,
como madres amorosas,
cavarán las tumbas
mordizco a mordizco
para los torturadores
del patrimonio humano
sin torturar la patria.
Aplanarán la tierra
y escribirán con un inmenso dedo de la girafa mecánica
el epitafio:
—"Yace aquí la Libre Empresa"—

about archeology
ecology
anthropology
antiquities
diseases
disasters
and even possibly history.
And those machines that in their hands
destroy and are fearsome
like modern dinosaurs,
like gigantic giraffes fed by gamma rays
will recover the noble thought
of the humble inventor
the one who intended to alleviate manual labor
to which the exploiter
subjected the worker
workers being the future mothers
who would serve everyone modestly and freely,
like loving mothers,
they will dig the grave
bit by bit
for the torturers
of human patrimony
without torturing the homeland.
They will level the land
and with an immense finger from the mechanical giraffe they will
write
the epitaph:
          "Here lies Free Enterprise"

AUDRE LORDE
VIRGIN ISLANDS

A Woman Speaks

Moon marked and touched by sun
my magic is unwritten
but when the sea turns back
it will leave my shape behind.
I seek no favor
untouched by blood
unrelenting as the curse of love
permanent as my errors
or my pride
I do not mix
love with pity
nor hate with scorn
and if you would know me
look into the entrails of Uranus
where the restless oceans pound.

I do not dwell
within my birth nor my divinities
who am ageless and half-grown
and still seeking
my sisters
witches in Dahomey
wear me inside their coiled cloths
as our mother did
mourning.

I have been woman
for a long time
beware my smile
I am treacherous with old magic
and the noon's new fury

with all your wide futures
promised
I am
woman
and not white

Coast Market

Hibiscus bright
the sun is rising over Christiansted.

Gouts of plastic litter
along the delicate shoreline
building shadows lengthen
but the sand is going away
sea corals hauled to build a pier
for cruiseships
a racetrack instead of a Junior High School
mud flows from the schoolyard fountains
our seniors fail or emigrate.

At sunset the ginger weeps
for what is growing
and the precious coin
we pay
for making
change.

The Woman Thing

The hunters are back from beating the winter's face
in search of a challenge or task
in search of food
making fresh tracks for their children's hunger
they do not watch the sun

they cannot wear its heat for a sign
of triumph or freedom.
The hunters are treading heavily homeward
through snow that is marked
with their own bloody footprints.
Emptyhanded the hunters return
snow-maddened, sustained by their rages.

In the night after food they may seek
young girls for their amusement. But now
the hunters are coming
and the unbaked girls flee from their angers.
All this day I have craved
food for my child's hunger.
Emptyhanded the hunters come shouting
injustices drip from their mouths
like stale snow melted in sunlight.

Meanwhile the womanthing my mother taught me
bakes off its covering of snow
like a rising blackening sun.

DELORES MCANUFF-GAUNTLETT
JAMAICA

The Last Child . . . Sold

Ancestors tears
filter the gauze
which bandaged time
and rivers of liquid salt
rust the nails
hammered by slavery

Ancestors whisper

through weeping wind
their tongues
too heavy for screams,
and the nothingness
within their souls
weighted torment on their hearts

Ancestors wrestle with sleep
in night clothes washed in sweat
and the patterns
brushed from bruise

Music instrumented their will
Sorrow masked in rolls of laughter,
refuge from pain
in the bosom of drums

Big trees with strong barks
gather and listen
to the wind of freedom
while branches bend
from bearing all memories

Rocks lament
on the well of strength
pooled by ancestors tears
which flow the river of hope
and the cascade of prayers
for the future that
misplaced
its past

AHDRI ZHINA MANDIELA
JAMAICA

In the Canefields

her mind has
become
my mouth . . . her
eyes & ears/my
teeth/my tongue
her feet now planted
in the ground
our stories unsung
except
in the canefields

no more messages in letters
home/no more
sleeping on sultry subways
no more chillblain-boned winter days
only sweet rest in the canefields.

my/aunt vida: lithe
bird of youth
took off to canada/surfaced
on a river called don, circled
under dundas bridge: docked
on an edge, lived on a ledge
like the pigeons
no news/papers caught the landing
no taxman demanding
a cut of her nearly unpaid/earning
bread, cooking &
cleaning, making beds
morning & evenings
tending kids she couldn't care about

shopped at *zellers*
woolco & *biway*
shipping a barrel home each holiday
time/pass/new season
spring/summer/finding new
reasons to stick around
no matter that it's underground

she was young, willing &
able/learning french
from food labels
polishing well her accent
for special events/a game
show or lottery winnings:
really only a dream,
in the beginning
& the frayed hopes end
caught her with the same
dream/spent/her bags stamped-
sent home by air/
presents
wrapped in gauze.

unpacked her luggage
in the canefields
buried her baggage
in the canefields: fell
dead/sugar/they said
filled the blood in her head

her mind
has become
my mouth/her
hands & foot & teeth
& tongue/
her tendrils

clinging under-
ground
our story now sung
in the canefields

LELAWATTEE MANOO-RAHMING
TRINIDAD / BAHAMAS

Full Moon Healing

Chaan Mama, Mother Moon
sits in the sky
veiled in her *sari,*
pale yellow, delicate,
like *sari* on fresh milk.
Veiled like a virgin
she sits and smiles.
She has never been touched
like how I've been touched by the one
who writes his name in stone
with my blood,
the one who smiles
when my nine year old pain
pours forth.

Chaan Mama, Mother Moon
sits in the sky;
pale yellow, delicate, she flirts
with silhouettes of coconut trees;
caressing shoulders of mountains,
she plays her girlish games.
She has never been touched
like how I've been touched by the one
who laughs in my hair as I cup

my nine year old virginity blood
in hands
that would not close,
in hands like baskets,
open-weave, useless.
Hands stained with blood,
shameful blood, a forbidden blood,
an incestuous blood. I promise
to keep the secret.
The secret I tie with rope;
with thick rope I bound up
this secret in my belly.
I scrub my hands
with lye but the blood
still flows and stains
blood-red my hands.
I scrub with lye
but the blood still stains
my hands.

Chaan Mama, Mother Moon
sits in the sky,
pale yellow, delicate veil,
tonight blushed with rose,
tinted with blood
I know she knows the secret
in my belly: I have been touched.
Touched by the one who writes
his name in stone with my blood.
The one who laughs
in my hair as I cup
my blood in hands
that would not close.

Chaan Mama, Mother Moon
sits in the sky.
Chaan Mama knows the secret.

She has seen this forbidden thing,
this incestuous love,
every Full Moon Night.
She has wept in darkness
for stains that would not wash,
for hands that would not stop
bleeding.

But *Chaan Mama*, Mother Moon
returns every Full Moon Night
and veils me and my sisters,
her daughters,
with love, pale yellow, delicate:
a healing veil
she spreads on the hurt
every Full Moon Night.

---

sari is, in Hindi, a Indian female garment. It is also cream that forms on
top of boiled fresh milk.

Woman Truths

Woman things
Of womanhood
In woman heart

I hide these truths
Under the bed
Among cobwebs
Encased in dust
Like panties soiled
With dry blood
Of first period

Flimsy nothingness

Stiff with dirty
Brown fear
Hidden for years
Forgotten in the
Dark musty corners
Of my mind

Spider like hands
That grabbed my
Groin my breasts
Tongue like leeches
Which clung to my
Lips in lecherous
Love clothed lust

But the bruised
Lips breasts groin
Could never mirror
The slashes
On my soul
The silenced anger
Of shattered trust

Until one day
I become brave
Daring pulling
The bed I
Expose the dust
Cobwebs and soiled
Panties of truths

The woman things
Which burst out
Of my woman heart
Shrieking shuddering
Wild like demons
In the sunlight
Of my womanhood

CARMEN NATALIA MARTÍNEZ BONILLA
DOMINICAN REPUBLIC

Canto a los niños sobre el tejado

Arriba contra el cobalto ensangrentado,
rostros y brazos y puños hacinados.
Arriba, contra las estrellas en asombro,
niños atormentados desafiando a los brutos.
Corazón contra balas.
Coraje contra odio.
Voces contra metralla.

Eran tan sólo niños.
Sencillos como las piedras
que arrojaron sus manos.
Niños atravesados por puñales de angustia.
Carne sin aire donde poder crecer,
sin aire donde madurarse.
Carne buscando aire en los tejados.

Arriba, muy más allá del suelo
erizado de duras bayonetas cobardes,
niños creciendo hasta alcanzar
la talla de gigantes.
Creciendo hacia el cobalto ensangrentado.
Creciendo hacia la luz.
Creciendo hacia la ruta de los mártires.

Eran tan sólo niños.
Claros como el rocío
que mojó sus cabezas
en la azul madrugada.
Niños llenos de sueños y de espinas.
Niños con la infancia atropellada,
bajo el pecho desnudo.
Niños sin aire, sin risa, sin palabras.

Song to the Children On the Rooftop

Up against the bloodstained cobalt,
faces and arms and fists accumulated.
Up there, against the stars in astonishment,
tortured children challenging the brutes.
Heart against bullets.
Courage against hate.
Voices against gunfire.

They were just children.
Plain like the stones
that their hands threw.
Children pierced by daggers of anguish.
Flesh without air to be able to grow,
without air to mature.
Flesh looking for air on the rooftops.

Up there, way above the ground
spiked by hard cowardly bayonets,
children growing up to reach
the size of giants.
Growing toward the bloodstained cobalt.
Growing toward the light.
Growing toward the route of martyrs.

They were just children.
Clear like the dew
that dampened their heads
in the blue dawn.
Children full of dreams and thorns.
Children with their childhood trampled,
under their naked chest.
Children without air, without laughter, without words.

Arriba, como banderas, como palomas.
Como nubes, como astros.
Arriba, con sus desesperadas piedras
y sus gritos anegados.
Arriba, con tu sueño y mi sueño
sangrándole la frente.
Con tu dolor y mi dolor llegándole al costado.
Desde arriba cayeron. Cayeron desde arriba
igual que frutos en sazón, desparramándose
en sangre y dulzura sobre el suelo.
Cayeron del tejado hacia el asfalto.

Eran tan sólo niños.
Cayeron como mártires.
No lloreis ni una lágrima
sobre el asfalto duro.
Llorad hacia el tejado,
hacia las estrellas en asombro,
hacia las verticales rutas, hacia la luz.
Llorad hacia el cobalto ensangrentado.

Zona de la libertad, ganada con su sangre.
Con tanta sangre y tanto llanto.
Zona de la libertad, ganada al odio,
ganada al crimen, ganada al plomo.
Zona de la libertad, ganada a los traidores,
ganada a los serviles, ganada a los cobardes.
Zona de la libertad, ganada para siglos
con ardientes claveles en la carne.
¡Zona de la libertad, ganada en los tejados
por los niños-gigantes!

Up above, like flags, like doves.
like clouds, like stars.
Up above, with their desperate stones
and their drowned cries.
Up above, with your dream and my dream
bleeding on their forehead.
With your pain and my pain reaching their sides.
From up above they fell. They fell from up above
just like fruits in season, scattering
in blood and sweetness over the ground.
They fell from the roof to the asphalt.

They were just children.
They fell like martyrs.
Don't cry even a tear
on the hard asphalt.
Cry up toward the rooftop,
toward the astonished stars,
toward the vertical routes, toward the light.
Cry up toward the bloodstained cobalt.

Zone of liberty, won with their blood.
With so much blood and so much weeping.
Zone of liberty, won from hate,
won from crime, won from lead.
Zone of liberty, won from the traitors,
won from the servile people, won from the cowards.
Zone of liberty, won for centuries
with burning carnations in the flesh.
Zone of liberty, won on the rooftops
by the children-giants!

MARIANELA MEDRANO
DOMINICAN REPUBLIC

El ombligo negro de un bongo

La abuela de ojos azules
       oreja negra retinta
Cuentos de cuco
        de cuco negro
historias de pañitos bordados
        sábanas blancas
        sexo virgen
        secretos de ollas y habichuelas
        —bastón mágico para cocinar la dicha—
Perdí la zapatilla de cristal en el polvo
y no vino el príncipe a acariciar las magulladuras
Luego fueron los cactus no los tulipanes
fue el encierro no la libertad
En las horas fijas de la guerra abuela
sus cuentos resbalaron por la piel
—negra no trigueña abuela—
—mujer no muñeca abuela—
Vino el trueno se desgarró en rayo sobre la isla
        —retumbando en el cuero—
    La carcajada del sarcasmo en los rizos
    bucles duros resistiendo químicos
    canturreando grifos y felices en el aire
La majestad tersa oscura negra bella
Le miré a los ojos
       geografía extensa e indivisible
Desde entonces soy una duda clavando interrogantes
       flecha aguda la lengua el cuerpo entero
Antes del óxido recobré la voz
       las pestañas sacudieron al tiempo
Soy heroína dentro de la jungla abuela
    veo la ronda
        el palmar

The Black Bellybutton of a Bongo

The blue-eyed grandmother
                blue-black ears
Used to tell tales of boogey men
                   of black boogey men
Stories of embroidered linen
                white sheets
                virginal sex
                secrets of pots and beans
                —magic wand to cook good fortune—
I lost my glass slipper in the dust
and the Prince did not come to soothe my bruises
Later it was all about cactuses, not tulips
It was about locking me in, not about freedom
In the time set for war, grandmother
your stories slid down my skin
—black, not olive, grandmother
—woman, not doll, abuela
Thunder came and lightning frayed the island
                    —beating the drum—
       Cynical laughter bursting in curls
       tough curls fighting chemicals
       singing kinkily and happily in the air
Black mellow dark beautiful majesty
I stared it in the eye
             a wide and indivisible geography
Since then I am a doubt planting questions
           sharp arrow is my tongue my entire body
Before the rust I found my voice
          my eyelashes dusted time
I am a heroine in the jungle, grandmother,
      I see the night patrol
             the palm trees

el fuego
Yemayá la del vientre de agua
el areíto
Yocahu—vaguá
Una negrita ruega por agua
elbaquini redobla las banderas
la cajita de colores abuela la olvidabas?
La mano pegada a su esqueleto
agita un ramito de Ruda
—no tema abuela—
es Lembá que le saluda bonachón.

JEANNETTE MILLER
DOMINICAN REPUBLIC

Utopía

Si nos piensan parcelar para placer de sus viciosos
no nos dejaremos
Si planean hoteles para bombearnos a sus jugadores
no los construiremos
Si Gulf—Alcoa—Grenada—Rosario—Falconbridge
son los nombres que compran
no nos venderemos
Si la droga la llevan a la escuela y la reparten en la
calle El Conde
no la aceptaremos
Si los políticos, los educadores, el propio Presidente,
los líderes de izquierda y de derecha fraternizan con ellos
nosotros no lo haremos
Si las agencias de publicidad y los editorialistas
entronizan la imagen de consumo
no la seguiremos
Si cada amanecer temido un adolescente tibio
aparece convertido en cadáver

the fire
Yemayá with her belly made of water
the areito
Yocahu—vaguá
A little black girl begs for water
the baquini multiplies flags
the box of many colors, did you forget it, abuela?
The hand closed on your bones
shakes a sprig of rue
—don't be afraid, abuela—
it's Lembá greeting you kindly.

Utopia

If they are planning to parcel us out so they can enjoy their vices
we won't allow it
If they are planning resort hotels to supply us to their gamblers
we will not build them
If Gulf—Alcoa—Grenada—Rosario—Falconbridge
are the names that they are buying
we will not sell
If they take drugs to the schools and distribute them on
El Conde Street
we won't accept them
If the politicians, the educators, the President himself,
the leaders of the left and the right fraternize with them
we won't do it
If the publicity agents and the editorialists
praise the image of consumerism
we won't follow it
If each feared dawn a warm adolescent
appears transformed into a cadaver

y su cuerpo delgado
sin conocer la vida
se cubre de rosas negras, violetas, rojas como la sangre
que tenía
nosotros gritaremos
Si el dinero es el precio del hombre
aquí no lo queremos
Si es necesario crujir, morder, roer, matar, brincar
culpar, desenmascarar
en contra de la sensatez de los cobardes
por sobre los consejos de nuestros vecinos
frente al mar invadido de acero restallante
sin armas, sin noches, sin días, sin cielo,
con sólo la culpa del cobarde
con sólo la herencia que llevamos de frente
con manos, uñas, dientes, lengua, vientre, alma, sexo, labios
ojos,
ánimo de siglos,
fuerza del pasado y del presente
herencia de este pueblo que ha luchado por siempre
contra todo el que quiere quitarnos la esperanza
¡óiganlo bien!
no nos someterán ni con napalm
porque nosotros.
sí,
nosotros
venceremos.

A medida que la oscuridad crece . . .

La tristeza como la tarde y estos pedazos de gente en el camino
donde tanto hemos puesto
después de los acordes falsos y la herrumbre.
Esta tristeza sin abertura ni hendija
sobre huecos de secas arboledas o de avenidas sin nombre.
Los dedos en continuo ritmo,
en continua cadencia de rito,

and his thin body
having never known life
is covered with roses, black, violet, red like the blood
he had
we will yell
If money is the price of man
we don't want it here
If it's necessary to crush, bite, gnaw, kill, attack
to blame, to expose
against the prudence of the cowards
over the advice of our neighbors
facing the sea invaded by cracking steel
without arms, without nights, without days, without a sky,
with only the guilt of the coward
with only the inheritance that we carry before us
with hands, fingernails, teeth, tongue, belly, soul, sex, lips
eyes,
the spirit of centuries,
the strength of the past and the present
the inheritance of our people who have always struggled
against all who want to take hope from us
listen well!
you won't subdue us even with napalm
because we,
yes,
we
will overcome.

As the Darkness Grows . . .

Sadness like the afternoon and these bits of people on the road
where we have placed so much
after the false agreements and the rust.
This sadness without an opening or a crack
over holes of dry trees or nameless avenues.
Fingers in continuous rhythm,
in continuous cadence of ceremony,

de muerte aglomerada en los atardeceres estrechos.
Residuos de las épocas augustas seguimos arriba como fardos
amontonados por el hambre y la muerte,
despreciando las líneas de esperanza mentira
en las tardes desesperadas del amor,
que continúa apareciendo
como si en verdad existiera,
mientras el ruido sigue,
el de la canción triste y sucia
forjada por alguien que como yo no olvida.

of death amassed on narrow dusks.
Remnants of illustrious eras, we keep rising like bundles
piled up by hunger and death,
disdaining the lines-of-hope lie
in the desperate afternoons of love
that keeps appearing
as if it really existed,
while the noise continues,
the noise of the sad and vile song
made by someone who like me doesn't forget.

MARINA AMA OMOWALE MAXWELL
TRINIDAD—TOBAGO

Caribbean Woman Birth Song

I am stuck in THE PASSAGE
I was different you see, about to be a breach
and so, it is (sometimes) difficult.
Thirty-how-much-years of labour
in
this archipelago of stones
still pebbles
peed on by history
fissured by Reagan
breaking . . .

My head is out (with a caul on my face)
But I had to be
torn
laterally
and horizontally
(like a crucifixion cross)
to get my big head out.

I am breathing
but it is difficult—
There is no obstetrician present at the moment
or camel
to free my shoulder, my body
stuck
sticking
in the PASSAGE, the passage, the middle
          PASSAGE, the passage

To be
obstetrician
in the very needed moment

You have to be
There
stimulating the movements
controlling the convulsions
pushing
only when necessary
Caressing the belly
Gently
turning the breach
Gently, gently as the head presents.

The amniotic waters rush over my face
And I have tasted (too often)
my own blood.

Someone, friends, cleared the clots away.
The mucus in my throat from the knotting tears
The umbilical which was wrapped tight
about my neck
I have removed.
But my navel (still unfree)
tugs
at an afterbirth
still
to be
expelled.

I remember
floating
in the amniotic
and the reverberations
and vibrations
that shimmered
my earliest waters
entered my sleeping soul.

I remember
both shac shac, shekkere

drum
and violin
and later the melting moments
of fusion—
drummed in my gut
injected in my chakra
ping-ponged
pinioned in my wing.

To come out of pebble—WHOLE
to BE
Born
healthy
is all
I ask/ed

To be free-ed
of the passage / tunnel
the passage, the passage, the MIDDLE passage, the
          passage
arms flailing
free
for I had already learnt the rudiments
of swimming.

The head is out
The terrible orchestration is past
It is to fly
(or cry)
now.

MOLLY MILLS
VIRGIN ISLANDS

Games

Wolf like I played the ageless game
of mock submissions to ritual
dominance

Throat bared, belly exposed, I learned
All games are not the same

Injured now, I retreat to heal
And smile, wolf like
Waiting for the kill.

Wolf Woman Dream

At times, through time, many times again
In mists I stand cloaked in grey

On a hill under a barren oak in
the night
Waiting

I watch myself, then enter and turn
feeling whole
One with myself and those who stand
beside me,
Brother wolves
Walking through my mind on
Silent paws
Waiting.

FLORETTE MORAND
GUADELOUPE

Reconnaitront-ils?

Vous des matins de mangos maraudés,
Vous des midis de fruit-à-pain—morue
Et vous qui soupez de contes créoles
d'air marin, de chant . . .
Vous des labours noirs;
Vous qui partagez avec l'attelage
le labeur, les tiques;
Vous des cases—nègres ou des ajoupas,
Vous des chemins creux pétris dans l'argile
par la spatule de vos pas vaillants,
Pauvres gens à pian,
Pauvres gens à chiques . . .
Citernes vivantes promises à la soif
d'affreux maringouins,
Proie de malaria,
Vous de marigots,
Vous des champs de canne basculant des mornes,
Vous des ports perdus rivés aux falaises,
Reconnaîtront-ils dans le sang du verbe
Vos nez écrasés et vos bras superbes?
Reconnaîtront-ils
Errant sur la plage des jours de soleil
Le cuir de vos mains
De vos mains crevées d'accusateurs calmes devant la misère.
Reconnaîtront-ils
Marchant vers l'amour
Vos humbles pieds, nus,
Marqués par la bouse verte des zébus . . .
Reconnaîtront-ils jamais dans mon cri,
Le temps d'un regard,
Votre vérité?

Will They Recognize?

You of the mornings of plundered mangos,
You of the middays of breadfruit and cod
And you who dine on creole tales
On sea air, on songs . . .
You of black labours;
You who share with the team of horses
the labour, the ticks;
You from the shacks—of blacks or Ajoupas,
You of the sunken paths moulded in clay
by the prints of your brave steps,
Poor people with yaws,
Poor chewing tobacco people . . .
Living vessels destined for the thirst
of frightful sand flies,
Prey to malaria,
You of the channels
You of the canefields toppling over in the mornings,
You of the deep harbours against the cliffs,
Will they recognize in the blood of the word
Your flat noses and your strong arms?
Will they recognize?
Wandering on the beach on sunny days
The leather of your hands
Of your hands blistered by accusers, calm before your poverty.
Will they recognize
Walking towards love
Your humble feet, bare,
Covered with the green dung of the oxen . . .
Will they ever recognize in my cry,
The time of a glance,
Your truth?

PAMELA MORDECAI
JAMAICA

Island Woman

I am a woman
of a fierce green place

my brows are mountains

tendrils of winding rivers
coil through my hair
short muddy black
with rapids and meanders

you may drink at the
springs of my eyes

I sing many songs
I am silent only
when the winds turn
upon me

sometimes for fear
I shiver

winds rumble in my belly
blow hot blow cool

paths vein my hands
well trod

Each year after the rains
I blossom

Kingdoms grow in my dark womb.

Poem

It grows inside you
like a child
its meanings secret
like the peal of bells
heard
and their music
long after

The rubric scratches
on the retina
the drums sound
but no spirit starts

Until
the fingers of the blood
assort the images
the wind remembers
sifting the long grass
the womb impulses
summoning
the beast

In a new testament
the Word

Protest Poem

An ache is in a man: towns do not ache,
nor ghettoes fester; the ravening gnaws
at bellies one-one; hurt is personal.
On the corner again and again see me
me sit with my needle and spoon, see me
puffin my spliff, see me splittin my mind,
see me teenager dead from the flows of your

your words that baptize me according to
Lenin and Marx: 'You are no one, no one."

Blessed be the proletariat whom
                we must mobilize
                we must motivate
                we must liberate
                we must educate
                to a new political awareness

Is di ole chattel ting again: di same
slavery bizniz, but dis time di boss
look more like we and him does be smarter.
Not a damn soul going mobilize my ass
to rass; dem joking. Any fool can read
Das Kapital: what is dat to di poor?

We the people propose
the abolition of you
and us: we propose
an acknowledgement
of our persons and
an alliance of poverty
we propose to share the little
that breeds on these
antilles one mango
to one mouth:
we propose to speak
your language
but not abandon ours:
we insist that you
understand
that you do not
understand us.
You may begin
by not shouting—
we are tired of noise.

On the corner again and again see
me stand with my pride and my children, my
quiverful, lot, my portion of life; see
me labour and wait; see me plan and scratch
dust for a yamroot, a corn, bellyful.

See me—
Look!
I am
here
I am
here
I am
here.

NANCY MOREJÓN
CUBA

Amo a mi amo

Amo a mi amo,
recojo leña para encender su fuego cotidiano.
Amo a sus ojos claros.
Mansa cual un cordero
esparzo gotas de miel por sus orejas.
Amo sus manos
que me depositaron sobre un lecho de hierbas:
Mi amo muerde y subyuga.
Me cuenta historias sigilosas mientras
abanico todo su cuerpo cundido de llagas y balazos
de días de sol y guerra de rapiña.
Amo sus pies que piratearon y rodaron
por tierras ajenas.
Los froto con los polvos más finos
que encontré, una mañana,
saliendo de la vega.
Tañó la vihuela y de su garganta salían
coplas sonoras, como nacidas de la garganta de Manrique.
Yo quería haber oído una marímbula sonar.
Amo su boca roja, fina,
desde donde van saliendo palabras
que no alcanzo a descifrar
todavía. Mi lengua para él ya no es la suya.

Y la seda del tiempo hecha trizas.

Oyendo hablar a los viejos guardieros, supe
que mi amor
da latigazos en las calderas del ingenio,
como si fueran un infierno, el de aquel Señor Dios
de quien me hablaba sin cesar.

I Love My Master

I love my master,
I gather wood to start his day's fire.
I love his blue eyes.
Gentle as a lamb,
I rub drops of honey on his ears.
I love his hands
that once threw me down on a bed of grass:
My master bites me and subdues me.
He tells me secret stories while
I fan his body, swollen with sores from bullet wounds
from long days of hot sun and pillaging.
I love his feet that have roamed and pirated
through foreign lands.
I rub them with the soft powders
I found one morning,
coming back from the tobacco fields.
He strummed his guitar and from his throat emerged
sweet ballads, as if born of Manrique's throat.
I longed to hear the sound of a marimbula.
I love his fine red mouth
that speaks words
I can't comprehend
Still. My language has never been his.

And the silk of time is now in shreds.

Hearing the old black overseers talking, I found out
that my lover
doles out whiplashes in the belly of the sugarmill
as if it were the hell of his Lord God
of whom he always spoke.

¿Qué me dirá?
¿Por qué vivo en la morada ideal para un murciélago?
¿Por qué le siervo?
¿Adónde va en su espléndido coche
tirado por caballos más felices que yo?
Mi amor es como la maleza que cubre la dotación,
única posesión inexpugnable mía.

Maldigo

esta bata de muselina que me ha impuesto;
estos encajes vanos que despiadado me endilgó;
estos quehaceres para mí en el atardecer sin girasoles;
esta lengua abigarradamente hostil que no mastico;
estos senos de piedra que no pueden siquiera amamantarlo;
este vientre rajado por su látigo inmemorial;
este maldito corazón.

Amo a mi amo, pero todas las noches,
cuando atravieso la vereda florida hacia el cañaveral donde a
hurtadillas hemos hecho el amor,
me veo cuchillo en mano, desollándolo como a una res sin culpa.
Ensordecedores toques de tambor ya no me dejan
oír ni sus quebrantos, ni sus quejas.
Las campanas me llaman . . .

Mujer negra

Todavía huelo la espuma del mar que me hicieron atravesar.
La noche, no puedo recordarla.
Ni el mismo océano podría recordarla.
Pero no olvido al primer alcatraz que divisé.
Altas, las nubes, como inocentes testigos presenciales.
Acaso no he olvidado ni mi costa perdida, ni mi lengua ancestral.
Me dejaron aquí y aquí he vivido.
Y porque trabajé como una bestia,

What might he say to me?
Why do I live in this hovel fit for a bat?
Why do I serve him?
Where does he go in his fine coach
drawn by horses more fortunate than I?
My love for him is like the weeds that overrun my small garden
the only possession I can call my own.

I curse

this muslin robe he put on me;
these frivolous laces he mercilessly made me wear;
those chores he made me do late in the evening;
this language so hopelessly hostile I can't mouth it;
these breasts so hardened they won't be suckled;
this belly lashed by his age-old whip;
this unlucky heart.

I love my master, but every night,
when I go down the flower-lined path toward the canefield where
we secretly make love,
I see myself knife in hand, flaying him like an innocent calf.

Deafening drumbeats now drown
his cries, his struggle.
The bells from the sugar mill are calling me . . .

Black Woman

I can still smell the spray of the sea they made me cross
I don't remember the night.
Not even the ocean itself could remember it.
But I still remember the first gull I saw in the distance.
The high clouds were there above like innocent witnesses.
I have not forgotten my lost coast, nor my ancestral language.
They brought me here and here I have lived.
And because I worked like a beast

aquí volví a nacer.
A cuánta epopeya mandinga intenté recurrir.

                                              Me rebelé

Su Merced me compró en una plaza.
Bordé la casaca de Su Merced y un hijo macho le parí.
Mi hijo no tuvo nombre.
Y Su Merced, murió a manos de un impecable *lord* inglés.

                                              Anduve.

Esta es la tierra donde padecí bocabajos y azotes.
Bogué a lo largo de todos sus ríos.
Bajo su sol sembré, recolecté y las cosechas no comí.
Por casa tuve un barracón.
Yo misma traje piedras para edificarlo,
pero canté al natural compás de los pájaros nacionales.

                                              Me sublevé.

En esta misma tierra toqué la sangre húmeda
y los huesos podridos de muchos otros,
traídos a ella, o no, igual que yo.
Ya nunca más imaginé el camino a Guinea.
¿Era a Guinea? ¿A Benín? ¿Era a Madagascar? ¿O a Cabo Verde?

                                              Trabajé mucho más.

Fundé mejor mi canto milenario y mi esperanza.
Aquí construí mi mundo.

                                              Me fui al monte.

Mi real independencia fue el palenque
y cabalgué entre las tropas de Maceo.

Sólo un siglo más tarde,

here I was born.
I have relied on many a Mandigo epic.

I rebelled.

His Master purchased me in a public square
I embroidered His Master's shirt and bore him a male child.
My son had no name.
And His Master died at the hands of an impeccable English lord.

I walked.

This is the land where I suffered degradation and beatings.
I traveled the length of all its rivers.
Under its sun I planted and gathered crops I did not eat.
A slave's shack was my home.
I myself carried the stones to build it,
but I sang along with the rhythm of the native birds.

I rose up.

In this very land I touched the damp blood
and the rotting bones of many others,
maybe brought here like me.
I never again thought about the road to Guinea.
Was it to Guinea? To Benin? Was it to Madagascar? Or to Cape Verde?

I worked harder.

I strengthened my ancient song and my hope.
Here I built my world.

I went off to the mountains.

My real independence was the maroon hideout
and I rode with Maceo's troops.

Only a century later,

junto a mis descendientes,
desde una azul montaña,

                                    bajé de la Sierra

para acabar con capitales y usureros,
con generales y burgueses.
Ahora soy: Sólo hoy tenemos y creamos.
Nada nos es ajeno.
Nuestra la tierra.
Nuestros el mar y el cielo.
Nuestras la magia y la quimera.
Iguales míos, aquí los veo bailar
alrededor del árbol que plantamos para el comunismo.
Su pródiga madera ya resuena.

Renacimiento

Hija de las aguas marinas,
dormida en sus entrañas,
renazco de la pólvora
que un rifle guerrillero
esparció en la montaña
para que el mundo renaciera a su vez,
que renaciera todo el mar,
todo el polvo,
todo el polvo de Cuba.

alongside my descendents,
from a blue mountain,

I came down from the Sierra

to put an end to capital and usurers,
to generals and bourgeois.
Now I exist: only today do we have and create.
Nothing is foreign to us.
The land is ours.
Ours the sea and the sky,
Ours the magic and the vision.
My equals, here I watch you dance
around the tree we are planting for communism
Its harvest of wood is already celebrated.

Rebirth

Daughter of the sea water,
asleep in its womb,
I am reborn from the gunpowder
spread over the mountain
by a guerrilla rifle
so that the world might be reborn in its turn,
that the sea would be reborn,
all the dust,
all the dust of Cuba.

Madrigal para cimarrones

La cabeza y las manos colgadas, llameantes,
burlando el rastro del Perseguidor.
Los cuerpos sudorosos se lanzan a la manigua húmeda.
Qué belleza tan dura tienen sus corazones.
Sobre sus machetes, como sobre ramales,
anidan palomas y jutías,
y el tiempo de sol,
y el tiempo de luna,
y el tiempo de la voluntad
haciéndolos renacer como a niños,
como a dulces niños de una libertad ya conquistada.

Requiem

Como si fuera la manzana de Eva,
Grenada te ha tentado,
ranger de los infiernos
y desembarcas en su costa
harto de whisky y marihuana.
Ya Point-Salines te embiste,
ya la hiel de la noche te aguarda,
ya los brazos del pueblo
te enseñarán su fiel venganza.
El Mar Caribe reconoce tu porte.
El Mar Caribe reconoce tus mañas.
Tu casco sobre la sangre.
Tu bota sobre la arena.
Tus huesos sobre las conchas
y la nuca en el estiércol.
Tu boca, entre los palmares,
clama y aúlla en su saliva derrotada.
Ranger del mal,
tu vientre sirve de pasto al águila.

Madrigal For Runaway Slaves

Head and hands hanging, flaring
mocking the Slave Tracker's pursuit
The sweaty bodies dive into the swampland
What a hard beauty their hearts have!
On their machetes, as though they were branches
Nest doves and field mice,
and the time of the sun,
and the time of the moon,
and the time of the will
making them live again like children,
like the sweet children of a liberty already won.

Requiem

As though it were the apple Eve picked,
Grenada has tempted you,
ranger from hell
and you disembark on her shore
full of whiskey and marihuana.
Point-Salines has already struck at you violently,
now the bitterness of the night waits for you,
now the arms of the people
will teach you their faithful revenge.
The Caribbean recognizes your stance.
The Caribbean recognizes your cunning tricks.
Your helmet over the blood.
Your boot on the sand.
Your bones on top of the shells
and the nape of your neck on the dunghill.
Your mouth, among the palm-groves,
rages and howls in its worn-out spittle.
Ranger of evil,
your belly serves as food for the eagle.

GRACE NICHOLS
GUYANA

I Coming Back

I coming back "Massa"
I coming back

mistress of the underworld
I coming back

colour and shape
of all that is evil
I coming back

dog howling outside
yuh window
I coming back

ball-a-fire
and skinless higue
I coming back

hiss in yuh ear
and prick in yuh skin
I coming back

bone in yuh throat
and laugh in yuh skull
I coming back

I coming back "Massa"
I coming back

Night Is Her Robe

Night is her robe
Moon is her element

Quivering and alert
she's stepping out behind
the fields of sugarcane

She's stepping out softly
she's stepping out carefully
she's bending / she's stalking
she's flitting / she's crawling

Quivering and alert
she's coming to the edge
of her island forest

Now with all the care
of a herbalist
she's gathering strange weeds
wild root
leaves with the property
both to harm and to heal

Quivering and alert
Quivering and alert
she's leaving the edge
of her island forest

Skin-Teeth

Not every skin-teeth
is a smile "Massa"

if you see me smiling
when you pass

if you see me bending
when you ask

Know that I smile
know that I bend
only the better
to rise and strike
again

Dark Sign

Yet even now
the Gods of my people
grow cold, turning
with anger

I have not forgotten
them
I have not forsaken
them

But I must be true
to the dark sign
of my woman's nature
to the wildness of my
solitude and exile

Circles round the moon
I can feel

hurricane months
fast coming

can see

tempestuous gathering
her rains and winds around

her like howling children
can see

palms rooting closer
to the earth

Nanny

Ashanti Priestess
and giver of charms
earth substance woman
of science
and black fire magic

Maroonic woman
of courage
and blue mountain rises

Standing over the valleys
dressed in purple robes
bracelets of the enemy's teeth
curled around your ankles
in rings of ivory bone

And your voice giving
sound to the Abeng
its death cry chilling
the mountainside
which you inhabit
like a strong pursuing eagle

As you watch the hissing
foaming cauldron
spelling strategies
for the red oppressors' blood
willing them to come
mouthing a new beginning song
Is that you Nanny—Is that you Nanny?

This Kingdom

This Kingdom Will Not Reign
Forever

Cool winds blow
softly

in brilliant sunshine
fruits pulse
flowers flame

mountains shade to
purple

the great House
with its palm and orange
groves
sturdy

and the sea encircling
all
is a spectrum of blue
jewels
shimmering and skirting

But Beware

Soft winds can turn
volatile
can merge with rains
can turn hurricane

Mountains can erupt
sulphur springs
bubbling quick
and hot

like bile spilling
from a witch's cauldron

Swamps can send plagues
dysentry, fevers

plantations can perish

lands turn barren

And the white man
no longer at ease
with the faint drum /
beat

no longer indifferent
to the sweating sun /
heat

can leave exhausted
or
turn his thoughts
to death

And we
the rage growing
like the chiggers
in our feet

can wait
or
take our freedom

whatever happens

This Kingdom Will Not Reign
Forever

DALIA NIEVES
PUERTO RICO

de *En el diario asombro de lo humano*

Sobre este oficio
dije,
sobre esta profesión
con materiales
que no nos cuestan
que les cuesta a otros
subir la voz
volar montañas
y morirse dignamente
para nosotros poder hablar
bajar la voz
y ejercer el oficio
del poeta.

                 *   *   *

Los periódicos de mi país
se indignan
se retuercen
se muerden la lengua
cada vez que tienen que decir algo importante
los periódicos
—debo decir los mantenedores de la palabra requerida—
se extravían en las manos del trabajador
se estrujan
se engrasan las vocales abiertas de suspiro
y se lanzan a la vida del zafacón
después de revisadas las cómicas
los chismes
los empleos
los desempleos
los garaje sales

From *The Daily Wonder of Being Human*

About this business
I said
about this profession
made with materials
that cost us nothing
but it costs others
to raise their voice
to fly over mountains
and to die with dignity
so that we can talk
to lower our voice
and to exercise our business
as poets.

*　　*　　*

The newspapers of my country
get indignant
they squirm
and bite their tongue
each time they have to say something important
the newspapers
—I should say the keepers of the required word—
fall into the hands of the worker
they sell out
they grease the open vowels of a sigh
and they are tossed into the life of the trash can
after the comics are scanned
the jokes
the jobs
the unemployment
the garage sales

y las ventas especiales
de los miércoles
los periódicos
que mantienen silencio en mi país
no dicen cosas que los poetas hablamos
nunca leí en un periódico de esta clase
que el gobernador de mi país había asesinado
la voz de dos jóvenes
que iban a volar el silencio
nunca leí la emboscada del grito
el desahucio de las maderas
los pescadores encerrados sin mar
por ser pescadores
y querer su tierra
y querer su mar
no he visto letras formando palabras de verdad
sólo vemos cristos llorando sangre
cada vez que le atravesamos un grito al sistema
imágenes que hablan
—hijos míos
mantengan el silencio y la paz
que el final se acerca
y el mundo es de los callados
y de los humildes—
iconografías mal usadas
para usarse mal
a propósito
insistiendo en desbordar las gentes
a cobrarle un día de luto al día
por los crímenes que comete el gobierno.

*   *   *

Mi ciudad tiene un silencio
de ritmo
de voz escondida
tiene crucifijos
colgando en las paredes de los cuartos

and the special sales
on Wednesdays
the newspapers
that keep the silence in my country
don't say the things that we poets say
I never read in a newspaper of this kind
that the governor of my country had assassinated
the voice of two young people
who were going to explode the silence
I never read about the stifling of the cry
the eviction from the woods
the fishermen kept from the sea
for being fishermen
and wanting their land
and wanting their sea
I haven't seen letters forming words of truth
we only see christs crying blood
each time we cast a cry against the system
images that speak
—my children
keep the silence and the peace
because the end is coming
and the world belongs to the quiet ones
and to the humble—
badly used iconography
to be used badly
on purpose
insisting on going beyond the people
to charge a day of mourning for each day
of crimes committed by the government.

*   *   *

My city has a silence
of a rhythm
of a hidden voice
it has crucifixes
hanging on the doors of the rooms

santos escondidos
debajo de los matres en las casas
y niños llorando de hambre
en los cuartos de la esquina de silencio
Mi ciudad tiene un cerro
donde hay un aroma
de silencio volado
un sonido lento
de pasos escondidos
un ritmo de marcha
de fuego
una antorcha encendida
y un agujero
por donde sale el grito guerrillero
del silencio.

SOLANGE NININI
GUADELOUPE

Assez ! ça suffit !

Je suis la faim . . .
Mais je suis la peur !
L'effroi dans l'obscurité cachée !
Spectatrice muette de ma mère.
Ecrasée ! piétinée ! de coups et d'injures
Rouée !

Je suis de mes frères et de mes soeurs
Les regards,
A jamais gravés dans ma mémoire.
Vers luisants dans la savane obscure,
Tapis comme eux puis bondissants
A ces coups retentissants.

saints hidden
under the mattresses in the houses
and children crying from hunger
in the corner rooms of silence
My city has a hill
where there is an odor
of silence exploded
a slow sound
of hidden footsteps
a rhythm of marching
of fire
a lighted torch
and a hole
through which the revolutionary's cry comes
out of the silence.

Stop ! That's Enough !

I am hunger . . .
But I am fear!
Terror in hidden darkness!
Silent onlooker of my mother.
Crushed! trampled! from blows and obscenities
Thrashed!

I am with my brothers and sisters
The glances,
Forever engraved in my memory.
Glowworms in the dark savannah,
Crouched like them and then springing up
At these resounding blows.

Je suis dans le silence de la nuit,
Nos mains en transe . . .
Nos bras tendus pour parer . . .
" Baguettes à jazz " qui affolées
Voltigent impuissantes dans l'espace.

Je suis nos voix rentrées
Jamais entendues,
Du vacarme muet de nos :
" Assez ! ça suffit !
Assez ! ça suffit ! "

OLGA NOLLA
PUERTO RICO

Datos atmosféricos

En Puerto Rico las mujeres viven
una doble opresión:
la del imperio
y la del macho.
Me dirán que esto es cierto
de casi todos nuestros países
de América Latina.
¡Pero mucho ojo aquí!
Los puertorriqueños somos
ciudadanos de Estados Unidos de Norteamérica.
Viajamos con pasaporte norteamericano
muy verde, muy brillante,
se siente siempre nuevecito entre los dedos
Disfrutamos de grandes privilegios
como el dólar,
cupones de alimentos,
el seguro social,

I am in the silence of the night,
Our hands in trance . . .
Our arms held out to stop us . . .
"Jazz drumsticks" which crazily
Fly helplessly about in space.

I am our returning voices
Never heard,
From the silent uproar within us:
Stop! that's enough!
Stop! that's enough!

Atmospheric Data

In Puerto Rico women live
a double oppression:
from the empire
and from the male.
You will tell me that this is true
of almost all our countries
in Latin America.
But pay attention here!
We Puerto Ricans are
citizens of the United States of North America.
We travel with a North American passport
very green, very shiny,
it always feels new between our fingers
We enjoy great privileges
like the dollar,
food stamps,
social security,

salario mínimo.
Hemos eliminado el analfabetismo.
¡Este es un gran país!
¡Lo mejor de dos mundos!
El puente, exclaman, nos martillan,
entre las dos Américas!
Somos los únicos latinoamericanos ciudadanos,
en bloque,
de los Estados Unidos de Norteamérica.
Esto es notable, nos apuntan.
¡Nos hemos ganado la lotería universal!
Díganme entonces, podrían explicar,
¿Por qué nos duelen las espaldas,
arrastramos los pies
y el mal humor nos retuerce la lengua?
¿por qué los adolescentes no saben distinguir
entre la yerba mala
y la caña de azúcar?
¿por qué desconfiamos hasta de quien comparte
nuestra mesa
y aún el lecho nupcial?
¿por qué nos contemplamos unos a otros
como fieras enemigas
y entendemos el amor
como una forma de dominio?
¿por qué nuestros funcionarios gubernamentales
viajan semanalmente a Washington
para que les informen
qué carajo es lo que pasa aquí
y recibir las instrucciones pertinentes
con la cuota de pan prensada al dorso?
¿por qué nuestra vegetación
y aún el mar
a duras penas se levantan gimiendo de cansancio
bajo capas y capas de basura
y desperdicios químicos?
¿por qué consideramos

minimum wage.
We have eliminated illiteracy.
This is a great country!
The best of two worlds!
They forge the bridge for us, they exclaim,
between the two Américas!
We are the only Latin Americans who are citizens,
in block,
of the United States of North America.
This is notable, they point out to us.
We have won the universal lottery!
Tell me then, you could explain,
why do our backs ache,
why do we drag our feet
and why does our bad humor twist our tongue?
why do the young people not know the difference
between the bad weed
and sugar cane?
why do we distrust even those who share
our table
and even our nuptial bed?
why do we look at each other
like fierce enemies
and understand love
as a form of dominance?
why do our government officials
travel weekly to Washington
to find out
what the hell is happening here
and to receive relevant instructions
with the bread quota printed on the back?
why does our vegetation
and even the sea
rise up with difficulty moaning from weariness
under layers and layers of trash
and chemical waste?
why do we consider

en el fondo,
que aquellos que se esfuerzan en hacer bien su trabajo
son unos pendejos?
¿que lo ideal es vivir del Welfare?
Alto aquí.
Alto aquí.
Los funcionarios gubernamentales
están muy preocupados con la agitación obrera,
con el estancamiento de la economía
En Washington sospechan
que tal vez sea mejor
reemplazar estos funcionarios nativos
con un equipo un poco, aunque sea una fracción,
más eficiente.
A los actuales funcionarios puertorriqueños,
esa idea no les cabe en la cabeza.
Confían en el agradecimiento
de aquellos a quienes sirven.
¿Qué pasa aquí?
¿Qué pasa aquí?,
gritan, silban,
desgarran las sirenas el aire,
las bombas grandes fábricas.
¡Esto es un verdadero campo de batalla!
Inexplicablemente,
un barrunto nos muerde los talones,
aquí, en Puerto Rico, en,
ni más ni menos territorio de,
los Estados Unidos de Norteamérica;
¡ni más ni menos en la corteza cerebral
del mecanismo de control!
Inexplicablemente,
ese barrunto en formación,
ese murmullo de tiñosas aves que se cuela
hasta el lecho nupcial,
ya no puede ignorarse por más tiempo
En Puerto Rico las mujeres viven

deep down,
those who work hard to do their job well
to be fools?
that the ideal is to live off Welfare?
Stop here.
Stop here.
The government officials
are very worried about labor unrest,
about the stagnation of the economy
In Washington they suspect
that perhaps it would be better
to replace these native officials
with a team a little, although just a fraction,
more efficient.
That idea doesn't fit in the heads
of the present Puerto Rican officials.
They trust the gratitude
of those whom they serve.
What is happening here?
What is happening here?
they shout, they whistle,
sirens rip through the air,
bombs through great factories.
This is a real battlefield!
Inexplicably,
a north wind bites at our heels,
here, in Puerto Rico, in,
nothing more nor less than a territory of,
the United States of North America;
nothing more nor less than in the cerebral cortex
of the control mechanism!
Inexplicably,
that north wind forming,
that murmur of mangy birds that sneaks
into the nuptial bed,
can no longer be ignored.
In Puerto Rico the women live

una doble opresión:
¿triple dicen?
¿multiplicada y al cuadrado dicen?
¿Por qué entendemos el amor
como una forma de dominio?
Doble opresión, dos veces sometida
y doblemente y al cuadrado agente
de cambio.
Ya no diremos cual.
Sobra y basta escuchar:
¡Qué pasa aquí!
¡Qué pasa aquí!
y ver cómo se arrugan las frentes
de los burócratas de gobierno,
cómo la mesa de controles en la oficina
de Washington
prende y apaga la lucecita roja
DANGER ZONE
bajo la jurisdicción de
(¿error de cálculo?)
asuntos internos.

Los nombres de la diosa

Conocí eras extensa
en la escarpada sierra de Cataluña:
estabas rodeada de velas encendidas,
de muchedumbres de devotos.
Tu rostro era negro; tu traje era de oro
y eras perfecta.
Eras hermosa y poderosa como la tierra.
Un recuerdo antiguo me habitaba,
como si comprendiera la imagen de tu fuerza
por la herencia del cuerpo.
Ahora te reconozco en los altares
de Africa y Europa;
en las suaves, sensuales, iglesias del Caribe

a double oppression:
triple they say?
multiplied and squared they say?
Why do we understand love
as a form of dominance
Double oppression, twice subjected
and doubly and squared agent
of change.
Now we won't say which.
It's enough and more than enough to listen:
What's happening here!
What's happening here!
and to see how the foreheads wrinkle
of the government bureaucrats,
how the control table in the office
in Washington
switches on and off the little red light
DANGER ZONE
under the jurisdiction of
(an error in calculation?)
internal affairs.

The Names of the Goddess

I knew you were vast
in the steep mountain of Cataluña;
you were surrounded by lighted candles,
by crowds of the pious.
Your face was black; your gown was golden
and you were perfect.
You were beautiful and powerful like the land.
An ancient memory dwelled in me,
as if I understood the image of your strength
by the inheritance of the body.
Now I recognize you in the altars
of Africa and Europe;
in the soft, sensual churches of the Caribbean

canto tu nombre;
y cuando dicen Yemayá y me hundo
en las aguas del mar como en tu cuerpo;
cuando dicen Ochún voy y me entrego
al río y su corriente.
Sé que tu cuerpo es uno con mi cuerpo.
Sé que he vivido mucho;
me conozco vestida de serpientes;
me recuerdo guerrera de los griegos;
me recuerdo gritando de dolor
al parir el mundo.
El tiempo tiene tanto mundo dentro
y es tan sólo un hilo de la vida.
Por eso
con tus nombres construyo mi alegría,
por eso.

ANA NÚÑEZ MACHÍN
CUBA

Guatemala

Dicen que el corazón le duele de bananas,
de "United Fruit", de monopolios fríos;
pero no está asustada.

Su sangre se batió en 1954
contra las hordas de las fieras,
y las cenizas y el chicle y la moda "made in USA",
y el espanto y la garra del águila.

Y todavía la semilla de la revolución
está escondida en la tierra guatemalteca
como un corazón enterrado en vida
que anda sobre sus frutos, despertando.

I sing your name;
and when they say Yemayá I sink myself
into the waters of the sea as into your body;
when they say Ochún I go and surrender myself
to the river and its current.
I know that your body is one with my body.
I know that I have lived long;
I know myself clothed in serpents;
I remember myself a warrior of the Greeks;
I remember myself screaming with pain
upon giving birth to the world.
Time has so much of the world within
and it is only a thread of life.
For this
I construct my happiness with your names,
for this.

Guatemala

They say her heart aches from bananas,
from "United Fruit," from cold monopolies;
but she isn't afraid.

Her blood fought in 1954
against the hordes of beasts,
and the ashes and the chewing gum and the style "made in USA,"
and the threat and the claw of the eagle.

And still the seed of the revolution
is hidden in the Guatemalan earth
like a heart buried alive
that walks over its fruits, awakening.

En Guatemala
corren ríos de sangre subterráneos;
rugen sus llamaradas
como fieras palomas de combate,
y caminan sus héroes hacia la eternidad y la vida.
Y al fin, habrá de verse libre sobre el cielo y la tierra,
porque no está asustada.

Bajo las aguas de incontenibles cauces,
en su suelo de plátano
rompe la rebeldía fiera,
porque en definitiva,
pueblo con rifles, con uñas y con dientes,
pueblo entero de hombres sobre puños crispados,
saltará hacia los vientos con su bandera henchida.

Sobre su fértil nombre se alzará Guatemala.

Canto a Puerto Rico

De cenizas heroicas,
de cenizas cadentes como llamas,
de corazones mártires,
pujante, como un fiero ciclón de las Antillas,
resurge Puerto Rico.

Es la tierra explotada en manos de los yankis,
la tierra de los hombres de coco y de palmera,
la tibia tierra heroica de Puerto Rico pobre,
como un puerto olvidado en el centro de América.

Borinquen, tierra virgen:
las plantas extranjeras recorren tu dulzura
con botas y fusiles;
y van sembrando el llanto de tus nobles mujeres
envueltas en el luto que dejan sus zarpazos.

In Guatemala
run rivers of subterranean blood;
the outbursts rage
like fierce doves of combat,
and her heroes walk toward eternity and life.
And finally, she will be seen free over the sky and the earth,
because she isn't afraid.

Under the waters of her uncontainable riverbeds,
in her soil of plantains
the fierce rebellion breaks,
because definitely,
a people with rifles, with fingernails and with teeth,
an entire people with men their fists tense,
will leap toward the winds with their swollen flag.

Above its fertile name Guatemala will rise.

Song to Puerto Rico

From heroic ashes,
from ashes smoldering like flames,
from martyred hearts,
powerful, like a fierce cyclone of the Antilles,
Puerto Rico rises again.

It's the land exploited in the hands of the Yankees,
the land of men of coconuts and palm trees,
the warm heroic land of poor Puerto Rico,
like a forgotten port in the center of America.

Borinquen, virgin land:
the foreign plants run over your sweetness
with boots and guns;
sowing the tears of your noble women
wrapped in the grief left by the blows.

De todas las semillas renacen las banderas,
una aurora de luz, cruza tu frente mártir . . .

Esclava no, Borinquen:
simplemente esperando;
despierta, como un mundo que va hacia la ternura.

Tu corazón de oro, tus palmeras,
tu estrella que resurge, tu frente de paloma,
todo tú, Puerto Rico,
rico en sangre rebelde, en patriotismo alzado,
como un mar renaciendo.
Todo tú como un pecho que se da al sacrificio,
surgiendo de los ríos claros de Albizu Campos.

Esclava no, Borinquen de cenizas heroicas,
sino tierra en espera,
surgiendo de cenizas candentes como llamas,
de corazones mártires,
pujante, como un fiero ciclón de las Antillas,
como una voz gritando al mundo su esperanza . . . !

From the seeds the flags are reborn,
a dawn of light crosses your forehead, martyr . . .

Slave, no, Borinquen:
just waiting;
awake, like a world moving toward tenderness.

Your heart of gold, your palm trees,
your star that rises again, your forehead of a dove,
all of you, Puerto Rico,
rich in rebel blood, in raised patriotism,
like a sea being reborn.
All of you like a chest offered in sacrifice,
rising from the clear rivers of Albizu Campos.

Slave, no, Borinquen of heroic ashes,
but a land waiting,
rising from the smoldering ashes like flames,
from martyred hearts,
powerful, like a fierce cyclone from the Antilles,
like a voice shouting its hope to the world . . . !

SOLITAHE YASMIN ODLUM
BARBADOS

Bonnie's Poem

Amid
the safe hills
I walked,
A poet searching for
metaphors, for truths
in the untouched,
uncreated world
before me.
Driven by polemics,
politics and
poetics
I sat among the grassroot
part of their very lives
like the coconuts skillfully
opened,
soothing our thirst;
Those ladies of the Valley
head-tied, voluptuous
skirts caught
between the soft
hills of their thighs,
much used,
much abused,
fertile like banana soil.
I see Teronah
hiding woe
like the hard beads
in a shac-shac,
her broken ribs
freshly healed—
It was a man of the drums

The man of her heart,
who fired with passion
and rum
danced the drum
on her belly.
I watched them,
Madonnas of the Malaway
cheek-bones like
mountain ridges,
arched high
with poverty
and peasant
beauty.
Complacently washing
their lives away
in the Sarotte river,
that witness
of generations of women
washing,
beating their hardship on
the frustrated
stones . . . .
I marvel at their warm
humanity:
"Bon Jour dou-dou"
The sound rich
as river water
busying itself
about the rocks.

Now I walk through
another world,
descending the hills
into a Ghetto . . .
At first
a man plays
a single note;
a clear, pure, clean

note
A man on his pan,
then each man on each pan
in the Diamon' Steel ban'.
The notes
tinkle like laughter
scattered in the air,
And junkies halt to hear
men spill their guts
into the sensuous hollow
of a pan;
Notes clear
like the tears
of God himself
squeezing out
of this panyard,
this Ghetto
of human life.

Trapped
in the reverie of pan music,
pied-piper style
men gyrated to another;
the maestro, a dealer in death
sat indomitable,
mercurial,
flamboyant with idiosyncrasy—
looking around
the garbage dump
of lives accumulated here,
testimony of his life
should the stickfighter
falter
in the stickfight
with Chance.

"My Delilah,
ah like yuh, yuh know."

Eyes of a Ba' John;
hard, unforgiving eyes—
"Buh ah doan trus' yuh!"
for might was right
in this devil dance
and may the better man win,
"My life ain' nutten
tuh write about . . . .

Eyes of a father;
Raison d'être;
Softly, "Sis,
everyting ah do
is fuh muh kids.
'Ave fore kids an'
ah love muh kids, Sis.
Ah ehn like yhuh, have eddication,
Buh ah eddicatin' muh kids.
Dey mus' never be like me, No Sis!"

And I hear, spilling
like the voice of conscience
into my memory;
my own father
who came from a family
of barbers,
hand-me-downs and a poor
man's dreams;
His voice paternal and afraid:
"This chap is your friend?
Child, have you even seen
a junkie?
A junkie is the worst form
of life on earth,
a person, crying in agony
'cause he can't stop
himself from destroying himself!"

But father, you've never lived
in the Ghetto,
carried around like your birthright,
a ghetto of your own
in that void
people call your soul.
Your mother was a peasant woman,
feeding husband and eleven joys
from her pot of humanity,
with the simplicity of her peasant dreams.
His was poor, impoverished to her soul
struggling, sinning, alone
without even the comfort of simplicity . . . .

"Ah done tuh much, arready,
tuh much. Ah tek jail, Sis."
I look at those hands, rough
used hands, ugly
hands with a history . . .
"Ah tired mahn, ah tired,"
His face lined, weary,
"Ah doan tek no shit see,
I is a big fuckin mahn!"
The cry of the Warrior
wanting to be man
in a world
which pawns
your vulnerable balls,
and unmanned,
you must stand and smile.

I rose to leave,
he looked at me,
naïve poet
searching for beauty
in a Ghetto.

Unlike them, I could leave
and he said,
"Hey, tek it easy, eh Sis."
I nodded.

MARCELLE PEPIN
GUADELOUPE

Jeunesse Realiste, Jeunesse Folle

Sous ton regard éperdu de réves
Elle a éclaté la bombe germée
Depuis des antans, la frousse s'est prise
A ton cou, à tes jambes, à ton corps en transes
Et tu parles de soutien, de communiqués
Tu crois avoir fermé l'embryon-révolution
Malgré son rire démoniaque dans tes hôtels
Gavés de touristes où ma peau noire brille
D'un reflet d'ombre rare.
Dans tes bars feutrés aux coins de la ville
Où ma voix joue un air faux,
Dans tes magasins de luxe
Où mon âme vomit de malaise
Dans tes boîtes de ripailles
Où le poil du chien a plus de valeur
Que mon argent noirci
Dans tes bureaux complexes
Où j'enfante la mort
Sous ton regard d'ailleurs,
Dans tes restaurants
Où ma gaucherie s'étale comme le plat du chef
Et pourtant tes mains de candeur fouillent mes poches
Jusqu'à n'avoir plus de contenu
Ton état a bàillonné ma bouche de politique paradisiaque
Je traîne dans les rues en tes habits de théâtre
Mais je te chante cet air:
"N'OUBLIE pas de désamorcer la bombe de tes abus
La peur acculée remonte à la gorge d'un goût de révolte
Et son cri n'a plus de maîtrise pour bluffer, pour calmer
à toi de lutter de ma lutte, de trembler de ma peur
Contre ce serpent lové en ton sein

Realistic Youth, Foolish Youth

Under your eyes lost in dreams
The germinated bombshell burst
Long ago, fear grabbed you
By the neck, by the legs, your body convulsing
And you talk of support, of communiques
You think you have closed the embryonic revolution
In spite of its demonic laughter in your hotels
crammed with tourists where my black skin shines
With a rare shimmer,
In your muffled bars on the corners of the city
Where my voice sings an off-key tune
In your luxury stores
Where my soul vomits with discomfort
In your food joints
Where the hair of a dog is worth more
Than my blackened money
In your complex offices
Where I give birth to death
Under your eyes,
In your restaurants
Where my clumsiness is displayed like the chef's special
And still your candid hands search my pockets
Until they no longer hold anything
Your state has gagged my mouth with paradisiacal politics
I hang about the streets in theatre clothes
But I sing you this song:
"DON'T FORGET to dismantle the bomb of your abuses
Cornered fear seizes the throat with a taste of revolt
And its cry no longer can bluff or calm
it is up to you to fight my fight, to tremble with my fear
Against this serpent coiled in your breast

Si persiflant, si menaçant, las de détours
Et d'une gueule grande d'attaques renaissantes
QUI A COMMENCE?
C'EST LE RACISME LATENT HEURTE SUR LES
ECORCURES DE L'ILE"

So mocking, so threatening, weary of detours
And with a big mouth ceaselessly attacking
WHO STARTED?
LATENT RACISM STRIKING EVERY CORNER
OF THE ISLAND"

JOYCE PETERS-MCKENZIE
ST. VINCENT

Yes, Me Child

Your Lord is risen
indeed! Yes, me child,
risen on the wings
of *your* votes to
luxurious comfort
in hotel suites.
Remember the days
on the bridge, me child?
you in your drudging
clothes, dirty and smelly,
he in his washed-out
jeans, T-shirt and sling-backs,
rapping with you like
friend to friend,
quenching your thirst
in socialist style,
cool, cool so!

Now he busy, busy,
chasing fast planes,
(first class at that!)
his lounge suit and
his briefcase heavy, heavy,
. . . . just like
my taxes.
He change-up, eh me child?
hair slick-back nice, nice,
like backra own, and his
dark glasses make the
insignificant you
appear like a floating

lump of human waste.

Then hear him at the
conference tables, me child,
big talks fo so! and the
gathering applauds loud, loud,
standing ovation, me child!

And you,
what did you have
for breakfast this morning?
a promise that tomorrow
will be better than today,
but *that* tomorrow may
never dawn because

Your lord is risen indeed!
risen above your minimum
wage, the same one which
the supermarket sharks
rejected last weekend.
And now you scrunt in
the garbage with dogs
and rats, to appease
those growling worms,
and stay that gaping
"pot-hole" in your
aching brain.

NOURBESE PHILIP
TOBAGO

Discourse on the Logic of Language

English
is my mother tongue.
A mother tongue is not
not a foreign lan lan lang
language
l/anguish
  anguish
—a foreign anguish.

English is
my father tongue.
A father tongue is
a foreign language,
therefore English is
a foreign language
not a mother tongue.

What is my mother
tongue
my mammy tongue
my mummy tongue
my momsy tongue
my modder tongue
my ma tongue?

I have no mother
tongue
no mother to tongue
no tongue to mother
to mother
tongue
me
I must therefore be tongue
dumb
dumb-tongued
dub-tongued
damn dumb
tongue

EDICT I

*Every owner of slaves
shall, wherever possible,
ensure that his slaves
belong to as many ethno-
linguistic groups as
possible. If they can-
not speak to each other,
they cannot then foment
rebellion and revolution.*

WHEN IT WAS BORN, THE MOTHER HELD HER NEWBORN CHILD CLOSE: SHE BEGAN THEN TO LICK IT ALL OVER. THE CHILD WHIMPERED A LITTLE, BUT AS THE MOTHER'S TONGUE MOVED FASTER AND STRONGER OVER ITS BODY, IT GREW SILENT—THE MOTHER TURNING IT THIS WAY AND THAT UNDER HER TONGUE, UNTIL SHE HAD TONGUED IT CLEAN OF THE CREAMY WHITE SUBSTANCE COVERING ITS BODY.

Those parts of the brain chiefly responsible for speech
are named after two learned nineteenth century doctors,
the eponymous Doctors Wernicke and Broca respectively.

Dr. Broca believed the size of the brain determined
intelligence; he devoted much of his time to 'proving' that
white males of the Caucasian race had larger brains than,
and were therefore superior to, women, Blacks and other
peoples of colour.

Understanding and recognition of the spoken word
takes place in Wernicke's area—the left temporal lobe,
situated next to the auditory cortex; from there relevant
information passes to Broca's area—situated in the left
frontal cortex—which then forms the response and passes it
on to the motor cortex. The motor cortex controls the
muscles of speech.

THE MOTHER THEN PUT HER FINGERS INTO HER CHILD'S MOUTH—GENTLY FORCING IT OPEN; SHE
TOUCHES HER TONGUE TO THE CHILD'S TONGUE, AND HOLDING THE TINY MOUTH OPEN, SHE BLOWS
INTO IT—HARD. SHE WAS BLOWING WORDS—HER WORDS, HER MOTHER'S WORDS, THOSE OF HER
MOTHER'S MOTHER, AND ALL THEIR MOTHERS BEFORE—INTO HER DAUGHTER'S MOUTH.

but I have
a dumb tongue
tongue dumb
father tongue
and english is
my mother tongue
is
my father tongue
is a foreign lan lan lang
language
l/anguish
   anguish
a foreign anguish
is english—
another tongue
my mother
     mammy
     mummy
     moder
     mater
     macer
     moder
tongue
mothertongue
tongue mother
tongue me
mothertongue me
mother me
touch me
with the tongue of your
lan lan lang
language
l/anguish
   anguish
english
is a foreign anguish

EDICT II

Every slave caught speak-
ing his native language
shall be severely pun-
ished. Where necessary,
removal of the tongue is
recommended. The offending
organ, when removed,
should be hung on high
in a central place,
so that all may see and
tremble.

A tapering, blunt-tipped, muscular, soft and fleshy organ
describes
(a) the penis.
(b) the tongue.
(c) neither of the above.
(b) both of the above.

In man the tongue is
(a) the principal organ of taste.
(b) the principal organ of articulate speech.
(c) the principal organ of oppression and exploitation.
(d) all of the above.

The tongue
(a) is an interwoven bundle of striated muscle running in
    three planes.
(b) is fixed to the jawbone.
(c) has an outer covering of a mucous membrane
    covered with papillae.
(d) contains ten thousand taste buds, none of which is
    sensitive to the taste of foreign words.

Air is forced out of the lungs up the throat to the larynx
where it causes the vocal cords to vibrate and create sound.
The metamorphosis from sound to intelligible word requires
(a) the lip, tongue and jaw all working together.
(b) a mother tongue.
(c) the overseer's whip.
(d) all of the above or none.

The Grammar of Love

I never heard the word
love in my house;

it lived there though
a deaf mute

with a sign language
complex as my own.

I never mourned the word
love in my home;

I had learnt its declensions
of violent silence.

Byeri

Fang woman of the flying hair,
behind the plexiglass enclosure,
you sweat palm oil and copal;
or is it tears that create
a patina of grief on your body wood?

In the ordinary course of things,
I should have come upon you
as a child maybe . . .
on some ancestor's box of bark
guarding her bones, her skull.

What do you guard now
Fang woman of the flying hair,
who sweats palm oil and tears
for us, who lost the ordinary course and
now seek you at the Art Gallery of Ontario?

What bones, whose skull do you now guard,
but those of my future, present and past?
Fang woman with the flying hair,
your mouth stretched wide in a silent scream,
is that palm oil or is it your pores that weep?

A hair's breath millennium away from you,
my mouth stretches wide as yours,
in a scream that shatters the glass
and your complicit silence remains
to haunt my questions.

Guardian of relics, keeper of bones,
Fang woman of the flying hair,
you stand on my grave
and become what you once guarded.
You stand on my grave
while two tears of palm oil
creep slowly down my screaming face.

_____

*Byeri are reliquary figures of the Fang people in Gabon.

MARILENE PHIPPS
HAITI

Maneenee

Maneenee was queen of the coal kitchen,
standing within six square feet of soot,
in front of four pits glowing with embers
churning the bubbling bean sauce, beaming

the yellow kernels of her smile at the chickens
flapping in the loose ashes below, strung
together by the feet with sisal,
and their furious claws resembling the old

people's toe nails. She sighed as she sat
on a low straw chair, the heat-lacquered
columns of her black legs folded in a squat,
her soiled apron caught between her knees

forming a valley just below the wrinkled
mound of the belly, to sort out
peas, the good, the diseased, though all
grew round together in the same pod.

When she took off the flowered scarf she wore,
Maneenee's hair resembled rice paddies,
with traced avenues on her scalp that
glistened like the moist red earth

of Kenskoff Mountain in soft fog. The remnants
of frizzy white down were gathered
into inch-long, upright, puffed-up braids
which, in the darkness of the windowless

kitchen, seemed the luminous gathering
of her ancestors' will-o'-the-wisps, filled

with murmurs about the secrets of her strength,
joy, and the sweetness of the food she cooked.

Out For Some Bread on Flatbush Ave.

With open lips like a gray rose,
a cloud hung over the church
of St. Rose of Lima in Miragoane.
Sunday Mass . . .

> *Damn! That day is right there*
> *in front of my eyes!*

    . . . our prayers
went to heaven. God . . . We were
poor . . .
Faith was a stained-glass-window blue
in our eyes.

> *Where the hell is that bakery? I*
> *could die*
> *just looking for it!*

I could sing in those days!
I am sure my prayers went to heaven
too . . .

> *FUCK YOU TOO,*
> *the sidewalk is for everybody,*
> *what's the problem?*
> *I SMELL MAYBE?!*

That fat priest really startled us:
"Would the family of the old woman
on the beach, go out and get her!"

. . . NO! I am NOT talking to you.
HEY! So what if I'm talking TO MYSELF!
You don't like it? WHAT'S YOUR PROBLEM!?
Shit . . .

She had been gone for years.
With all this gelatinous green stuff and webs
of ocean mucus on her hair, undone,
her body, naked, my mother looked like
something the sea spat.

　　　Spat!

She had been underwater. People do.
And you don't have to wait till you are dead
to live in that cold world. *Voye mo amba dlo—*
send the dead underwater—just for a while . . .
should have believed her in those days
when she took me to those ceremonies.
Ha! What difference? She still would have left us.
The family listened to Spirits then.
That's why she had gone underwater—
following a mermaid who beckoned to her, really?!
"The Spirits pulled me. It's because
they love me, they pulled me down.
I did not know I was down—everything
was the same, I saw houses, trees, roads, people
walking, eating bread, talking to each other.
The Spirits taught me how to make baths to heal,
I learnt all about spells . . ."

OH SHIT! Sorry . . .
what d'you mean CRAZY?! Fout LOUGAROU!
That's right LOUGAROU! D'you look at
yourself LATELY!?
Goddamn WEREWOLF, get a comb in your
OWN hair!

. . . Wish my mother had taught me a few spells.
Too many people, clean those streets,
Get rid of some population . . .

> *I COULD BLOW SOME NASTY POWDERS*
> *OVER THESE New-York streets, GET RID*
> *OF YOU PEOPLE!*

For all these hours I spent listening to my mother,
what'd I learn?: "wash the stone the Spirits gave me,
don't you be sassy and disrespect it! Make
a bath with lots of flowers, basil, the kind
with large leaves and *monbin fran* and *zo devan*
and lots of Florida cologne. When people come to me,
I will caress it, talk to it and it will talk back."
Boy! Did I get scared the day I caressed it too
and the wind whistled in the breadfruit tree . . .

> *Scared! Scared! And HUNGRY too!*
> *where the HELL is that bakery, where am I?*
> *YOU scary, YOU ugly, not me! LOUGAROU!*
> *mpa peu'ou se moun ou ye—no, I'm not afraid,*
> *you people—you people, you too-goddamn-many*
> *people. My mother could take care of you people!*
> *A Mambo, yea, a MAMBO! Nine years*
> *she spent under water, nine*
> *NINE GODDAMN YEARS!*

> > . . . They pulled her down.
> They pulled her down. Did she ask for it?
> Pretty mermaid smiled. She wanted to get closer . . .
> Pulled her down. And what about us?
> And what about me?
> Maybe that's why she was mad at them.
> Still, she shouldn't have converted—"Jesus,
> I only want to hear Jesus"—shouldn't have
> ignored their warnings, shouldn't have. She'd still

be alive. Wouldn't have choked. Just like that . . .
wasn't even ill . . . Ooh I miss you Mama!
If you could see me now! I crossed over!
I was the lucky one. My roof is concrete
not coconut straw, I buy my food in supermarkets,
wrapped in cellophane, I stroll in underground malls.
Yet my body burns in this cold. Loneliness in a red coat.
But . . . I AM the lucky one. I crossed over . . .

NEW-YORK!

This stretch of pavement is my gray beach.
Where is that bakery? Let me sit on my beach . . .
right here

> *HEY! Get your hands off me!*
> *GOT A PROBLEM? What's your problem!*

                . . . I close
my eyes to see a small pool I can enter,
find my bodyshoreless, at ease . . . breathe.
I undress to go home . . . be home . . . aah, that's better.
Gray sand is wet and cold. I close my eyes
to let my family come to me . . . I close
my eyes to shut out the voices, screams, sirens . . .
I close my eyes to feel my body,
come close, my arms,
close, my shoulders,
close, my face,
close, my home, touch
close, my mother, close . . . close . . .

VELMA POLLARD
JAMAICA

British Museum and After

Guardian of the Great Tradition
those volumes stood
in sturdy black
and through their golden teeth of leaves
sent whispers down:
pass gently gently
touch me not
touch me not for I am holy

Guardian of a great tradition
those statues stood
remembering Egypt
and from the stone lips of the sphinx
the silent whisper
touch me not
and pass me gently
I am cold and I am lonely
I am freezing naked poorly
for I need the golden desert
need its parching on my stone

From the hollow of that sound
from the screaming of that rape
to the shelter of my nothing . . .

Then the voice of that other
took my hand in his invisible hand
and led me to the bed of the river
where little banks like dunes of sand
sit waterless in the river's lap
and over my head his inaudible voice:

this is the voice of the waterless river
this is the voice of the shallow peaks
these are the books of endless unbinding . . .

And the voice of his hand
held my hand firm and led me
to my timeless children
who played in their present
Tannique and Tungi
Kamau and Abenna

Show them your river
said his soundless voice
show them the dunes
the dry sanded bank-heads
the clear mountain trickle
that tomorrow will fall
white foam falls of beauty
let them play in this present
where the grass greens low
and the silt land is ready

And these books of endless unbinding
will fatten with the leaves of their reaping
and the seamless wide open wall sides
will green with the pages of their toil . . .
tomorrow belongs to the children.

Drake's Strait

Half-sunken mountains
or half-risen plains
you choose the metaphor
or truth
this humbling moment
while the boat

slices the blue
between volcanic
pellets (the king of Danes had named them)
in this Virgin sea

But what of Drake?
Why is this passage his?
except to note his passing pirating
from Tap Hus
to that sleeping Turtle
where his spirit still
in British English
over US coins
four centuries later
yet invites
Lord Nelson to come tumble up . . .

How like a toothless lion here
this Drake who with his
brother Hawkins
now mere names
put on our best designs
hobbles around
grand ancestor of terrorists everywhere
their job description
pirate buccaneer
naming hotels and beaches
teeming with those
who this time come
for other conquest
sun and sea and brown
shrouding their need
to conquer and to own.

MAGALY QUIÑONES
PUERTO RICO

La nueva gesta

Si Cervantes viviera en este fin de siglo
haría un Quijote guerrillero,
un individuo raro y peligroso, un barbudo siniestro.
Y si hubiera nacido en esta tierra pobre,
a orillas de esta América,
la leyenda hablaría de un líder campesino
o un citadino obrero, de los de machete en la manga,
uno que se llamara Juan o Pedro.
Y una mañana hecha de sol, toda hoguera,
poblada de bandidos mercenarios,
poblada de bandidos con metrallas,
hecha de salteadores y tecatos sonámbulos,
de esbirros militares en acecho,
el loco marginado, el héroe nuevo,
cruzaría amanecido las ciudades, vejado y esposado
como un vulgar galeote moderno.

Habría que comenzar . . .
Sin casa, sin frontera, hizo el pan con sus manos.
Sin dama, sin adarga, sin escudo, sin yelmo,
salvó sudando todo lo que era suyo y era mío,
no anduvo ni a caballo ni en carroza,
donde vivió, creció cuanto el alma tocaba,
su patria fue el valor y el sacrificio.
O habría que decir . . .
En sangre, no en granizo, el de figura triste, el elegido,
dejando una vez más en brazos de la incierta Fortuna
el devenir de un natural oficio,
partió desde un rincón de la galaxia
y llegó a nuestro mundo, al Caribe
y se internó tristísimo en zaguanes oscuros,
en selvas derribadas en luto, en poblados pobrísimos.

The New Epic

If Cervantes lived at this century's end
he would create a guerrilla Quixote,
a rare and dangerous individual, a sinister bearded figure.
And if he had been born in this poor land,
on the shores of this America,
legend would tell about a peasant leader
or an urban worker with a machete up his sleeve,
named Juan or Pedro.
And one sunny morning, the sun at full blaze,
inhabited by mercenary bandits,
inhabited by bandits with machine guns,
made up of assailants and sleepwalking junkies,
of military henchmen in ambush,
the crazy outcast, the new hero,
would cross the cities at dawn, humiliated and shackled
like a common modern galley slave.

It would have to begin . . .
Without a home, without a border, he made bread with his hands.
Without a lady, without a shield, without a helmet,
sweating he saved all that was his and all that was mine,
he didn't travel on horseback or in a carriage,
where he lived, he grew spiritually,
his homeland was his valor and his sacrifice.
Or it would have to say . . .
In blood, not in hail, the one with a sad countenance, the chosen one,
once more leaving to Uncertain Fortune
the future of a natural profession,
he departed from a corner of the galaxy
and arrived in our world, the Caribbean
and moved sadly into dark doorways,
into forests tragically felled, into poverty stricken towns.

Yo que lo conocí lo vi bajando como piedra en el río.
Yo que lo presentí lo vi retando al resplandor más fiero.

Y si fuera posible,
si la Poesía fuera el ojo de la lucha,
si quedara de ella la flor, el canto, el hueso,
América tendría una nueva gesta
y andaría en la boca de todos, firme como sus ídolos,
buscando el aire de su corazón,
despeñando enemigos como estrellas
sobre la vibración de la Palabra . . .

I who knew him saw him descending like a rock into the river.
I who sensed him saw him challenging a fiery blaze.

And if it were possible,
if Poetry were the eye of the struggle,
if the flower, the song, the bone were left from it,
America would have a new epic,
and it would be on the lips of everyone, steadfast as their idols,
searching for the air of their hearts,
throwing enemies like stars
on the vibration of the Word . . .

JENNIFER RAHIM
TRINIDAD—TOBAGO

Still Birth

Lying in the safe waters
of a Caribbean belly,
these islands beat out
their own rhythms
while they await birth signals
that will call them out
into a new beginning, until
opportunistic obstetricians
armed with conquest's forceps
invaded the sanctity of womb-
space, clamping iron prisons
around the necks of innocents,
forcing labour pains that
yanked them into a civilization

> not their own
> not their time
> not their way.

The pain of artificial labour
stretches across drum rolls of time,
while this unwanted surrogate mother-land
squeezes sugar-labour and life
from the blood and sweat of islanders.

This Mother crying for her
children, still feels the cold
steel grip tearing life
from her womb as forceps change
into the hands of children who
became monsters bearing the
triple six seal that reads:
Duvalier, Batista, Burnham.

She's waiting, this Mother
silent in her secret knowing
for the right moonface and tide
to begin the re-birthing of her
island children in their own time,
in their own way.

Haiti,
the contractions begin
the water bag bursts
crying freedom
Cuba,
the movement down
the passageway
taking deep breaths
the pain sharper, faster
Grenada,
we coming
reaching for the door
that will end one journey
and begin another.

Anticipating the life-cry
the Mother searches
her brain for a name . . .
Walter
Maurice

We still waiting.

Before Speech

Before the word

                                spoken
from the centre womb of being
there are only the pained cries
of silence

                                the anguished absence
of sounds playing upon sounds—
a music that can give meaning
to one yet unformed

Before the birth of speech
I am / am not myself
even with name

                                I am the one busy
with the business of trying to find
other ways of waiting
no longer able to bear the blows
of my tongue's unrooted lashings

I   must   speak
lest this tongue's rebellion
against / within the tight-lipped prison
of infancy where I hold it
in spite of / because of my desire
to possess the word

(and I know that)
when a tongue rebels
against its own self
a language is born
that sounds as hard   as death

The Felling of a Tree

When the air is a sharpened blade,
cutting nostrils clean like cutlass steel,
the bush-planters pass the sleeping houses.
Sometimes alone, sometimes in pairs,
they lumber up the mountain road tall-
tops pounding the asphalt smooth.

Sometimes I awake and follow them,
knowing they go beyond the road's end
into the depths of bearded trees,
where tallness is not neighbours' fences
and bigness is not the swollen houses
that swallow us all.

I follow—slowly—my thinking measured;
my steps behind clobbering boots, steady,
knowing that if I stay in neat clearings
I will never see, and I want to see the trees,
I want to hear their long silences speaking,
leaves whispering secrets in my starved ears.

I follow, drinking the air like water,
my steps a soft conversation with blades
that cut paths for themselves through asphalt.
I follow, the strength in my thighs a newness
that makes my feet sprout roots,
and I think: This is what tall means.

Just when my lips begin to savour my salt,
he looks back, and seeing me growing branches
draws out his cutting steel and slashes my feet,
since girls can never become trees.

Turning, I run down the mountain weeping,
weeping like leaves after lashings
from rain-forest showers.

GLADYS do REGO
CURAÇAO

Poem

M'a buskabu
den memoria di mi pueblo
graba pa mannan blanka
Ku leter preta
riba papel

M'a buskabu
den kurasou di nos patria
riba borchi
riba estatua
bida eterua p'esuan
K'a sobresali

M'a buskabu
den memoria di nos mama
plama mane chemene
den tur nachi
den tur skina
te ora m'a bin komproude
muhe
muhe
UNDA b'a keda?!

Poem

I have searched
through my people's memory
recorded by white hands
Words printed
on paper

I have searched
in the soul of my nation
the streetnames
the statues
eternal life for those
who excelled

I have searched
through my mother's memories
dispersed like soot
In every nook
and every cranny
until I understood well

woman
woman
what has become of you?!

SOLEIDA RÍOS
CUBA

Pájaro de La Bruja

1

El pájaro nació del filo de un machete.
Nada tiene que ver con el sinsonte
el choncholí o la torcaza triste.
Nació del filo de un machete
no de la hueva blanca de una pájara vieja.

Ni alondra he dicho
ni quetzal
ni el aura ansiosa tras las últimas huellas.
Vive en el canto de La Bruja.
            Allí es su nido.
Canta como los pájaros del mar y los del monte.
Arrea las mulas. Y en mal tiempo
vuela implacable sobre los guanos de un bohío
y entonces alguien tiene que morir.

De marzo a octubre el pájaro es culpable.
Si cae un rayo en medio de la palma
si se desborda el río
sí una décima viene lejanísima
con el aroma del último café
siempre—de marzo a octubre—
el pájaro es culpable.

2

Dicen que como fiesta mágica hace tiempo
unos compadres se vieron una noche
cerca del canto de La Bruja.
Que allí sacaron la enorme botijuela
que era un secreto de los dos

Bird of La Bruja

1

The bird was born of the blade of a machete.
It has nothing to do with the mockingbird
the woodcock or the sad ringdove.
It was born of the blade of a machete
not of the white egg of an old bird.

Not a skylark I have said
nor a quetzal
nor the anxious buzzard after the last traces.
It lives in the big rock of La Bruja.
        Its nest is there.
It sings like the birds of the sea and those of the mountain.
It harnesses the mules. And in bad weather
it flies relentlessly over the palm trees of a shack
and then someone has to die.

From March to October the bird is to blame.
If lightning strikes in the middle of the palm tree
if the river floods its banks
if a ballad comes from far away
with the aroma of the last coffee crop
always—from March to October—
the bird is to blame.

2

They say that like a magic festival long ago
some compadres were seen one night
near the big rock of La Bruja.
That there they took out the enormous jug
that was a secret between them

en nombre de los hijos.
Dicen que algo se puso en el lugar
donde la hombría se rompe, no se sabe.
Que halaron los machetes.

3

El pájaro nació en el último escalón
violento del corazón dentro del pecho.
Nadie lo puede ver
pero ha volado por todas las lomas de la Sierra.

De la sierra

No se había dicho de la Sierra
que es el altar de la sonrisa
que el viento nunca pudo desgreñar las lomas
cuando subía en la madrugada del sinsonte
que el carro de mulas y el grito del guajiro
chillaban su abstinencia
repartiendo el pan de pocos días
que la costa negó su sitio al cementerio
porque un yate descargó esmeraldas
que la palma arregló su peinado
cuando las barbas besaron la ciudad.

Ya de la Sierra
el brigadista su abecedario de Arma Nueva
la zafra del café
el onomástico de mayo en el Uvero
con las banderas en la loma del primer disparo.

Cuando se abre la ventana del sol
un niño su libreta en mano
salta de piedra en piedra el arroyuelo
ordena las flores del camino que pregona historias
sonríe allá en la escuela.

in the name of their children.
They say that something was put in its place
where integrity is broken, no one knows.
They say that they pulled out their machetes.

3

The bird was born on the last violent
rung of the heart inside the chest.
No one can see it
but it has flown throughout the hills of the Sierra.

From the Sierra

It had not been said about the Sierra
that it is the altar of the smile
that the wind could never dishevel the hills
when it rose up in the dawn of the mockingbird
that the mule cart and the peasant's cry
proclaimed their abstinence
sharing a few days' bread
that the coast denied the cemetery its place
because a yacht unloaded emeralds
that the palm tree straightened its hairdo
when the beards kissed the city.

Now from the Sierra
the brigadista's New Weapon the alphabet book
the harvest of the coffee
the May celebration in Uvero Park
with the flags on the hill where the first shot was fired.

When the window of the sun is opened
a child his notebook in hand
jumps from rock to rock across the stream
arranges the flowers along the road that celebrates history
smiles there at the school.

Entrevista

Aquí el sillón
la vieja abanicando los recuerdos.
El viejo que murió allá en la Guerra
cuando el machete aullaba rescatando
el vértice sonoro de la tierra.

Aquí también el pañuelito burdo
de todos los domingos,
el traje—tanto remendarlo—del día de las bodas.

El son en los ojos
aun cuando tanta muerte nunca los apagaron.
Las arrugas no caben en las manos.
El retrato mambí y todos los enseres
en el viejo baúl,
la última carta que llegó después
"no te sofoques, vieja
los tataranietos van a tener escuela".

Caray, el tiempo no se acuesta
mira que carreteras en la loma
y Fidel
y escuelas de ésas secundarias en el campo
y jovencitos rayando la guitarra
diciendo que la trova no se acaba.

Y hay que ver lo que suena el machete
en manos de Victoria.
Hay que ver lo que canta el gallo ahora.

Interview

Here the chair
the old woman fanning her memories.
The old man who died there in the War
when the machete howled rescuing
the singing vortex of the land.

Here also the course handkerchief
from every Sunday,
the suit—mended so many times—from wedding days.

The sound in her eyes
even when so much death never extinguished them.
The wrinkles don't fit on her hands.
The rebel portrait and all the things
in the old trunk,
the last letter that arrived afterward
"do not despair, old woman
your great-grandchildren will have a school."

Goodness, time does not rest
look what highways in the hills
and Fidel
and those secondary schools in the country
and youngsters strumming the guitar
saying that the verse is not over.

And you must see how the machete sings
in Victory's hands.
You must see how the rooster sings now.

ETNAIRIS RIVERA
PUERTO RICO

El velero vaporoso

Llevo un mapa de hoja para cruzar la vida
hoja amarilla de bordes rojos
que se dió a mi mano mientras pasaba
la isla es una hoja caída
de un árbol de estrellas

Espero la confidencia de las mariposas
alfombra de pétalos que trae el día
en el día una concha para escuchar al Caribe
una flauta marina para llamar al amado
sobre el Caribe caen hojas estrelladas
luego el viento trajo semillas y habitantes
luego por el bagua empezaron a llegar
malacaña de extranjeros

Llevo un mapa de hoja de constelaciones hecha
día venusino de arpas
y la luz roja que emana de aquel astro
y la orquídea blanca creciendo
en el territorio del corazón
melodía de las nubes por el transcurrir antillano

Tengo un mapa también de país colonizado
acá las mujeres trabajan duro
y sus hombres poco duermen
acá los niños
nacen a respirar sus días contaminados
playas invadidas, bases atómicas
radares para detectar los pájaros que viven
para salvar la tierra

Tengo un mapa de ríos por liberar

The Ephemeral Sailing Ship

I carry a leaf map to traverse life
a yellow leaf with red edges
that fell into my hand as I passed
the island is a fallen leaf
from a tree of stars

I long for the secrets of the butterflies
a carpet of petals that brings the day
a conch in the day to hear the Caribbean
a sea flute to call a loved one
starry leaves fall over the Caribbean
later the wind brought seeds and inhabitants
later they began to arrive by sea
a bad crop of foreigners

I carry a leaf map made of constellations
a Venusian day of harps
and the red light that emanates from that star
and the white orchid growing
in the territory of the heart
melody of clouds through the Antillean passage

I also have a map of a colonized country
here the women work hard
and their men sleep little
here the children
are born to breathe their contaminated days
invaded beaches, atomic bases
radar to detect the birds that live
to save the land

I have a map of rivers to be liberated

en el Caribe vivimos los que conocemos esta canción
en el Caribe tenemos malacaña de invasores
el árbol de este mapa crece indio y cimarrón
acontecen los días antillanos
sobre el vuelo esperado de una mariposa verde
fosforescente.

*   *   *

Sabemos que el viento viene del mar
y que las rejas carcelarias caerán
porque las haremos caer
bandadas de toda nacionalidad de pájaros
esperan al convite
el pueblo celebra diremos entonces
el ritual mayor
suene la danza de las islas libres

Saldrán los que en carnaval fueron arrestados
el amanecer distinto sobre las blancas arenas
iremos de toda ola en el Caribe
por la alfabetización haitiana
¡cuántas niñas nacerán para llamarse Lolita, Yemayá
velero vaporoso que asciende en la noche tropical
y liberada!
¡cuántos conucos sembraremos por cada compañero
vilmente asesinado!
fue también a la tierra a quien desangraron
los ríos recogieron su sangre
y cantaron una nana comprometida
los pájaros que estuvieron allí

Sabemos que el viento viene del mar
y sobre nuestro mar hay barcos invasores
buques de guerra constante en la bahía
canto porque estoy amando
en medio de la guerra contra mi pueblo
y mi canción es brava

in the Caribbean live those of us who know this song
in the Caribbean we have a bad crop of foreigners
the tree of this map grows Indian and Maroon
Antillean days befall
the awaited flight of a phosphorescent
green butterfly

*   *   *

We know that the wind comes from the sea
and that the imprisoning bars will fall
because we will make them fall
flocks of birds from all nationalities
are awaiting the feast
the people are celebrating, we will say then,
the greatest ritual
may it sound the dance of the free islands

Those who were arrested in carnival will be free
the clear dawn over the white sands
we'll go full surge ahead in the Caribbean
for Haitian literacy
how many girls will be born to be called Lolita, Yemayá
an ephemeral sailing ship that rises up in the tropical night
free!
how many gardens will be sown for each comrade
vilely assassinated!
they also bled the land to death
the rivers absorbed its blood
and the birds that were there
sang a dedicated lullaby

We know that the wind comes from the sea
and on our sea there are invading ships
ships of constant war in the bay
I sing because I am loving
in the midst of the war against my people
and my song is brave

Sabemos que el viento viene del mar
y que el zapato que calzas se originó en las manos
sustentadoras de algún hermano obrero
y por lo que mi hermano en algún campo del mundo sembró
nos alimentamos en las ciudades
que habitamos en la poesía de sobrevivir
a toda costa y playa invadida
y nos atrevemos a tanto
dígase que por las flores del Borikén
que por los niños y para que tengan un cielo
límpido libre como batey de juego
dígase que por las antillas
único y mismo pájaro volando sobre el mar
dígase que por la danza misma de la vida.

REINA MARÍA RODRÍGUEZ
CUBA

Cuando una mujer no duerme

cuando una mujer no duerme
la magia se ha regado entre sus pechos
y hay que temer a ese desvelo
a ese mito que comienza
entre el sueño y la oscuridad.
no habrá conjuros ni espíritus.
se está llenando de mieles el silencio
y ha vuelto otra vez al tiempo de sus pamelas
a reconciliarse con las nubes
y todo el aire tendrá el peligro de sus ojos
cazadores de estrellas.

anoche no dormí y te prevengo:
cuando una mujer no duerme
algo terrible puede despertarte.

We know that the wind comes from the sea
and that the shoe you wear was made by the nourishing
hands of some worker brother
and by what my brother in some field of the world sowed
we feed ourselves in the city
we live in the poetry of survival
on every coast and invaded beach
and we dare so much
say it's for the flowers of Borikén
for the children and for them to have a sky
untroubled and free like a playground
say it's for the Antilles
the one and only bird flying over the sea
say it's for the very dance of life.

When a Woman Doesn't Sleep

when a woman doesn't sleep
the magic has been sprinkled between her breasts
and you should fear her attentions
to that myth that begins
between sleep and obscurity.
there will be no spells or spirits.
she is filling herself with the honey of silence
and she has returned again to the time of her summer hats
to reconcile with the clouds
and all the air will contain the danger of her eyes
hunters of stars.

last night I didn't sleep and I warn you:
when a woman doesn't sleep
something terrible can wake you.

Emelina

de vez en cuando vienes por el barrio.
el pueblo que te escucha, de piedras y palmas,
comprende el mal que te volvió tan loca,
tan cuerda de sufrir,
tan desagarrada por el viento.

el mundo de mis negros
como tambor abierto a la noche
se oye tras de ti
y empieza a caer sobre la calle:
fantasmas de lamentos hacinados
barracones escapados a su entierro
cimarrones eternos
Ochún y Yemayá contigo se levantan
en los pisos fregados con tu cuerpo,
por las encías negras, penosas de los techos.
no hay rincón que no cruja con tu verso
mientras a la tierra vuelven con un beso
los que no fueron sepultados.

Emelina

from time to time you come through the barrio.
the town, of stones and palms, that listens to you,
understands the evil that made you so crazy,
so sensible from suffering,
so torn apart by the wind.

the world of my black people
like a drum open to the night
is heard behind you
and begins to fall over the street:
ghosts of accumulated grief
shacks escaped to their grave
eternal runaway slaves
Ochún and Yemayá arise with you
on the floors scrubbed with your body,
along the arduous black parapets of the roofs.
there isn't a corner that doesn't creak with your verse
while those who weren't buried
return to the earth with a kiss.

ASTRID ROEMER
SURINAME

zij zien ons vergaan als mislukte oogst
schudden de christelijke hoofden
wij zwijgen als velden
jammeren niet
gij hebt het gedaan
zien verbaasd elkaar in de ogen
hijgen in de smog van verval
Laten Wij Liefhebben
Laten Wij Liefhebben

trouble in mind cry me the blues sister
blus de hitte van mijn pijn
cover me spread your love all over me brother
hoofden vol vlechten en krullen
onthullen de zalvende schijn
stir it up stir it up people
laten we verstrengeld moisty en hot
samen de laatste plebejers zijn
we are the toughest we are the toughest
Laten We Nobelnaakt Maar Nooit Bang Zijn

be black and be proud
brult de panter in afrika
uhuru, jankt mijn ziel
white christmas lord a wonderfull white world
rinkelt santa claus in het westen
uhuru, jankt mijn ziel

they watch us go down like a harvest that failed
shaking their christian heads
we are silent as fields
we don't complain
thou hast done it
see the amazement in each other's eyes
panting in the smog of decay
Let Us Love
Let Us Love

trouble in mind cry me the blues sister
extinguish the heat of my pain
cover me spread your love all over me brother
heads full of curls and braids
revealing an unctuous appearance
stir it up stir it up people
leave us unto each other moist and hot
together the last ordinary people
we are the toughest we are the toughest
Let Us Be Naked But Never Afraid

be black and be proud
screams the panther in Africa
freedom, cries my soul
white christmas lord a wonderful white world
tinkles santa claus in the west
freedom, cries my soul

geen revolutie is volbracht
geen eeuw voorbij

reeds klinkt geen keten aan mijn nek
en zelfs het brandmerk is geen teken
want ik loop lieflijk in de ban
van wet en kerk
ik ben echt
mijn man zwaait met zijn rechterhand

wij zijn gelijk (ik draag zijn naam)

tijd is slijtage van bezwaar
zolang de was zweet in de zon en slaap
dag in dag uit het hart opwindt
staan rozen aan mijn schaduwkant
zijn nageslacht voert schijngevechten met de wind

alleen het haardvuur smoort in mij
geen slavernij gaat ooit voorbij
waar staat mijn winst
waar staat mijn vlijt

mijn hand maakt zijn bezit smet-vrij

(vanochtend vroeg ik een gast aan tafel
ik gaf gul melk
ik gaf gul brood
in het journaal van dezelfde avond sprong hij
eruit—mijn gast, maar dood
hoe kan ik miljoenen honger stillen hoe
kan ik miljoenen doden aan hoe kan
ik miljoenen moeders troosten)

geen revolutie is volbracht—geen eeuw voorbij
ik leg me bij mijn witman neer
en vrij

no revolution is accomplished
no century passed

no sound of the chain around my neck
no sign of the burn mark
i walk lovely under the spell
of law and church
i am real
my man waves with his right hand

we are equal (i carry his name)

time is wear and tear as a drawback
long as the laundry sweats in the sun and sleep
winds up the heart day in day out
roses are on my side
his posterity fights with the wind

only the fire glows in me
no slavery ever passes
where my profit stands
where my diligence stands

my hand makes his property stainless

(this morning i invited a guest to my table
i served milk freely
i served bread freely
in the evening news my guest
appeared, but dead
how can i alleviate the hunger of millions how
can i take millions of dead and how can
i comfort millions of mothers)

no revolution is accomplished—no century passed
i give in to the white man
and free

heel d' aarde is de mens gegeven
tot één een lap wond om een stok
toen waren natiën geboren en sinds
dien houdt geen oorlog op

waren ze wit te paard mensen met baarden
die het goud vergaarden met het mes op de
keel van roden en gelen van bruinen en zwarten
ontheemden die roepen: wij eisen ons deel

een ziel onrustiger dan water
zoekt her en der naar liefd' en rust
beklimt de levensboom der aarde tot
dat een godenhand haar plukt

hoort naar het migrantenlied
dat luide klinkt langs elke keerkring:
zoekt tot gij vindt—gegroet gij vreemd' ling
god schiep de mens kosmopoliet

heel d' aarde is de mens gegeven
tot één een lap wond om een stok
toen waren natiën geboren en sinds
dien houdt geen oorlog op

the whole earth has been given to peoples
men turned a piece of cloth around a stick
nations were born and ever since
the war has not stopped

they were bearded white men on horses
they took the gold with a knife at
the throat of the red, the yellow, of the brown and the black
displaced persons who shout: we demand our share

a soul more restless than water
searches everywhere for love and peace
climbs the earth's tree of life until
a goddess' hand takes her away

listen to the migrants' song
heard in every tropic
seek till you find it—greetings, stranger
god created the human cosmopolis

the whole earth has been given to peoples
men turn a piece of cloth around a stick
nations were born and ever since
the war has not stopped

NADINE ROGERS
BARBADOS

"When one chile die . . . an'ther one does cry"

Yuh know we eh Man yet,
Ah mean we eh Mankind yet at all.
Everyone ah we is still a chile,
Frighten an' hidin' from the world.
       Hidin' from Gorbachev & Reagan
       wondering who more mad than who;
       Ah' frighten 'bout if what dey
       say 'bout de year 2000 is true.
An' watchin' . . .
       Watchin' dem in sout' Africa
       bleeding an' hurting an' not free yet.
       Jus' like how we eh Man yet.
Den I does realise dat we eh
       no different from dem—
None ah we eh free yet!
Dem trap in Namibia
An' we trap in de World.
Dem trap in dey skin
An' we trap in we head.
       An' is dis dat make me get
       to see, dat de only difference
       is . . .
Dat when one chile die
An'ther one does cry.

CARMEN ROGERS-GREEN
ANGUILLA

Sarah Seh

Ah was ah happy woman—
At leas dats what I tought.
Ah had everyting ah could wish for,
Plus mi husban, George was sexy and smart.

But las week mi fren Sarah
Whisper dat di news was out:
While I busy earnin a livin
Mi husban busy romancin bout.

At fus ah could only laugh
An brag pon George loyalty.
But when ah reconsider, ah start fret
Cause George was always so sleepy!

Mi member di strange phone calls
An special Valentine card las year,
An ah swear ah was goin kill George—
An go prison—right den an dere!

Sarah sey, "Not so fas gal,
Wait, dohn murder di man
Cause husban wid rovin eye
Dem plentiful like san pon dis lil islan."

She know one obeah doctor
who cure all problems of di heart.
An ask how I tink her Robert
Come ti mek cookin an cleanin a art?

Ah was still a lil hesitant
When Sarah sey, "Gal dis is no lie

Is di same ting Paula usin ti control
Sweet Mout Bobby, di playboy!"

Well, when she mention Bobby,
Ah know it mus be true.
Bobby used to fall in love so!
Like how yuh ketch di commom flu.

So, ah give Sarah $1,000
Ti buy di compellance medcin.
But when ah get di obeah tings
Ah nearly dead, ah was so frighten.

Di snake oil and di frog oil green.
Di oil ah love mi long an strong
Look like mud—it tick an brung,
An smell so bad, it knock mi dung!

A yella spendtriff powder
Would mek George buy me jewelry bright,
An one slimy octopus oil
Would mek him hole mi tight-a-night.

"Sarah dis medcin cahn wuk.
If jus seein it mekin mi sick,
Den how mi ah get mi husban
Ti stay normal an drink it?"

Sarah sey, "Put six drops
each in two big nana dumplin
An no need ti worry yuh head, gal,
Dumplin an Caribbean man besta fren."

Di moon was a sight ti see dat night
An while George was busy eatin
Ah was chantin an doin a wicked obeah dance
Ti control he heart, ina di kitchen.

But George hardly eat two good mout fulls,
When he flare up wid a shout,
He swear di dumplins full a poison
Dash pass me, an outa di house.

Ah dumplin was still on di plate
But before ah could grab it up,
Dis big, ugly, dawg name Benji
Swallow di ting dung in one gulp!

Lawd, ah sorry ah listen to Sarah.
Time pass—after twelve o'clock.
Mi ah wonder if George still love mi,
An worse, if he ever comin back.

Ah was cryin an prayin,
When a soun disturb di night.
Twas comin from di bedroom door,
So ah rush in an turn on di light.

Ah reach out quick to embrace George,
When someting sof touch me.
Sarah was right, di obeah wuk
Twas di ole, mangy dawg Benji!

ALTHEA ROMEO-MARK
ANTIGUA

Tropic Dimensions

Tropic sun pervades,
its strong head smothers
like black smoke
of burning coal heap;
there is no escape.
Even throats seem to hold
thick air that chokes
in the midst
of dust evoked
by cars traveling
on red dirt roads.
Wheels churning rapidly
spit out gravel
and more dust
hiding those
who walk the roads
in a mist of dirt
which settles unto sweat
clinging to bodies.

On the road,
there are those
who brave the heat
to sell food fried
in brown fat that smokes.
Potatoes, plantains
and dried fish
lie in open trays.
They, too, are subject
to red dust
which coats bodies

inside and out
after food, sold,
is swallowed hungrily
and hurriedly
in a quick roadside feast.

There are those
who bear the burden
of heat,
walk aimlessly
with hands outstretched
with hope that someone
would pity their plight.
The blind and the cripple
remain in corners
and doorways
where they were left
in the morning
to battle the heat
between the shifting of shades
and are picked up in the evening
with coins jingling
in pockets patched many times over.

Sand-coated land
parch feet like peanuts;
the tar-coated streets
bear a heat
steaming into a noon-day mirage
which waves
like a curtain in the wind.
It puts the mind to sleep
and bodies succumb
to the hovering spirit of heat.
All is soon forgotten
on sweat-soaked pillows, mats,
sidewalks lined with perspiring bodies.

SEKETI
SURINAME

Poem

Mujercita caribena
Desde las Guyanas alumbrantes
Hasta las aguas infinitas de las mares azules
Cuantos lenguas sabes hablar!
Cuantos bailes sabes bailar!
Cuantos cantos sabes cantar!
Si no son tradicionales
Que sean al menos nacionales
O tal vez regionales
No me presente una opera en una noche de rumba afrocubana
No quiero nada del norte en la tarde de samba bajo el sol
de Brasil
Prefiero un reggae cuando la luna es Jamaiquina
Y necesito un calipso en las calles de Trinidad Tobago
No necesito "Made in England" durante vacaciones en Grenada
Me quitas el "Rock and Roll" cuando huelo lluvias Vicentinas
Mujercita caribeña
Baila kawina con la nigra Surinamesa
Canta la Cancion de una Guyanesa
Lucea con la Sudafricana por la solidaridad
Abrasa la Argentina por la fuerte amistad
Diga hermana a la guerrillera Nicaraguense
Diga Panameno al Canal de Panama
Libertad eterna a la Chilena
Mais para Guatemala para que no sea guatepeor
Mujercita Caribena
Si tus lenguas no sabes hablar
Y tus bailes no sabes bailar, ni tus cantos cantar
Perdoname que te lo digo! Pero asi no vas a triunfar

Poem

Dear Caribbean woman
From the shining Guyanas
To the infinite waters of the blue seas
How many languages you know how to speak!
How many dances you know how to dance!
How many songs you know how to sing!
If they aren't traditional
At least have them be national
Or perhaps regional
Don't give me an opera on a night for Afro-Cuban rumba
I don't want anything from the north on an afternoon of samba
under the Brazilian sun
I prefer a reggae when the moon is Jamaican
And I need a calypso in the streets of Trinidad—Tobago
I don't need "Made in England" during vacations in Grenada
Take away the "Rock and Roll" when I smell Vincential rains
Dear Caribbean woman
Dance the kawina with the black Surinami woman
Sing the Song of a Guyanese woman
Fight for solidarity with the South African woman
Embrace the Argentine woman for strong friendship
Say sister to the Nicaraguan revolutionary woman
Say Panamanian to the Panama Canal
Eternal freedom to the Chilean woman
Corn for Guate"mala" so it doesn't become Guate"worse"
Dear Caribbean woman
If you don't know how to speak your languages
And you don't know how to dance your dances, or sing your
                                                            songs
Pardon me for telling you! But that's not the way you're going to
                                                            triumph

OLIVE SENIOR
JAMAICA

Colonial Girls School

Borrowed images
willed our skins pale
muffled our laughter
lowered our voices
let out our hems
dekinked our hair
denied our sex in gym tunics and bloomers
harnassed our voices to madrigals
and genteel airs
yoked our minds to declensions in Latin
and the language of Shakespeare

> Told us nothing about ourselves
> There was nothing about us at all

How those pale northern eyes and
aristocratic whispers once erased us
How our loudness, our laughter
debased us

> There was nothing left of ourselves
> Nothing about us at all

Studying: *History Ancient and Modern*
Kings and Queens of England
Steppes of Russia
Wheatfields of Canada

> There was nothing of our landscape there
> Nothing about us at all

Marcus Garvey turned twice in his grave.
'Thirty-eight was a beacon. A flame.
They were talking of desegregation
in Little Rock, Arkansas. Lumumba
and the Congo. To us: mumbo-jumbo.
We had read Vachel Lindsay's
vision of the jungle

> Feeling nothing about ourselves
> There was nothing about us at all

Months, years, a childhood memorising
Latin declensions
(For our language
—'bad talking'—
detentions)

> Finding nothing about us there
> Nothing about us at all

So, friend of my childhood years
One day we'll talk about
How the mirror broke
Who kissed us awake
Who let Anansi from his bag

For isn't it strange how
northern eyes
in the brighter world before us now

Pale?

Amazon Women

Gardening in the Tropics, sometimes
you come across these strong Amazon
women striding across our lands—

like Toeyza who founded the Wori-
shiana nation of female warriors
in the mountains of Parima—of whom
the missionary Brett and Sir Walter
Raleigh wrote. Though nobody believed
them, I myself could tell a tale or two
(though nothing as exotic as the story
of Toeyza and her lover Walyarima who
swam the river disguised as a black
jaguar whenever he visited her). Now
we've got that out of the way let me
hasten to say I'm not into sensationalism,
I merely wished to set the record
straight by averring that the story
of Amazon women might have begun
because when the warriors went away
—to war or voyages—it was the
women who kept the gardens going
and sometimes if the men were not
heard from again (as occasionally
happened) they banded together and
took up arms to defend the territory.
So somebody—like Cristobal Colón
or Sir Walter Raleigh—could have
come along and heard these (marvellous)
tales of (fabulous) lands full of
(pure) gold and fierce (untamed,
exotic) women (you know how men stay!)
And the rest (as they say) is history.
Mark you, the part about Toeyza's
husband sending her and the other
women to gather cassava for a feast
while he ambushed and killed her lover
is true (at least, my auntie says so
and her husband's uncle's grandfather
told him as a fact—and he got it
from someone who knew). I don't know

about you but the part I find
disgusting is that while they were
away, the husband (a chief at that)
skinned and hung the lover up
in the women's hut as a lesson
to faithless wives. (Though if men
go around in jaguar disguise, what
can they expect?) If you ask me,
that husband got what was coming
(poisoned with bitter cassava juice
mixed in with the beer) though
I can't see what the rest of the men
did to deserve equal treatment.
But that Toeyza (with liberated words)
led all the wives in flight and they
managed (despite pursuit) to fight
their way across the jungle to the
heights and freedom in their own
nation which ever since has been
justly celebrated as the Land of
the Amazon. The best part (I hear)
is that they allow men to visit them
once a year. Boy children they send
back to the land of their fathers,
girls they keep to rear (though
I'm not sure I would want my girl
raised by a band of women outlaws
keeping company with jaguars). But
you see my trial! I'm here gossiping
about things I never meant to air
for nobody could say I'm into
scandal. I wanted to tell of noble women
like Nanny the Maroon queen mother
or the fair Anacaona, Taino
chieftainess who was brutally
slain by the colonists, or of
the Carib women whom the said Colón

relied on for navigation
through the islands. I hadn't meant
to tell tall tale or repeat exotic
story for that's not my style.
But we all have to make a living
and there's no gain in telling stories
about ordinary men and women.
Then again, when gardening
in the Tropics, every time you lift
your eyes from the ground
you see sights that strain your
credulity—like those strong
Amazon women striding daily across
our lands carrying bundles of wood
on their heads and babies strapped
to their breasts and calabashes of
water in both hands.

Gardening On the Run

I

Gardening in the Tropics for us
meant a plot hatched quickly,
hidden deep in forest or jungle,
run to ground behind palisade or
palenque, found in cockpit, in
quilombo or *cumbe.* In Hispaniola,
where they first brought me
in 1502 in Ovando's fleet,
as soon as we landed I absconded
and took to the forest. Alone,
I fell in with runaways who
didn't look like me though
(I took this as a sign) their
bodies were stained black (with

grey markings)—in mourning
they said, for the loss of their
homeland, else they would have
been painted red. The bakras
called them wild Indians, me they
called runaway, maroon, cimarron.
No matter what they called, I
never answered. As fast as they
established plantations and brought
millions like me across the sea,
in chains, to these lands, the
dread of mutilation, starvation,
transportation, or whip, counted
less than the fear of life
under duress in the Americas.
The brave ones abandoned plantation
for hinterland, including women
with children and others waiting
to be born right there in the
forest (many mixed with Indian),
born to know nothing but warfare
and gardening on the run. With
the children, no opportunity
to teach lessons was ever lost;
nothing deflected them from
witnessing:

Copena, charged with and convicted
of marronage . . . is sentenced to
having his arms, legs, thighs, and
back broken on a scaffold to be erected
in the Place du Port. He shall then
be placed on a wheel, face toward
the sky, to finish his days, and
his corpse shall be exposed. Claire,
convicted of the crime of marronage
and of complicity with maroon Negroes,

shall be hanged till dead at the gallows
in the Place du Port. Her two young
children, Paul and Pascal, belonging
to M. Coutard, and other children
—Francois and Batilde, Martin and
Baptiste—all accused of marronage,
are condemned to witness the torture
of Copena and Claire.

2

Some have said that, compared
to many, when my time came, I
got off lightly. The first time
they recaptured me they cut off
my ears and branded me with a
fleur-de-lis on my right shoulder.
I ran away again. The second time,
they branded me on the left side
and hamstrung me. I crawled back
to the forest. The third time,
they put me to death. Released
from all my fears now I feel free
to enter their dreams and to say:
You might kill me but you'll never
bury me. Forever I'll walk all
over the pages of your history.
Interleaved with the stories
of your gallant soldiers—
marching up the mountainside
in their coats of red, running
back (what's left of them) with
their powder wet, their pride
in tatters, their fifes and drums
muted, their comrades brutally
slain by the revolting savages

(who cowardly used guerrilla
tactics, sorcery, stones for shot,
and wooden replicas for rifles)
—you will be forced at least
to record the presence of their
(largely absent) adversaries:
from Jamaica, Nanny of the
Windward Maroons, Cudjoe and
Accompong who forced the English
to sign treaties; in Mexico,
Yanga and the town of San Lorenzo
de los Negroes; all the *palenques*
of Cuba; in Hispaniola, le Maniel;
the Bush Negroes of Suriname;
the many *quilombos* of Brazil,
including the Black Republic
of Palmares. And so on . . .

3

Although for hundreds of years
we were trying to stay hidden,
wanting nothing more than to be
left alone, to live in peace,
to garden, I've found
no matter what you were
recording of plantations and
settlements, we could not be
omitted. We are always there
like some dark stain in your
dairies and notebooks, your
letters, your court records,
your law books—as if we had
ambushed your pen. Now I have
time to read (and garden), I who
spent so many years in disquiet,

living in fear of discovery,
am amazed to discover, Colonist,
it was *you* who feared *me.* Or
rather, my audacity. Till now,
I never knew the extent to which
I unsettled you, imposer of order,
tamer of lands and savages,
suppressor of feeling, possessor
of bodies. You had no option
but to track me down and
re-enslave me, for you saw me
out there as your own unguarded
self, running free.

SISTA ROOTS
TRINIDAD—TOBAGO

The Great Escape

Fifteen million
Dead souls
     Alive
Never thought
They would
     Survive
Come back again
To clean the stain
     Left behind
Come back again
To heal the strain
     In your mind
Go forward again
And you will find
     Fifteen million
You'll see those slaves
Are not in their graves

EINTOU PEARL SPRINGER
TRINIDAD—TOBAGO

Freedom Child—Tilla's Lullaby

And as I rock you
gently
I will sing.
I will sing to you
of skies dawning
to the bright lights—
of hope.
I will lull
I will lull
your slumber
not to the hollow
sounding thuds
of lash
on raw black flesh,
not to the clank
of chains,
but to a roar
from throats
sounding freedom.
Sound freedom
into the ears
of generations,
pile edifices
to deeper freedom
truer freedom.

Sound freedom
won by Ogun's
reddened machetes
sound freedom
won in open war

in subterfuge.
And I will soothe
I will soothe
your sleep
with tales
of Toussaint, Dessalines
Cuffy, Cudjoe
Nanny and Boukman

I will show you
your ancestors
labelled warrior
and not victim.
I will teach you
a history of resistance.
Suck from my breasts
the will
to fight
the strength to
hope.

Suck from my breasts
my love.
It is a season
to bind
in
love

It is a season
to sow seed
plant fruit
spawn fruit
spawn nations
I will sing . . .
sing to you of
freedom

The Speech Band Song

Ah want to tell allyuh a story
about the ills in we society,
why young people feel leave out completely.
They not allowed to make a statement,
so they landing up on the pavement.
Draw you bow Mr. Fiddler.

Stop you bow Mr. Fiddler.
Is drugs and unemployment
incest, homelessness and lack of achievement
the education system so shallow
like it have no hope for tomorrow,
cause we leaders done give way we future,
with all whey they borrow.
Draw you bow Mr. Fiddler.

Stop you bow Mr. Fiddler
IMF, World Bank come like we leaders addiction.
To all we people they bringing affliction
they go once, twice, they get pain
still they wouldn't look for a different solution.
They only going back again and again.
Draw you bow Mr. Fiddler.

Stop you bow Mr. Fiddler.
And they keep talking bout youth and pregnancy
yet economic vultures come here
breed we and leave we
double standards and immortality
have so much sickness in we society
and we leaders still want respect from we!
Draw you bow Mr. Fiddler.

Stop you bow Mr. Fiddler.
Every day they talking bout youth being the future

yet all the society leave for dem is departure;
filling dey head with a foreign culture
not involving the people in development here
making we aliens in we own atmosphere
Draw you bow Mr. Fiddler.

Stop you bow, Mr. Fiddler
So what you expect, it must have explosion,
when people backs dem against the wall.
You setting a time bomb in motion
when you doh listen when we call and call
you bringing destruction on one an all
Draw you bow Mr. Fiddler

Stop you bow Mr. Fiddler
I beg you, teach we we history and culture.
The strength within we, leh we nurture
leh we love we Caribbean brother
cause is the same ship bring all ah we here
whether through slavery or indenture.
Draw you bow Mr. Fiddler.

LYNN SWEETING
BAHAMAS

Living on the Lee

Today the ocean took me
east against the tide,
past gabled mansions
the rum runners built,
past town houses and yards
naked of trees,
to the place where

the bones of Lucayans lay,
Lucayans who drowned themselves
so as never to die
in the pearl beds
of Columbus' Cuba,
their bones forever bleaching
in a sun older
than the oldest soul.

Clearly now,
I see you,
mooncolour
skeletons
alive,
inches
beneath the blue.
I see you now,
spirit dust in search of
bits of flesh and
black hair lost
among breathing coral heads,
piecing your bodies together
even as the wind
blows them apart
again.

From rain forests you came to a shallow sea of islands
and found them bejeweled, rich with life and the moon
spun round you and inside you and was born of you
as you were born of earth and sea's memory.
Searching for the lee you settled
secret coves, sacred inlets, gateways to the East
and open ocean, where the sun was always rising.

I remember you,
offering prayers of thanks
for every sweetwood taken,

accepting from earth and sea
only that which was painlessly given,
and your hair grew long as
wild cinnamon grew high.
You named these islands
by the nature of tides.

I remember you,
burying your dead
in dark watery caves,
birthing in the woodland
inheritors of your knowing,
and your songs were like
the waves that whispered and crashed
according to the wind
and a goddess' whim.

You waited
for the coming of a people
who believed
you had no religion,
who razed to limestone
all you keepers of the Cacique.

The successor to the Chief
was not his son
but the eldest son of the eldest sister
or other sons of that sister.
Failing that, the sons of the other sisters inherited.
If there were none
the brother inherited.
The son of the Cacique
was the last choice.

Last cacique,
believers in the Motherblood,
when drums were sounding

foretelling your apocalypse,
did you understand?
When they cracked the horizon
did you think only of what you could give,
never what would be taken from you?

This sandstone zemi,
this web of cotton,
this wide-winged parrot
starving to death
on a bloody deck,
cannot be the end of you.

I see you now,
in the year of a lord
not your own,
greeting the gods
with hair like yellow
sea grass flying
and eyes cold
as locust lobster crawling
from the belly
of a rotten blue hole.
I see you clearly,
falling before the men
who left you ravaged
like the heart
of the last virgin forest.
Clearly, I see you,
dispossessed and enslaved,
raping, at the point of a knife,
the ocean floor, your mother,
until your final
earthly breath.
I see you
dead
but never

crying.

Because you were not
truly dead.

When the last son drowned
on Fernandina's weeping reef,
and every daughter flung herself
from the farthest bluff,
and every island was a shallow grave,
strange silence trembled
in the heart of the rock,
and the killers fled
in fear of something
they could not kill nor keep
like a trophy.

Today the heart
of the rock
still trembles.
Today is the day
of your resurrection,
from the ground we walk on,
from the sandy flats we sail,
from beyond the pages
of histories written by people born
to pretend all lost peoples
deserved to be lost.

Here, between megalith hotels
and neon signs proclaiming
burgers, chicken, pizza to go,
here, past the condos and the airstrips
and the shell-shocked harbour,
here, beyond the houses of parliament
and the private beach pavilions
and the ramshackle ghetto streets,

you are still alive.

I see you now,
moon colour skeletons,
inches
beneath the blue.

Prayer For The Nameless

Who are you, barefoot maiden walking
the honeycomb cliff, gathering the gold,
the lucina, the whelk, the sandstone heart?

Who are you, daughter of azulene shallows,
seeker of cave and watery labyrinth, of
open sea, what is your mother's name?

What colour, your magic?
Like the wild cinnamon leaf, a mosaic
of emaraude and serpentine?
Like the manioc field, a vision
of cream, of pebble, of olivesheen?

No-name woman, speak.
To languish now without a name
is to mother a people of poverty.

Lucayan queen, what name
would some chickcharnie breathe
invoking you?

Some hidden mystery,
my own dark-shadowed ancestry,
is dead until you speak.

ELEAN THOMAS
JAMAICA

Before They Can Speak of Flowers

Some
are born into
lush green fields
of trees and
flowers ever-blooming
Unplanted by themselves.

Some
are born into wildernesses
of poisonous weeds
tough choking vines
greedy parasitic growths
staunching their life-blood-flow
strangling their breath.

Some
can wander
unthinking
in ready-made gardens
speak with each other
of daffodils
delicate lillies
rare orchids.

Some
must grasp cutlasses
to chop away
the choking vines
hoes to dig out
poisonous parasitic
roots

channel healing waters
to flush and irrigate
the land
sprinkle seeds
of rebirth
Plant the Tree of Life
Before They
can speak of flowers.

Litany of A Housewife

I stay in this house
                              from morn till night
And cook and clean and wash
                              Mountains of shirts
                                    and pants
                                    and nappies
                                    and dresses
                                          Then you say
                                          I am only fit to do domestic work

I stay in this house
                              from morn till night
And kitchy-kitchy coo
                                    da da
                                    ma ma
                              With the children
                              Then you wonder
Why I only talk baby-talk

I stay in this house
                              from morn till night
And share all the gossip
                                    and woes
with my sister across the fence
                                    who stays in that house

                              from morn till night
Then you ask
Why do I nag and gossip so

I stay in this house

                     from morn till night
                          Oblivious
           of national production targets
                foreign exchange deficits
                     neutron death
                          MX missiles
                     Star wars at the door

American boots of death
Over new-born Nicaragua
Ten million feet
One hundred million hearts
Beating for peace and life
Multi-coloured hordes of

                     mankind shouting yes to
                     Social Revolution.

                     Social Revolution
                          which alone
                          can free me
                     from staying in this house
                          from morn till night
                     And the making of which
                          is demanding
                               demanding
                               demanding
                          That I no longer stay
                               in this house
                          from morn till night

PATRICIA TURNBULL
ST. LUCIA / VIRGIN ISLANDS

Corpus Christi

in this new land
en route to Magian bliss
blessed merchants do not give
at end of year
those almanacs
upon which humble people count
to reckon with the next

these are for sale instead
impressions of new age
commercial blow-ups
leave no space for the small print
of *temp passé*
the fickle faces of the moon
are slapped by stronger tides
and there's no liturgy for saints
decanonized

so one tends to forget
what day it was
when Peter's pilgrims cast their tackle
upon Conway shores
anchored their drift of grind and grog
with mock gentility
fishwomen too
renouncing rage awhile
would flaunt respectability
like high folks proving class

and one tends to forget
what day it was

when hand-picked girls
immaculately bred
shed royal blue for convent white
to bear the wondrous lady
and her alabaster train
in litanies
around columbus square

yes one tends to forget
which magic moon it was
that humored growing things
purged undesirable stuff
transformed sweet darlings
into lunatics and peeves
and vice versa
back to front
they'd jam until guilt burn
whole forty days of grace
upon repentant brows

in this new land
where no flamboyant fisher's fete
no sacrament unveiled
proceeds outdoors
where every day is Lent
and moons are blocked by towers
stacked like children's toys
into the crowded sky

in this new land
where body and blood is lost
as fast as bread and wine is found
a soul too settled after sacrifice
tends to forget

MIRIAM VENTURA
DOMINICAN REPUBLIC

En una mano Dafne en la otra las heridas

A las Mirabal

Sentada en un diente de Zahori viajo sobre mismas
mil veces de nosotras hasta medrar en la ulterior
hazaña de los golpes antes que la historia me reduzcan
Vuelvo a resarcir la pluralidad que todo vientre habita
me transo en lo undoso donde oscilan la imagen el espejo

Recobra para mí todos los coros. La voz dejó de ser pequeña
Mucho más alto que mi tiempo vuelan los ojos al retrato
Tres heridas. La sangre de mi madre

Interludio.
Todas mis madres. Las hermanas y amigas que tengo
Las enemigas de fábula

Una "Dafne" transformada claridiurna deja caer
en su danzar bencina.

Preludio de taimados. Nombres antinombres. Joyas.

Zahori convertida viajo. Del poema ralo llanto sacralidad liorna
Oboes refrescanme la orilla. Mismas mil veces de nosotras
recobrando para mí todos los coros.

Nadie puede tronar sus pies sobre la tierra
si antes no damos la piel al fuego el tul también la mueca.

On the One Hand Daphne, On the Other My Wounds

To the Mirabal Sisters

Seated on a tooth of the Diviner I travel on the
backs of those we were a thousand times until I survive
the aftermath of the beatings before being diminished by history
I go back to making amends for the plurality to be found in our
being, I settle for the wave where the mirror and image hesitate.

It retrieves the choirs. The voice has ceased to be small
Higher than my times the eyes soar to the portrait
Three wounds. My mother's blood

Interlude.
All my mothers. The sisters and friends that I have
The enemies of legendary tales

A Daphne transformed, clear-sighted,
as she dances she spreads benzene

A prelude of the cunning. Names contradictions. Jewels.

The Diviner transformed, I travel. From the poem I breed tears of
        sacred confusion
The oboes make the shore new again. On the very backs of those
        we were
a thousand times, for my sake I recover all the choirs

No one can erase their footsteps on this earth
if we don't give up our skin, our veils, our face to the fire.

MARÍA DEL CARMEN VICENTE
DOMINICAN REPUBLIC

Abril

estoy entre las aguas de la noche
invadiendo tu territorio violando
la soberanía de tus montañas
sumergiéndome en tus bosques espesos bañándome
con tus ríos tibios sorbiendo
cada terruño para ensuciar mi boca
apoderándome de tus fusiles y embarrándolos
de sangre acorralándote en desembarcos
haciéndote sudar hasta oír tu gemido largo robando
tus semillas para hacer parir tierra invasora
hasta que entre humo y mordiscos me
expulses de tus
playas y me
retire
queriendo aún
triturarte con los dientes
y ladrillo a ladrillo
reconstruir tu
historia

April

I am within the waters of the night
invading your territory violating
the sovereignty of your mountains
plunging myself into your dense forests bathing myself
with your warm rivers sucking
each clod of earth to dirty my mouth
seizing your rifles and smearing them
with blood cornering you at disembarkations
making you sweat until I hear your long moan robbing
your seeds to give birth to invading land
until between smoke and bites
you drive me from your
beaches and I
retreat
still wanting
to grind you with my teeth
and brick by brick
reconstruct your
history

CHIQUI VICIOSO
DOMINICAN REPUBLIC

Un extraño ulular traía el viento

1

Antes la identidad era palmeras
mar, arquitectura
desempacaba la nostalgia otros detalles
volvía la niña a preguntarle a la maestra
y un extraño ulular traía el viento.

2

Antes el amor era reuniones
libros, trenes, oratoria
la pasión y el arte temas
y el auto-exilio . . . "la línea".
Sólo la niña, o cuando la niña
asomaba en torbellino la cabeza
rompía papeles, revolvía los libros
volteaba el café sobre la mesa
ignoraba al marido y escribía
en el blanco impecable . . .
volvía el mar como un rugido de epiléptico
en el amanecer de la conciencia
y la luz a desdoblar con palmeras las persianas
y un extraño ulular traía el viento.

3

Reinaban en el imperio del cuatro las paredes
pero llegó con la brusquedad de los tambores
con la lejanía sensorial de lo cercano
la insomne aparición de la extrañeza
se manifestaron los números y el siete
—como tenazas golpeando contra el cuatro—
como un hacha azul abriendo trechos
en la azul selva donde esperaban juntos

The Wind Bore a Strange Howl

1

Before, our identity was palm trees,
sea, architecture
nostalgia unwrapped other details
the little girl asked her teacher again
and the wind bore a strange howl.

2

Before, love was gatherings
books, trains, oratory
passion and art themes
and self-imposed exile . . . "the line."
Only the girl, or when the girl
poked her head into the whirlwind
she would tear up papers, overturn her books
spill the coffee on the table.
She would ignore her husband and write
on the impeccable white . . .
the sea would return like the bellowing of an epileptic
at the awakening of his consciousness
and the light filtered through the palm trees onto the shutters
and the wind bore a strange howl.

3

The walls ruled in the empire of the four
but the sleepless specter of strangeness
arrived with the brusqueness of the drums
with the sensory distance of that which is near
The numbers were revealed and the seven
—like pincers beating against the four—
like a blue axe opening expanses
in the blue jungle where they waited together

Ochún y Yemayá y la pregunta
anunció el séptimo imperio del lagarto.

4

Entonces la identidad era palmeras
mar, arquitectura
tambores, Yemayá y Ochún
y la temporaria paz del agua.
Agua-cero
como el circular origen de la nada.
Y un extraño ulular traía el viento.

5

Entonces el amor era reuniones
trenes, oratoria, Amílcar
la clara oscuridad del instinto
el ¿esto es? convertido en ¿quién eres?
y el cinco una serpiente con manzanas
y el cinco una gran S
silbando el nombre de una isla
. . . y otro nombre
como un trampolín de adolescentes esperanzas
¡Esto es! dijo el corazón
¡Esto es! repitieron por vez primera
conformadas la niña y la maestra
aferradas al avión
como de un lápiz.

6

Era el imperio mutable del cinco
con sus serpientes y manzanas
la identidad y el amor ya unidas
eran palmeras, mar, arquitectura
tambores, Amílcar, Yemayá y Ochún
la clara oscuridad del instinto
la promesa, el lápiz, la alegría
pero un extraño ulular traía el viento.

Ochún and Yemayá and the question
announced the seventh empire of the lizard.

4

Then our identity was palm trees,
sea, architecture
drums, Yemayá and Ochún
and the temporary peace of the water.
Water-zero
like the circular origin of nothingness.
And the wind bore a strange howl.

5

Then love was gatherings
trains, oratory, Amílcar
the clear darkness of instinct
the Is this it? changed into Who are you?
and the five a serpent with apples
and the five a big S
whistling the name of an island
. . . and another name
like a trampoline of adolescent hopes
This is it! said the heart
This is it! they repeated for the first time
girl and teacher agreeing
both clasping the airplane
as though it were a pencil.

6

It was the mutable empire of five
with its serpents and apples
identity and love united
There were palm trees, sea, architecture
drums, Amílcar, Yemayá and Ochún
the clear darkness of instinct
the promise, the pencil, the joy
but the wind bore a strange howl.

7

Subrepticio anunció el cuatro la vuelta de Saturno
sorpresivas descendieron las paredes
una inmensa red cuadriculó con tramas la isla
la S se convirtió en silencio
el cinco en talvia derretida
y entonces
la identidad y el amor eran palmeras
mar, arquitectura
tambores, Amílcar
Yemayá y Ochún
la oscura oscuridad del instinto
el lápiz, la tristeza
y la absurdidad del ¿esto es?
detenida en medio de la calle
como una niña en sobresalto.
¿Esto es? como una hormiga
es un transparente cubículo de plástico
¿Esto es? como un cadáver implorante
en guerra el cinco contra el cuatro
el universo se volvió un nueve
y un extraño ulular de voces trajo el viento.

8

Espejo proyectó la isla al cosmos su esfera
y la sombra, en reflejo
como una barrena gigantesca
redondeó los bordes
Se volvió la isla una pelota
en manos de una gran ronda de maestras
carpinteros, campesinos, muelleros, poetas,
médicos, choferes, vendedores, maniceros
ciegos, cojos, mudos, reinas de belleza
tráficos, policías, obreros, prostitutas
una pelota en manos de una gran ronda de escolares
¡Esto somos! ¡Esto eres! una rueda
aplastando—sin violencia—el ¿esto es?

7

Surreptitiously the four announced the return of Saturn
unexpectedly the walls descended
an immense net squared off the island
the S turned into silence
the 5 into a melted talvia
and then
identity and love were palm trees,
sea, architecture
drums, Amílcar
Yemayá and Ochún
the dark darkness of instinct
the pencil, sadness
and the absurdity of Is this it?
at a standstill in the middle of the road
like a frightened girl
Is this it? like an ant
in a transparent plastic cube
Is this it? like an imploring cadaver
the five at war with the four
the universe became a nine
and the wind bore a strange howling of voices.

8

A mirror projected the island to the cosmos its sphere
and its shadow, in reflection
like a gigantic sander
rounded the edges.
The island became a ball
in the hands of a great ring of teachers
carpenters, farmers, dock workers, poets
doctors, chauffeurs, vendors,
blind, lame, mute, beauty queens,
traffic police, laborers, prostitutes
a ball in the hands of a great ring of school children
This is what we are! This is what you are! a ball
smashing—without violence—the Is this it?

Doña Mariana

Tengo 63 año y tó lo veo ocuro
somo como un barco de carga
que se va undiendo de lao
¡si sólo lo levantaran un chin
pa permitirno balancearno!

Hoy se cumplen siete año de la muerte de Marino
quise aserle una horasanta
pero con la noticia no tengo ánimo ni pá comé
pa decile que venga a ocuparse de susijo
¡que ya ta bueno de tanta lagrima!

¿De qué no sirve ser tan rico?
tenemo mina de tierra, de oro, de café
y cuando yo era muchacho sembraba caña el campesino
ahora lo colono son lo guardia
¿se abrá vito cosa igual?

¡Y nuetra caña e tan dulce!
son capase de llevarsela en el avión
cuando se vayan . . . si se van
. . . si no nos van
Doña Mariana.

Algún día se irán todo pa'l monte
¡Ah!, ¡a mi me guta criar puerco y gallina!
mato uno, se lo aso y lo pongo en una bandeja
lo cubro con mucha ropa dobladita y con mucha sábana . . .
y le digo
que soy la lavandera de Don Fulano de tal . . .

¡Y allá arriba lo muchacho dándose banquete!
. . . ya eso del monte no se usa Doña Mariana
¡Eso te cree tú!
un día se alza ete pueblo como paloma
¡y no habrá guardia!

Doña Mariana

I am 63 years old and everything looks dark
we are like a cargo ship
that's listing to one side
if only they'd raise it a little
to allow us to balance ourselves!

Today it's been seven years since the death of Marino
I wanted to say a prayer
but with the news I don't even have the energy to eat
to tell him to come take care of his kids
that it's okay after so many tears!

What good does it do us to be so rich?
we have mines of land, gold, coffee
and when I was a kid the campesino sowed cane
now the planters are the guards
have you ever seen such a thing?

And our cane is so sweet!
they can take it with them on the plane
when they leave . . . if they leave
. . . if they don't leave
Doña Mariana.

Some day they will all go to the mountains
Ah! I like to raise pigs and chickens!
I kill one, I roast it and I put it on a tray
I cover it with a lot of folded linens and sheets . . .
and I tell them
that I am the washerwoman of Mr. So-And-So . . .

And there, above, the boys giving themselves a banquet!
. . . that business of the mountain isn't used anymore Doña Mariana
You better believe it!
one day this town will rise up like a dove
and there won't be any guards!

Y eso no lo veré yo
lo verán utede lo muchacho
a mi me lo contarán hormiga
me lo dirá la tierra, me lo dirá Marino
¡. . . y florecerán sonrisas Doña Mariana!

Reykjavik

Desplazada de mi tribu
encadenada bestia
al violento temor de los vencedores
decidí desatar mis velas
y construirnos un mar a la medida.

Allí el viento nos habló de la cañada
de los ríos y lagunas
donde aprendimos a sortear las piedras
de las flores y frutos silvestres
del animal amor de los animales
del sexo entre la hierba o entre corrientes
en baratos moteles para estudiantes
o en baratas habitaciones del Hotel
y la embriaguez nos hizo olvidar
el peso de la puerta sobre la espalda.

Reykjavik de formas y sonidos
con el solo desafío de la página
un pacífico mar comenzó a hablarnos del Caribe
de los techos desprendidos por el viento
de las calles vueltas charcos
de la oscuridad
solo rota por la rota luz

And I probably won't see that
you boys will see it
the ants will tell me about it
the earth will tell me, Marino will tell me
. . . and smiles will flourish Doña Mariana!

---

* Marino refers to Maximiliano Gómes, El Moreno.

Reykjavik

Displaced from my tribe
beast chained
to the violent fear of the conquerors
I decided to unfurl my sails
and build us a sea made to order.

There the wind spoke to us of the ravine
of the rivers and the lagoons
where we learned to dodge the rocks
of the flowers and the wild fruit
of the brute love of animals
of sex in the grass or in the currents
in cheap motels for students
or in cheap hotel rooms
and the intoxication made us forget
the weight of the doors on their backs.

Reykjavik in shapes and sounds
with the only challenge on the page
a peaceful sea began to speak to us about the Caribbean
of the roofs torn off by the wind
of the streets become puddles
of the darkness
only broken by the broken light

de dispersos cristales
del pavoroso silencio después del primer azote
y de la primera calma
furor de los verdes y los azules
guerra entre el agua y el aire
donde el cuerpo es lo firme
y es la víctima.

Desplazadas de la embriaguez y de sus éxtasis
encadenadas bestias
a la memoria del amor, del desamor y de sus lutos
la tercera edad nos acogió en sus asilos
y comenzó a éter-
                    minarnos
una
a
una.

of scattered windows
of the frightening silence after the first whip
and of the first calm
fury of greens and blues
war between water and air
where the body is solid
and is the victim.

Displaced by the intoxication and its ecstasies
beasts chained
to the memory of love, unlove and its grief
the third age sheltered us in its refuge
and began to ether-
                             ize us
one
by
one.

---

* "the weight of the doors on their backs" refers to a newsphoto of
Bosnian refugees, some carrying the doors from their homes.

MARGARET WATTS
TRINIDAD—TOBAGO

To a Correspondent Who Thought Before Seeing Me I Was Black

I am sorry to disappoint you so.
But you can't judge a horse by its colour,
And a rose by any other name
Would prick, you understand.
My circumstances are quite out of hand.

My mother, you see, is pale yellow with freckles,
And my father, a mottled pink,
I am a molding bleached-out bronze.
They don't care what the neighbours think.
My brother even turned purple once.

My children come in three shades—
Sepia, mauve and copper.
Never mind what people say.
Their father is ebony gone slightly bad,
His cousin, dusty white, really grey.

So, you see, with this motley array of hues,
Our lives are a limbo of off-whites and blues.
And although I should so like to please
And fit neatly into your assumed role,
Our chromatic situation is quite out of control.

Washerwoman

Washerwoman does share one dress
with her mooma, she so poor,
according to Minshall's tale.

Some say his white mooma
could not be a washerwoman.
Washerwoman is only those
who wash the clothes at the river.

Minshall's sister is washerwoman;
and when she graced the Savannah stage,
black woman, pure and prayerful, in white—
clothes dancing on trembling lines
like disembodied immigrants,
hips winding into music,

every woman rose and cheered
transcending the jooking board,
then reached for the nearest of woman kind,
embraced her, blind to social hierarchy,
touching ark and archangel,
and all the company of heaven.

For it was carnival, after all,
when woman may assume a myth,
escape constraint and enter art—
'dance like literature'.

The vision does not fade;
it remains as large as life,
however hard we scrub,
despite the river's pollution
and Washerwoman's death.

PATRICIA BONNIE ZAMIA
GUADELOUPE

Tais-toi

Maman m'a dit "tais-toi"
Quand je commençais à parler

La maîtresse m'a dit "tais-toi"
Quand je voulais bavarder

La police m'a dit "tais-toi"
Quand j'ai voulu protester

La société m'a dit "tais-toi"
Quand j'ai voulu crier

Et aujourd'hui je ne sais pas parler
Seulement je pense.

Be quiet

Mama told me "be quiet"
When I would begin to talk

The teacher told me "be quiet"
When I wanted to talk

The police told me "be quiet"
When I wanted to protest

Society told me "be quiet"
When I wanted to shout

So today I don't know how to talk
But I do know how to think.

BIOGRAPHICAL & BIBLIOGRAPHICAL NOTES

Opal Palmer Adisa, from Jamaica, is a widely acclaimed performance poet, a novelist, short story writer and scholar. She holds a PhD in Literature and Ethnic Studies from the University of California at Berkeley. The poems here have been reprinted with special permission from the author. "A Run-Away," "We are Formed from Volcanoes" and "Market Woman" are from her collection, *Tamarind and Mango Women*, (Toronto: Sister Vision Press, 1992) for which she won the PEN Oakland / Josephine Miles Literary Award. She is currently an Associate Professor and Chair of the Ethnic Studies and Cultural Diversity Program at the California College of Arts ad Crafts.

Julia Alvarez was born in Santo Domingo and left with her family in 1960 during the notorious Trujillo regime. She is a poet, short story writer and novelist of considerable acclaim in the U.S. literary community; and, with the publication of her recent works on the Dominican Republic, she has earned the admiration of her colleagues throughout the Caribbean. She was awarded the PEN Oakland / Josephine Miles Award. She is currently on the faculty at Middlebury College. The poems presented here, "Audition" and "Bilingual Sestina" are from *The Other Side / El Otro Lado* (Copyright © Julia Alvarez, 1995, published by Dutton, an imprint of Dutton Signet, a division of Penguin Books USA) and are reprinted with special permission from the author.

Cira Andrés Esquivel (Cuba) studied literature at the Escuela Nacional de Instructores de Arte in Havana. The poem presented here was previously published in her collection, *Visiones*, published in 1987 by Editorial Letras Cubanas, La Habana. She has also published in *Cuba: En su lugar la poesía*, 1982, an anthology edited by Roberto Fernández Retamar and *Usted es la culpable*, 1985, an anthology edited by Víctor Rodríguez Núñez (La Habana: Editora Abril de la UJC). The translation is by Tracy Hudgins.

Marlène Rigaud Apollon was born in Cap-Haitien, Haiti, and emigrated to the U.S. in 1964. She is the author of two books of poetry, *Cris de colère, Chants d'espoir* and *I Want to Dance*. Her poems have appeared in *Panorama de la Littérature Haïtienne de la Diaspora*, *The Utah Foreign Language Review*, *Haiti-Progrès*, *Kiskeya* and a special Caribbean issue of *River City*, 1996. She has also written for the magazine *Girl's Life* and has been active with radio interviews and poetry readings for college students and other groups. "Mois de la femme" was published in 1994 by "Le Petit

Courier." The other poems presented here are from her collection, *Cris de colère, Chants d'espoir*, published in 1992 by CIDIHCA, Québec, and are reprinted with special permission from the poet. The translations from the French are by Raymonde Niel.

María Arrillaga is a poet and novelist born in Mayagüez, Puerto Rico. She has published extensively in both national and international magazines and anthologies. "To the Poets of My Generation" is from her prize-winning poetry collection, *Frescura 1981*, published by Ediciones Mairena, Río Piedras, in 1981, and "Sinfonía del todo y de la nada" is from *Vida en el tiempo*, her prize-winning collection published by the Ateneo Puertorriqueño, San Juan, in 1974. The translations are by Tracy Hudgins.

Vera Bell is from Jamaica. "Ancestor on the Auction Block" was originally published in 1948 in the second of Edna Manly's series of *Focus* anthologies.

Louise Bennett is one of Jamaica's best known performance poets. Among her collections are *Jamaican Dialect Poems*, 1948, *Anancy Stories and Direct Verse*, 1957, *Laugh With Louise*, 1961, *Anancy and Miss Lou*, 1979, and the following recordings: *The Honourable Miss Lou, Carifesta Ring-Ding, Listen to Louise*, and *Miss Lou's Views*. The selections presented here were published in *Jamaica Labrish* (Kingston: Sangster's Book Stores, 1966 © Louise Bennett). Throughout the 1960s and '70s "Miss Lou" presented her poems and her socio-political commentary on Kingston radio for the popular audience. A collection of these radio broadcasts appears in print under the title *Aunty Roachy Seh*, (Kingston: Sangster's Book Stores, 1993).

Marion Bethel (Bahamas) writes poetry, prose, drama and essays. She was the 1994 winner of the prestigious Casa de las Américas prize for her collection *Guanahani, My Love*, published as a bilingual English/Spanish edition. In 1991 she was the recipient of the James Michener Fellowship for the Caribbean Writers' Summer Institute of the University of Miami. Her work also appears in the anthologies *Junction*, 1987, and *From the Shallow Seas*, 1993, and in the following journals, *Lignum Vitae, WomanSpeak, The Massachusetts Review, The Caribbean Writer*, and a special Caribbean issue of *River City*, 1996. She is a Cambridge-educated lawyer working in Nassau, The Bahamas, where she was born. The poems presented here are from *Guanahani, My Love*, and all are reprinted with special permission from the poet.

Valerie Bloom of Jamaica has an Honours degree in English in African and Caribbean Studies from the University of Kent. She is the author of *Touch Mi! Tell Mi!*, 1983 and *Duppy Jamboree*, 1992. The poem presented here is from *Watchers and Seekers*, an anthology edited by Rhonda Cobham and Merle Collins and published by Peter Bedrick Books, New York, 1988. Her poetry has also been anthologized in *From Our Yard*, 1987, *Ain't I a Woman!*, 1988, *Black Poetry*, 1988, *Voiceprint*, 1989, *Caribbean Poetry Now*, 1992 and *Daughters of Africa*, 1992. She performs her work internationally.

Janet Bohac was a long-time resident of Bonaire. She has an M.F.A. in Creative Writing from Western Michigan University and was a Screenwriting Fellow at The America Film Institute's Center. She also received the Ila Rosenbaum Award for Scripwriting. Her book, *Evidence of the Outer World*, was published in 1992 by Paradigm Publishing Company. The poem presented here is from *The Caribbean Writer*, Volume 3, 1989.

Jean "Binta" Breeze, from Jamaica, is a widely acclaimed performance "dub" poet and short story writer. "We Speak Through the Silence of Our Stares" is from her collection *Riddym Ravings* (London: Race Today Publications, 1988, © Jean Binta Breeze) and "Red Rebel Song" is from her collection *Spring Cleaning* (London: Virago Press, 1992, © Jean Binta Breeze). Among the anthologies and journals in which her work appears are *Dub Poetry*, 1986, *Voiceprint*, 1989, *The Literary Review*, 1990, *Creation Fire*, 1990, *Caribbean Poetry Now*, 1992, and *Daughters of Africa*, 1992.

Jennifer Brown (Jamaica) has published her poems in *Caribbean Quarterly*, *Jamaica Journal*, *Arts Review* and in *The Caribbean Poem*, a 1976 anthology edited by Neville Dawes and Anthony McNeill. The poems presented here were published in *Jamaica Woman*, one of the first Caribbean-area anthologies dedicated to the work of women poets edited by Pamela Mordecai and Mervyn Morris (Kingston: Heinemann Educational Books, Caribbean, Ltd., 1980.)

Barbara Burford (Jamaica) is a poet and short story writer. The poem presented here was published in *A Dangerous Knowing*, a collective book of poems with Gabriela Pearse from Colombia, Grace Nichols from Guyana and Jackie Kay from Scotland, published in 1984 by Sheba Feminist Publishers, London. She has participated in two other collective publications, *Dancing the Rightrope*, 1987, and *Charting the Journey*, 1988.

Julia de Burgos (1914-1958) is one of Puerto Rico's most respected poets for her dynamic expressions of feminism and political justice. Since her untimely death in 1958, her work has become an inspiration to women throughout the Americas. Olga Nolla writes in her poem "Oración por Julia de Burgos" (*Dafne en el mes de marzo*, 1989), "Quiero que sepas / que tu sacrificio no fue en vano / Ahora lo importante / es abolir el sacrificio" ("I want you to know / that your sacrifice was not in vain / Now the important thing / is to abolish sacrifice.") Julia de Burgos' work has been widely anthologized in both Spanish and English. Among the most recent anthologies are *Poesía feminista del mundo hispánico*, 1984, *The Defiant Muse*, 1986, and *Making Face, Making Soul / Haciendo Caras*, 1990. The poems presented here are from *Obra poética*, Julia de Burgos, published in 1961 in San Juan by the Instituto de Cultura Puertorriqueña, and the translations are by Tracy Hudgins.

Aída Cartagena Portalatín (Dominican Republic) (1918-1994) was one of the 20th century's most remarkable writers who devoted her life and her career to raising political consciousness about her country and its historical struggles. She was a poet, short story writer, novelist and scholar. Among her several books of poetry are *Víspera del sueño*, 1944, *La tierra escrita*, 1967, and *En la casa del tiempo*, 1984. The selections of "Yania Tierra" and the translation are from a critical bilingual edition of *Yania Tierra* published in 1995, by Azul Editions, translation by MJ Fenwick.

Lourdes Casal (1936-1981) was born in Havana and left Cuba for the U.S. shortly after the Revolution. But a dramatic change in her political consciousness came as she confronted the contradictions of life in the U.S. In the 1970's she began to reestablish her relations with Cuba and returned many times before her death. She had a PhD in psychology and devoted her career to researching and writing about Cuba, its literature and people. The poem presented here is from *Palabras juntan revolución*, her poetry collection which merited the 1981 Casa de las Américas prize. The translation is by MJ Fenwick.

Merle Collins is a poet, novelist and short story writer. She was born in Aruba, but Grenada has always been her home. Among the many anthologies in which her poetry has appeared are *Watchers and Seekers*, 1987, *Creation Fire*, 1990, *Caribbean Poetry Now*, 1992, *Daughters of Africa*, 1992, and a special Caribbean issue of *River City*, 1996. "The Butterfly Born," and "Because the Dawn Breaks" are from her collection, *Because the Dawn Breaks!, Poems Dedicated to the Grenadian People*, (London: Karia Press, 1985, copyright © Merle Collins). The poems from this collection express the dreams and visions of the Grenada Revolution in 1979 and the disappointment suffered after the U.S. invasion and the murder of President Maurice Bishop in 1983."Chant Me a Tune" is from her 1992 collection, *Rotten Pomerack*, (London: Virago Press, copyright © Merle Collins). All the poems are reprinted here with special permission from the author. She is currently on the faculty at the University of Maryland.

Afua Cooper (Jamaica) refers to herself as a "Womanist." She is also a poet who views her work as "an art to be performed." "Breakin Chains" is the title poem of her first collection, *Breakin Chains*, published in 1984 by Weelahs Publications, Toronto. "Atabeyra" is from her third collection of poetry, *Memories Have Tongue*, (Toronto: Sister Vision Press, 1992). Her other collection is titled *Red Caterpillar on College Street*, (Toronto: Sister Vision Press, 1989). Her poetry has also appeared in *Harambee, Fireweed, Creation Fire*, the 1990 Caribbean anthology edited by Ramabai Espinet and published by Sister Vision Press, Toronto, and CAFRA, Tunapuna, Trinidad-Tobago, and a special Caribbean issue of *River City*, 1996.

Christine Craig (Jamaica) is a widely published poet and writer of short stories and children's literature. She was a founding member of the Caribbean Artists Movement in London. The poems presented here, "The Chain" and "Elsa's Version" are from *Quadrille for Tigers*, (Berkeley: Mina Press Publishing, 1984, copyright © Christine Craig). Among the many anthologies and literary magazines in which her works have appeared are *Creation Fire*, 1990, edited by Ramabai Espinet, *The Literary Review*, 1992, a special Caribbean issue edited by Pamela Mordecai and Betty Wilson, *Caribbean Poetry Now*, 1992, *Daughters of Africa*, 1992, *Savacou, Arts Review*, and *Callaloo*.

Melania Daniel, originally from St. Lucia, is a graduate in Economics from the University of the West Indies, Cave Hill, Barbados. She was the first place winner of the St. Lucia national poetry competition. "No Man's Land" is reprinted from the anthology, *Under We Sky*, 1987, edited by Nadine Rogers, and "Early Birds" is reprinted from the anthology, *My Slice of the Pie*, 1988. Both anthologies are publications of CREWA, the Creative Writers Association of the University of the West Indies at Cave Hill.

Mahadai Das (Guyana) has been one of the Caribbean's most militant poets. She has published four collections of poems. "Beast" and "The Growing Tip" are from *Bones* (Leeds, U.K.: Peepal Tree Press, 1989) and are reprinted here with the kind permission of the publisher. "My Final Gift to Life" is from *My Finer Steel Will Grow* (Quebec: Samisdat, 1982, copyright Mahadai Das). Her first collection was titled *I Want to Be a Poetess of My People*, published in 1976. Among the anthologies and literary magazines in which her works have appeared are *India in the Caribbean*, 1987, *Jahaji Bhai*, 1988, *Creation Fire*, 1990, *The Literary Review*, 1992, *Caribbean Poetry Now*, 1992, a special Caribbean issue of *River City*, 1996, *Kaie* and *Kyk-Over-Al*. She has a Masters' Degree in Philosophy from the University of Chicago and now lives in Georgetown, Guyana.

Tania Díaz Castro (Cuba) has published four books of poetry. The poems presented here are from her 1970 collection of poetry, *Todos me van a tener que oir* (La Habana: Cuadernos Unión). Her other collections are *Apuntes para el tiempo*, 1964, *Aguas de felicidad* and *De frente a la esperanza*. Her poems have appeared in the anthologies *5 poetas jóvenes*, 1965 and *Palabra de mujer*, 1982. The translations are by Tracy Hudgins and MJ Fenwick.

Maria Diwan (Curaçao) writes poetry and children's stories. Her collection of poems is titled *Suspiro*, and she has a collection of children's stories titled *Solo Ta Sali Pabo Tambe*. Her concern is for the children of Curaçao, as she says, "not those at home, but those who crossed the ocean to Holland looking for a better life." She works as a secretary in the private sector and is the producer of a local radio program, "At Daybreak" at CUROM-Z-86. "Yunan di solo" and its translation are presented here with special permission from the author.

Adeline Dorlipo was born in Sainte-Rose, Guadeloupe. The poem presented here is reprinted from *Karukéra Anthologie*, 1983, published in Guadeloupe by the Association Guadeloupèenne des Amis de la Poésie. The translation is by Raymonde Niel.

Marcia Douglas (Jamaica) is an exciting new writer whose poems represent the epitome of the contemporary Caribbean woman's voice. She is currently a PhD candidate in Creative Writing and in Afro-U.S. and Caribbean literature at the State University of New York in Binghamton. Her dissertation is a novel set in Jamaica where she grew up. "Voice Lesson From The Unleashed Woman's Unabridged Dictionary," "Electricity Comes to Cocoa Bottom" and "Murline" are part of an unpublished manuscript, *Electricity Comes to Cocoa Bottom*, and are printed here with special permission from the author. Among the literary magazines in which her poetry and fiction have appeared are *Tar River Poetry*, *Puerto del Sol*, *Sundog: The Southeast Review* and *APTE: Contemporary Fiction by Emerging Writers of African Descent*. Works are forthcoming in *Phoebe* and *Callaloo*.

Eugenie Eersel was born in Suriname. The poem presented here is reprinted from *Ordinary Women Mujeres Comunes*, 1978, an anthology of women poets living in New York, edited by Sara Miles, Patricia Jones, Sandra Maria Esteves and Fay Chiang.

Ramabai Espinet (Trinidad) is a poet, a writer of fiction and essays, a critic and an academic. She is the editor of *Creation Fire*, the first extensive multi-lingual anthology of poetry by Caribbean women, published in 1990 by CAFRA of Trinidad and Tobago and Sister Vision Press of Toronto. She has a PhD and is Professor of English in the School of English Studies at Seneca College in Toronto. She is also a part-time faculty member at York University where she teaches a course on Caribbean Women's literature and an Adjunct Professor in the Graduate Faculty of Interdisciplinary Studies. She is a feminist writer, activist and academic who is committed to the goals of women's empowerment in all quarters. She is is especially committed to developing strategies to combat the increasing violence against women globally. Her field of academic research is post-colonial studies, and she is particularly interested in the development of scholarship on

Indo-Caribbean studies. She has worked with a women's collective to write and produce the play, *Beyond the Kala Pani*, which deals with Indian women and indentureship in the Caribbean. She is currently editing an anthology of writings by South Asian (Indian) women in the diaspora, *Kala Pani: Crossing the Blackwater*. Her poetry has appeared in several anthologies and literary magazies including, *Jahaji Bhai*, 1988, a special Caribbean issue of *River City*, 1996, the *Trinidad and Tobago Review* and *WomanSpeak*. The poems presented here are from her collection *Nuclear Seasons* (Toronto: Sister Vision, 1990) and are reprinted with special permission from the author.

Sandra Maria Esteves was born in the Bronx, New York, the daughter of a Dominican mother and a Puerto Rican father, and is one of the most active poets in the Hispanic literary community there. Her work has been anthologized extensively, in *The Next World*, (Trumansburg, New York: The Crossing Press, 1978), *Nuyorican Poetry*, (New York: William Morrow & Co., 1975) and most recently in *Papiros de Babel*, edited by Pedro López-Adorno and published by Editorial de la Universidad de Puerto Rico, 1991. "1st Poem for Cuba" is from her book *Yerba Buena*, published in 1981 (New York: The Greenfield Review Press). "Puerto Rican Discovery #5, Here Like There" and "Anonymous Apartheid" are from *Bluestown Mockingbird Mambo* (Houston: Arte Público Press, 1990, © Sandra Maria Esteves). Another collection is titled *Tropical Rains: A Bilingual Downpour* (New York: African Caribbean Poetry Theatre, 1984).

Patricia M. Fagan was born in St. Thomas, Virgin Islands. She is a poet and writes short stories. She won Connecticut's 9th Annual Literary Award, and her work has been published in several magazines including *Sister Wisdom*. "Charcoal" appeared in *The Caribbean Writer*, volume 1, number 1, spring 1987, and is reprinted here with special permission from the author. She now lives in Arizona and, as a beautician, works to help women.

Honor Ford-Smith (Jamaica) is primarily known for her work in theatre. She is an actor, playwright and the founding Artistic Director of the Sistren Theatre Collective of Jamaica. As a feminist scholar she edited and co-authored *Lionheart Gal: Life Stories of Jamaican Women*, 1968. The poem presented here appeared in *Creation Fire* (Toronto: Sister Vision, 1990) edited by Ramabai Espinet.

Joan French (Jamaica) is a feminist scholar and is active in The Sistren Theatre Collective in Jamaica. The poem presented here appeared in *Creation Fire*, 1990, edited by Ramabai Espinet and published by Sister Vision Press (Toronto) and CAFRA (Trinidad and Tobago) of which she is a founding member.

Cornelia Frettlöh is originally from Germany but has lived in Barbados for the last decade. Her poetry has been published in several newspapers and magazines including BIM. The poem presented here appeared in *Creation Fire*, (Toronto: Sister Vision Press, 1990) edited by Ramabai Espinet.

Phillis Gershator is a long-time resident of St. Thomas, Virgin Islands. She has a poetry chapbook titled *Bang Bang, Lulu*, and her work has appeared in various journals and anthologies. The poem presented here is from *The Caribbean Writer*, volume 6, 1992.

Joya Gomez calls herself a "pelau," a Trinidadian spicy dish of rice, peas and salted meats simmered in coconut milk with hot pepper. She is an internationally known actor of the stage, television and film. She has been a broadcaster, editor, world traveller and poet. She has taught English, American, African and other Commonwealth Literatures, Theatre History and Performance arts in Trinidad, England, East and West Africa and Canada. The poems presented here, "New Woman" and "On Receiving An 'Ostrichian' Egg From Him," are reprinted with special permission from the author. They previously appeared in *Washer Woman Hangs Her Poems in the Sun*, the 1990 anthology of poetry by women from Trinidad and Tobago edited by Margaret Watts. "New Woman" has been set to music for baritone and piano and was composed by her son, German-based Conductor Kwamé Ryan. The premier performance was given in Cambridge, England, in 1992.

Lorna Goodison (Jamaica) is one of the Caribbean's most widely acclaimed poets. She is the author of five books of poems and short stories and received the Commonwealth Poetry Prize, 1986, and the Musgrave Medal in 1987. Among the many anthologies and magazines in which her work appears are *Jamaica Woman*, 1980, *One People's Grief*, 1983, *Caribbean Quarterly*, 1984, *Facing the Sea*, 1986, *From Our Yard*, 1986, *Voiceprint*, 1989, *Callaloo*, 1989, *Hinterland*, 1989, *Creation Fire*, 1990, *Tradewinds*,1990, *Caribbean Poetry Now*, 1992, *The Literary Review*, 1992, *Daughters of Africa*, 1992, *The Norton Anthology of World Masterpieces*, 1995, *Review: Latin American Literature and the Arts*, 1995, *The Garden Thrives*, 1996 and *The Vintage Anthology of World Fiction*, 1996. She was one of three Caribbean poets featured in *Come Back to Me My Language* a critical book on the new canon of Caribbean literature by J. Edward Chamberlin published in 1993 by The University of Illinois Press. "The Road of the Dread" is from *Tamarind Season*, (Kingston: Institute of Jamaica, 1979); "For My Mother (May I Inherit Half Her Strength)," "Guinea Woman" and "Nanny" are from *I Am Becoming My Mother*, (London: New Beacon Books, 1986); and "Mother, the Great Stones Got to Move" is from her 1995 collection, *To Us, All Flowers Are Roses*, (Urbana: The University of Illinois Press). They are reprinted here with special permission from the author.

Lucile Gottin was born in Basse-Terre, Guadeloupe. The poem presented here previously appeared in *Karukéra Anthologie* published in 1983 by the Association Guadeloupéenne des Amis de la Poésie. The translation is by Raymonde Niel.

Jean Goulbourne is from Jamaica. Her poems have been featured in several journals and anthologies, *Savacou, BIM, The Caribbean Writer, Facing the Sea*, 1986, *From Our Yard*, 1987, *Caribbean Poetry Now*, 1992, and *The Literary Review*, 1992, a special Caribbean issue edited by Pamela Mordecai and Betty Wilson. "Like a Bridge" appeared in *Dream Rock*, an anthology edited by Kamau Brathwaite (Kingston: Jamaica Information Service, 1987). "Jamaica: January 16, 1980" appeared in *BIM*, volume 17, June, 1983. "Shadow" is from her first collection of poems, *Actors in the Arena*, 1977, published in Kingston by the Savacou Cooperative. A forthcoming collection of poems will be titled *Woman Song*. She is a lecturer at the Church Teachers College in Jamaica.

Cynthia James (Trinidad) is a poet and short story writer and a graduate of the University of the West Indies in St. Augustine, Trinidad. Her poems were anthologized in *Washer Woman Hangs Her Poems in the Sun*, edited by Margaret Watts, 1990, and in a special Caribbean issue of *The Literary Review*, 1991, edited by Pamela Mordecai and Betty Wilson. The poems presented here, "New World Soldier," and "Port-of-Spain by Night" are from her collection, *La Vega and Other Poems*, Tunapuna, Trinidad, 1995, "Amerindia" is from her collection, *Vigil*, Tunapuna, Trinidad, 1995, and "A Street Vendor Goes Home" is from her first collection, *Iere, My Love*, Port of Spain, 1990. Iere is the Amerindian name for Trinidad, meaning Land of the Humming Bird. All the poems are reprinted here with special permission from the poet.

Meiling Jin is a poet and has written short stories for children. She was born in Guyana of Chinese parents. She lives in England. One of her "truths" for women is that we "have to fight to speak" before someone else speaks for us. Her poetry is her power, and her first book is *Gifts From My Grandmother*, published in 1985 by Sheba Feminist Publishers, London. "Strangers in a Hostile Landscape" is from *Gifts*, and it later appeared in two important anthologies of women poets, *Watchers and Seekers*, 1988, (New York: Peter Bedrick Books) and *Creation Fire*, 1990, (Toronto: Sister Vision Press). "Judgement" appeared in another anthology, *Black Women Talk Poetry*, published in 1987 by Black Womantalk Ltd, London.

Amryl Johnson (Trinidad) is a poet and short story writer. She has a degree in African and Caribbean Studies from the University of Kent. She has a book of essays on the Caribbean titled *Sequins for a Ragged Hem*, 1988, and three collections of poetry, *Shackles, Long Road to Nowhere*, 1982, and *Tread Carefully in Paradise*, 1991. "Far Cry" appeared in *Long*

Road to Nowhere, (Sable Publications and Virago, both London presses) and in *Tread Carefully in Paradise,* (Coventry: Cofa Press). "Watchers and Seekers" is the title poem for the 1988 anthology, *Watchers and Seekers,* edited by Rhonda Cobham and Merle Collins and published by Peter Bedrick Books, New York. Her work has also been anthologized in *News for Babylon,* 1984, *Facing the Sea,* 1986, *Let It Be Told,* 1987, *Voiceprint,* 1989, *Creation Fire,* 1990, *Caribbean Poetry Now,* 1992, and *Daughters of Africa,* 1992.

Marie-Ange Jolicoeur (Haiti) (1947-1976) published three collections of poetry, *Guitare de vers,* 1969, *Violon d'espoir,* 1970, and *Oiseaux de mémoire,* (Port-au-Prince: Seminaire Adventiste, 1972). The poem presented here is from her last book and was reprinted in *The Literary Review,* 1992, volume 35, number 4, a special Caribbean issue edited by Pamela Mordecai and Betty Wilson. The translation is by Raymonde Niel.

Barbara Althea Jones (Trinidad) (1937-1972) published one collection of poems, *Among the Potatoes,* (North Devon: Arthur H. Stockwell, Ltd., 1967) in which "West India" appeared. It is reprinted here with the kind permission of the poet's family.

Lucie Julia (Guadeloupe) is a poet, novelist and short story writer. Her poetry collection is titled *Chants, sons, cris pour Karukéra.* She has a bilingual (Creole and French) collection of short stories titled *Tim tim, bwa sek!,* 1992. The poem presented here appeared in *The Literary Review,* 1992. The translation is by Raymonde Niel.

Jane King was born in St. Lucia where she now teaches at the Sir Arthur Lewis Community College. She is a poet, an actor and a theatre director and is a founding member of the Lighthouse Theatre Company in Castries. Her work has appeared in several journals and anthologies including *Kyk-Over-Al* and *Graham House Review,* a special Caribbean issue, 1991. "Sad Mother Ballad" is from her collection, *In To the Centre,* published in 1993. Another collection, *Fellow Traveller,* was published 1994 by Sandberry Press, Kingston. She received a Witter Bynner Fellowship in 1992 and a James Michener Fellowship in 1993.

Christine Lara was born in Africa but lives in Guadeloupe. The poem presented here is from *Karukéra Anthologie,* published by the Association Guadeloupéenne des Amis de la Poésie in 1983. The translation is by Raymonde Niel.

Lolita Lebrón was involved in the Puerto Rican independence struggles of the 1950's and an ally of revolutionary, Pedro Albizu Campos. In 1954, she participated with Puerto Rican Nationalists in an attack on the U.S. Congress and spent twenty-five years in prison. Poet Sandra Maria Esteves calls her "Womanstrength / a mold to guide the dawn" (poem: "For Lolita Lebrón"). Lolita Lebrón's poems have been anthologized in *Antología de la poesía de la mujer puertorriqueña*, 1981, *Contemporary Women Authors of Latin America*, 1983, and *The Literary Review*, a special Caribbean issue, 1992. The poems presented here are from *Sándalo en la celda*, 1974, published by Editorial Betances in Cataño, Puerto Rico. The translations are by Tracy Hudgins.

Consuelo Lee Tapia de Corretjer (Puerto Rico)dedicated much of her life to the Puerto Rican struggle for independence from the U.S. She was arrested in 1969 for conspiracy against the U.S. government. She has poetry anthologized in *Antología de poetas contemporáneos de Puerto Rico*, 1946, and *Antología de la poesía de la mujer puertorriqueña*, 1981. The poem presented here is from her collection *Con un hombro menos*, published in 1977, © Consuelo Corretjer. The translation is by Tracy Hudgins.

Audre Lorde (1934-1992) was born in the U.S. but lived in St. Croix, Virgin Islands, during the last years of her life. She had degrees in literature and library science, achieved international literary acclaim for her poetry and fiction and wide admiration for her dynamic political stand on important feminist issues. Among the many anthologies in which her poetry appeared are *Charting the Journey*, 1988, *Creation Fire*, 1990, *Daughters of Africa*, 1992, and *Erotique Noire / Black Erotica*, 1992. "The Woman Thing" appeared in the anthology, *Black Sister*, (Bloomington: Indiana University Press, 1981), "A Woman Speaks" appeared in her poetry collection, *The Black Unicorn* (New York: W.W. Norton & Company, 1978), and "Coast Market" appeared in both *The Caribbean Writer*, volume 4, 1990, and *Creation Fire*, an anthology edited by Ramabai Espinet (Toronto: Sister Vision, 1990).

Delores McAnuff-Gauntlett is from Jamaica. Her "The Last Child . . . Sold" appeared in *The Caribbean Writer*, volume 9, 1995.

Ahdri Zhina Mandiela is a performance dub poet from Jamaica, living and working in Toronto. In addition to her own collections, her work has appeared in *Focus '85*, 1985, and *Creation Fire*, 1990. Her first book, *Speshal Rikwes*, was published in 1985, and "In the Canefields" is from her recent collection, *Dark Diaspora . . . in Dub*, 1990, both published by Sister Vision Press, Toronto.

Lelawattee Manoo-Rahming was born in Trinidad and now lives and works as a Mechanical / Building Services Engineer in Nassau, the Bahamas. She writes poetry and fiction and is a college lecturer. "Full Moon Healing" was previously published in *WomanSpeak*, volume 3, 1996. This poem plus "Woman Truths" will appear in her new manuscript in preparation, and all are reprinted here with special permission from the poet.

Carmen Natalia Martínez Bonilla (Dominican Republic) (1917-1976) was a poet, a novelist and wrote for the theatre. Among her books are *Alma adentro*, 1938, 1981, *Luna gitana*, 1944, and *La victoria*, 1945. The poem presented here is from the 1982 anthology *Antología de poetas petromacorisanos*, (Santo Domingo: Editora Taller, Ediciones de la Universidad Central del Este, San Pedro de Macorís). Other anthologies in which her work appeared are *Antología poética hispanoamericana actual*, 1969, *Antología literaria dominicana*, 1981, and *Sin otro profeta que su canto*, 1988, edited by Daisy Cocco de Filippis.

Marina Ama Omowale Maxwell was born and lives in Trinidad. She is a writer, singer, lecturer, playwright, and producer for theatre and television. She was founder of the Yard Theatre in Jamaica and the Writers' Union in Trinidad-Tobago. "Caribbean Woman Birth Song" is from the 1990 anthology, *Washer Woman Hangs Her Poems in the Sun*, edited by Margaret Watts, Trinidad-Tobago, and is reprinted here with special permission from the poet. Among the other anthologies and journals in which her work has appeared are *Breaklight*, 1972, *Poetic Tributes to Walter Rodney*, 1985, *Creation Fire*, 1990, *The Literary Review* special Caribbean issue, 1992, *BIM* and *Savacou*.

Marianela Medrano was born in the Dominican Republic. She has participated in the writers group, the Second Círculo de Mujeres Escritoras. Her poetry is designed to redefine the woman and her role in Dominican society. She has two collections, *Oficio de vivir* and *Los alegres ojos de la tristeza*. The poem presented here is previously unpublished. The translation is by Daisy Cocco de Filippis.

Jeannette Miller was born in Santo Domingo, and she is currently on the faculty of the Universidad Autónoma de Santo Domingo and the Escuela Nacional de Bellas Artes. She writes poetry, plays and movie scripts, and she has received many awards. Her work has been anthologized in *Antología de la literatura dominicana*, 1972, *Antología literaria dominicana*, 1981, *Contemporary Women Authors of Latin America*, 1983, *Mujeres poetas de Hispanoamérica*, 1986, *Sin otro profeta que su canto*, 1988 (edited by Daisy Cocco de Filippis), and *The Literary Review* special Caribbean issue, 1992 (edited by Pamela Mordecai and Betty Wilson). "Utopía" is from her 1985 collection, *Fichas de identidad*. "A medida que la oscuridad crece . . ." is from her 1972 collection, *Fórmulas para combatir el miedo*. Both books were published in Santo Domingo by Ediciones de Taller. The translations are by Tracy Hudgins and MJ Fenwick.

Molly Mills has been a resident of St. Thomas for twenty years. She is of Irish-Cherokee descent and now shares the warmth and beauty of "America's Paradise" and its people. She is a Special Educator and works for the U.S. Virgin Islands Department of Education in Federal Grants.

The poems presented here were originally published in her collection titled *One Woman's Song*, 1989. She also has work published in *The Caribbean Writer*.

Florette Morand (Guadeloupe) is a poet and short story writer. "Reconnaitront-ils?" is from her poetry collection, *Feu de brousse*, (Montreal: Editions du Jour, 1967). Her other books are *Mon coeur est un oiseau des îles*, 1954, *Biguines*, 1956, and *Chanson pour ma savane*, 1959. Among the anthologies and journals in which her work has appeared are *From the Green Antilles*, 1966, *La Poésie antillaise*, 1977 (edited by Maryse Condé), *La Littérature des Antilles-Guyane Française*, 1978, *Les Poètes de la Guadeloupe*, 1978, and *La Revue Guadeloupéenne*. The translation is by Michelle Thompson.

Pamela Mordecai (Jamaica) is an important presence in Caribbean literature. As both a poet and an editor she has worked hard toward establishing the new canon. Her work has appeared in essentially all the Caribbean-area literary magazines, including *BIM*, *Savacou*, *Jamaica Journal*, *Arts Review*, *Caribbean Quarterly*, *Kyk-Over-Al*, *Callaloo* and *The Caribbean Writer*. And among the many anthologies in which her work has appeared are *Carifesta: Anthology of 20 Caribbean Voices*, 1976, *Parang*, 1977, *New Poets from Jamaica*, 1979 (edited by Kamau Brathwaite), *Focus 83*, 1983, *Anansesem*, 1985 (edited by Velma Pollard), *Caribbean Verse*, 1986, *Black Poetry*, 1988 (edited by Grace Nichols), *Voiceprint*, 1989, and *Daughters of Africa*, 1992. She has been an editor of three important anthologies, *Jamaica Woman*, 1980 (co-edited with Mervyn Morris), *From Our Yard*, 1987, *Her True-True Name*, 1989 (co-edited with Betty Wilson), and the special Caribbean issue of *The Literary Review*, 1992 (also co-edited with Betty Wilson). The poems presented here are from her own poetry collection, *Journey Poem*, (Kingston: Sandberry Press, 1989.)

Nancy Morejón is contemporary Cuba's most internationally acclaimed poet. Among the many anthologies in which her work has appeared are *Con Cuba*, 1969, *Poesía cubana de la revolución*, 1976, *Writing in Cuba Since the Revolution*, 1977, *Sensemayá*, 1980, *Los dispositivos de la flor*, 1981, *Palabra de mujer*, 1982, *Breaking the Silences*, 1982, *Woman Who Has Sprouted Wings*, 1984, *Poesía feminista del mundo hispánico*, 1984, *Women Brave in the Face of Danger*, 1985, *The Defiant Muse*, 1986, *The Renewal of the Vision*, 1987, *Lovers and Comrades*, 1989, *Creation Fire*, 1990, and *Daughters of Africa*, 1992. Among the many literary magazines are *Casa de las Américas*, *El Caimán Barbudo*, *Revolución y Cultura*, *The Black Scholar*, *The Literary Review*, a special Caribbean issue, 1992, and a special Caribbean issue of *River City*, 1996. "Amo a mi amo" and "Mujer negra" are from her collection, *Octubre imprescindible*, (La Habana: UNEAC, 1982), and "Requiem" is from her *Grenada Notebook (Cuaderno de Granada)*, (New York: Círculo de Cultura Cubana, 1984). Her other poetry collections are *Mutismos*, 1962, *Amor, ciudad atribuida*, 1964, *Richard trajo su flauta*, 1967, *Parajes de una época*, 1979, *Where the Island Sleeps Like a Wing*, 1985, and *Ours the Earth*, 1990, published by the Institute of Caribbean Studies at the University of the West Indies in Mona, Kingston, Jamaica. In addition to these poetry collections, she has several scholarly books and essays. The translations to the poems presented here are by Rosabelle White and MJ Fenwick.

Grace Nichols (Guyana) is a poet, novelist and a successful author of children's literature. She is degreed from the University of Guyana in Georgetown and currently lives in East Sussex, U.K. The poems presented here, "I Coming Back," "Night Is Her Robe," "Skin-Teeth," "Dark Sign," "Nanny," and "This Kingdom" are from her first collection, *i is a long-memoried woman*, (London: Virago Press, 1983), which won the Commonwealth Poetry Prize. Her next collection was *The Fat Black Woman's Poems*, 1985, which was cited in the "Introduction" to this anthology. Her 1989 collection is *Lazy Thoughts of a Lazy Woman*, (London: Virago Press, 1989). Important anthologies in which her work has appeared are *News for Babylon*, 1984, *Walter Rodney: Poetic Tributes*, 1985, *Watchers and Seekers*, (edited by Rhonda Cobham and Merle Collins), 1987, *Let It Be Told*, 1987, *Black Poetry*, 1988, *Voiceprint*, 1989, *Her True-True Name*, (edited by Pamela Mordecai and Betty Wilson), 1989, *Tradewinds*, 1990, *Caribbean Poetry Now*, 1992, *Daughters of Africa*, 1992 and the special Caribbean issue of *The Literary Review*, (edited by Pamela Mordecai and Betty Wilson), 1992.

Dalia Nieves Albert (Puerto Rico) is a well-published poet, and in 1974 she received the Prize of the Ateneo Puertorriqueño. The selections presented here are excerpts from *La calle*, (Barcelona: Artes Gráficas, 1977) and from *En el diario asombro de lo humano*, (Puerto Rico: Ediciones Puerto, 1989). Her political challenge is expressed in these lines from *En el diario asombro*, "¿A qué no te comprometes / con la vida / hasta que te duela?" ("Why don't you commit yourself / with your life / until it hurts?")

Solange Ninini (née Naranin) is from Capesterre Belle-Eau, Guadeloupe. The poem presented here is from *Karukéra Anthologie*, published in 1983 by the Association Guadeloupéenne des Amis de la Poésie. The translation is by Raymonde Niel.

Olga Nolla is one of contemporary Puerto Rico's most acclaimed poets. "Datos atmosféricos" is from her collection, *El ojo de la tormenta*, (San Juan: Ediciones Palabra de Mujer, 1975) and "Los nombres de la diosa" is from her collection, *Dafne en el mes de marzo*, (Madrid: Editorial Playor, 1989). Her other collections are *De lo familiar*, 1973, *El sombrero de plata*, 1976, *Clave de sol*, 1977, and *Dulce hombre prohibido*, 1994. Among the many anthologies in which selections from her work have appeared are

Borinquen: An Anthology of Puerto Rican Literature, 1974, *Poemario de la mujer puertorriqueña*, 1976, and *Palabra de mujer*, 1982, and the very important literary magazines, *Zona de Carga y Descarga* and *Sin Nombre*. She currently directs the literary magazine *Cupey*. Her commitment to the power of poetry in history is expressed in these lines from *El ojo de la tormenta*, "Y aceptar lo que nos duele / y entender que estamos hechos / de actos pasados / semillas / Y ver claro / tratar de ver el camino / de la historia / Y provocar el derrumbe / E inventarnos otra vez." ("And accept what hurts us / and understand that we are made / from past acts / seeds / And see clearly / try to see the path / of history / And provoke the collapse / And invent ourselves again.")

Ana Núñez Machín is a poet of the Cuban Revolution. Her poetry publications are *Versos*, 1955, *Tiempo de sombra*, 1959, *Sangre resurrecta*, 1961, and *Metal de auroras*, (La Habana) 1964, the collection from which the selections presented here were taken. She has published internationally and in many of the magazines of contemporary Cuba, including *Bohemia* and *Verde Olivo*, Her work shows a strong commitment to the independence struggles throughout the Caribbean and Latin America. She was degreed as a teacher from the Escuela Normal para Maestros de La Habana in 1952, and contributed her skills to the rural literacy campaign during the years following the Revolution of 1959. The translations are by Tracy Hudgins.

Solitahe Yasmin Odlum is from Barbados. Her "Bonnie's Poem" is reprinted here from *Under We Sky*, 1987, an anthology edited by Nadine Rogers and published by CREWA, the Creative Writers Association of the University of the West Indies, Cave Hill, Barbados.

Marcelle Pepin Archelon was born in Lamentin, Guadeloupe, and has a collection of poems titled *Cri des conques*. The poem presented here, "Jeunnesse realiste, Jeunesse folle," appeared in *Karukéra Anthologie*, an anthology published in 1983 by the Association Guadeloupéenne des Amis de la Poésie. The translation is by Raymonde Niel.

Joyce Peters-McKenzie has been a teacher and administrator in St. Vincent. "Yes, Me Child" is reprinted from *The Caribbean Writer*, volume 3, 1989.

Nourbese Philip is a poet, novelist and writer of short stories. She was born in Tobago and has lived in Canada for the past twenty five years. Even as a child, she explains, she always knew she would have to leave the Caribbean because of the colonial economic structure and the scarce opportunities for writers and intellectuals. Today she is an accomplished writer and an attorney. In 1988 she won the prestigious Casa de las Américas Prize, in 1989 she won the Choice Award from the Canadian Children's Book Centre, in 1990-91 she was a Guggenheim Fellow, and in 1994 she received the Laurence Foundation Award. "Discourse on the Logic of Language" is from her highly acclaimed book *She Tries Her Tongue, Her Silence Softly Breaks*, (Charlottetown: Ragweed Press, 1989). "The Grammar of Love" and "Byeri" are from *Salmon Courage*, published in 1983 by Williams-Wallace, Toronto. Among the other anthologies and journals in which her work has appeared are *Sad Dances in a Field of White*, 1985, *A Shapely Fire*, 1987, *Imagining Women*, 1988, *Creation Fire*, 1990 (edited by Ramabai Espinet), *Daughters of Africa*, 1992, and *Kitchen Talk*, 1992, *The Black Scholar, Wasafiri* and a special Caribbean issue of *River City*, 1996. The poems presented here are reprinted with special permission from the author.

Marilene Phipps (Haiti) is a prize-winning poet and painter whose work features scenes of Haitian life and is "an invitation to viewers [and readers] to look into these people as they themselves are showing you the way in . . . into their culture, into their souls, into their minds, into their selves." Her poetry is written in English. Her work wants to show the enormous strength and resilience of the Haitian people in the face of economic scarcity and political violence. She was born in Port-au-Prince, spent her adolescence partly in Haiti, partly in France and has lived in the U.S. for the past ten years. She has an undergraduate degree in anthropology from the University of California at Berkeley and an MFA from the University of Pennsylvania. She was a Guggenheim Fellow in 1995. Her poetry has appeared in several important literary magazines, including *Grolier*, (winner of the Grolier poetry prize, 1993), *Callaloo, International Quarterly, Compost*, and is forthcoming in *Ploughshares*. "Maneenee" and "Out For Some Bread On Flatbush Ave." are from her manuscript *Haitian Masks* and are presented here with special permission from the poet.

Velma Pollard (Trinidad) is the author of several volumes of poetry and fiction. Her work merited the prestigious Casa de las Américas Prize in 1992. Further, she is a widely respected scholar and educator and is currently a Senior Lecturer in Language Education and Dean of the Faculty of Education at the University of the West Indies at Mona, Kingston. Her monograph titled *Dread Talk—the Language of Rastafari* is a product of her research in creole languages. She has a volume of short stories, *Considering Woman*, 1989, a novella, *Karl*, 1992, a novel, *Homestretch*, 1994, and two volumes of poetry. "Drake's Strait" is from her 1992 collection, *Shame Trees Don't Grow Here*, (Leeds: Peepal Tree Press), "British Museum and After" is from her 1988 collection, *Crown Point*, (Leeds: Peepal Tree Press). Other poems have appeared in the 1980 anthology, *Jamaica Woman*, (Kingston: Heinemann Educational Books), edited by Pamela Mordecai and Mervyn Morris. The poems are reprinted here with special permission from the author. Among the many other anthologies in which her poetry and stories appear are *Voiceprint*, 1989, *Her True-True Name*, 1989, (edited by Pamela Mordecai and Betty Wilson), *Caribbean New Wave*, 1990,

Creation Fire, 1990, (edited by Ramabai Espinet), *Green Cane and Juicy Flotsam*, 1991, and *Daughters of Africa*. Her work has also appeared in many of the important Caribbean journals, *BIM*, *Kyk-Over-Al*, *Jamaica Journal*, *Caribbean Quarterly*, *Arts Review*, *The Trinidad and Tobago Review*, and the special Caribbean issue of *The Literary Review*, edited by Pamela Mordecai and Betty Wilson.

Magaly Quiñones (Puerto Rico) is the author of seven books of poems and is active in the literary community in Río Piedras, Puerto Rico. In 1986, she received the prestigious Pen Club Award. In addition to her poetry, she has published critical essays, art reviews and travel accounts, and she has served as juror for many poetry prizes. She participates in a poetry radio program, Revista Oral de Poesía on WRTU, Radio Universidad, giving readings and talks on poetry. She is the Assistant Librarian at the University of Puerto Rico in Río Piedras. Her 1978 poetry collection is *Cantándole a la noche misma*, and her 1982 collection is *En la pequeña Antilla*, (San Juan: Ediciones Mairena). "La nueva gesta" is from her 1989 collection, *Razón de lucha, razón de amor*, (San Juan: Ediciones Mairena). Her other collections are *Entre mi voz y el tiempo*, 1969, *Era que el mundo era*, 1974, *Zumbayllu*, 1976, and *Nombrar*, 1985. Among the many anthologies and magazines in which her work has appeared are *Poemario de la mujer puertorriqueña*, 1976, *Antología de la poesía de la mujer puertorriqueña*, 1981, *Antología de la poesía puertorriqueña*, 1986, *Poetas del nuevo mundo*, 1991, *Voces femeninas del mundo hispánico*, 1991, *The Caribbean Writer*, *The New Voices*, *Callaloo* and *Nosotras*. The poem is reprinted here with special permission from the poet. The translation is by Tracy Hudgins and MJ Fenwick.

Jennifer Rahim (Trinidad) is a poet and a student of West Indian literature. She has previously published her work in the anthologies, *Washer Woman Hangs Her Poems In the Sun*, 1990, edited by Margaret Watts, *Creation Fire*, 1990, edited by Ramabai Espinet, and *Sacred Journeys*, 1995, and the literary magazines, *The Caribbean Writer*, the *Trinidad and Tobago Review*, the *Graham House Review*, 1991 (a special Caribbean issue), *The Malahat Review* and *The Literary Review*, 1992 (a special Caribbean issue edited by Pamela Mordecai and Betty Wilson). "Still Birth," and "Before Speech" are from her first collection, *Mothers Are Not the Only Linguists*, 1992; "The Felling of a Tree" is from her new anthology, *Between the Fence and the Forest*, forthcoming from Peepal Tree Press (Leeds, U.K.). The poems are all reprinted here with special permission from the author.

Gladys do Rego-Kuster is a social and cultural worker in Willemstad, Curaçao. She writes poetry and has written scripts for documentary films about women. Her work has appeared *Bosero* and *Chimichimi* and in the 1990 anthology of women writers, *Creation Fire*, edited by Ramabai Espinet and published by CAFRA, Tunapuna, Trinidad-Tobago, in collaboration with Sister Vision Press in Toronto, Canada. "Poem" is reprinted here with special permission from the author.

Soleida Ríos is a poet whose interest in poetry began in the years following the Cuban Revolution as she went from community to community as an elementary teacher in the Sierra Maestra mountains. Her first collection is *De la sierra*, a collection of poems born of this experience, published in 1977 by Ediciones Uvero in Santiago. The poems presented here, "De la sierra," "Pájaro de La Bruja" and "Entrevista" are from this collection. The translations are by Tracy Hudgins and MJ Fenwick. Her other collections are *De pronto abril*, 1979, and *Entre mundo y juguete*, 1987. She also edited an anthology of contemporary Cuban women poets titled *Poesía infiel*, (La Habana: Editora Abril, 1989).

Etnairis Rivera is one of Puerto Rico's most widely acclaimed contemporary poets. Her poetry and her political commitment have been closely allied in her work with popular theatre in New York and with political prisoner defense groups. Among the many anthologies and literary magazines in which her work has appeared are *Poesía nueva puertorriqueña*, 1971, *The Puerto Rican Poets / Los poetas puertorriqueños*, 1972, *Poesía rebelde de América*, 1978, *Poesía militante puertorriqueña*, 1979, *Puño de poesía*, 1979, *Inventing a Word*, 1980, *Antología de la poesía de la mujer puertorriqueña*, 1981, *Poetas hispanoamericanos contemporáneos*, 1989, *Papiros de Babel*, 1991, *The Literary Review*, special Caribbean issue, 1992, and *Zona de Carga y Descarga*. Presented here from her collection, *El día del polen*, (Mayagüez: Jardín de Espejos, 1980) are selected excerpts from her poem, "El velero vaporoso." Her 1974 collection, *WYDondequiera*, was published in Puerto Rico by Ediciones Puerto. The translations are by Tracy Hudgins and MJ Fenwick. Her other collections are *María Mar Moriviví*, 1976, *Pachamamapa takín*, 1976, and *El pulso de una estrella aguardándome*, 1981.

Reina María Rodríguez (Cuba) has received three important literary prizes, Premio 13 de Marzo in 1975 for *La gente de mi barrio*, Premio UNEAC "Julián de Casal" in 1980 for *Cuando una mujer no duerme*, and Premio Casa de las Américas in 1984 for *Para un cordero blanco*. Her work has appeared in numerous anthologies, *Breaking the Silences*, 1982, *Cuba: en su lugar la poesía*, 1982, *Poetisas cubanas*, 1985, *Usted es la culpable*, 1985, *Poesía infiel*, 1989 (edited by Soleida Ríos), *Lovers and Comrades*, 1989, and a special Caribbean issue of *The Literary Review*, 1992. She is degreed in Spanish American Literature from the University of Havana. "Cuando una mujer no duerme" is the title poem from her 1982 collection and "Emelina" is from her 1975 collection. The translations are by MJ Fenwick.

Astrid H. Roemer is a novelist, poet, and the author of short stories, theatre works, radio plays, recordings and essays. Her works are internationally acclaimed, and her style is impressive as is her commitment to social and economic justice. She was born in Parimaribo, Suriname, and presently lives and works as a family therapist in the Netherlands. She writes in both Dutch and Sranen. The long list of her titles includes poetry: *Sasa*, 1970, *En wat dan nog*, 1984, and *Noordzee Blues*, 1985; fiction: *Nergens ergens*, 1983, *Levenslang gedicht*, 1987, *Een naam voor de liefde*, 1987, *De wereld heeft gezicht verloren*, 1991, and *Niets wat pijn doet*, 1994, *Gewaagd Leven*, 1996, and *Maar ik blijf*, 1996; and theatre: *Purple Blues*, 1985, *Nestwarmte*, 1990, *Dichter bij mij schreeuw ik*, 1991, *Mert*, 1993, and *Dans dans dan*, 1994. Her works have been anthologized in *Green Cane and Juicy Flotsam*, 1991, *Daughters of Africa*, 1992, and *Callaloo*. The poems presented here are from *Noordzee Blues* and are reprinted with special permission from the author. The translations are by Joop Arends.

Nadine Rogers was born in England but is a long-time resident of Barbados. "When one chile die . . . an'ther one does cry" is from the anthology, *Under We Sky*, published in 1987 by CREWA, the Creative Writers Association of the University of the West Indies, Cave Hill, Barbados.

Carmen Rogers-Green (Anguilla) has printed her poems in an Anguillan anthology, *Conchs by the Sea*. "Sarah Seh" previously appeared in *The Caribbean Writer*, volume 9 (1995).

Althea Romeo-Mark (Antigua) writes poetry and short stories. "Ole No-Teeth Mama" was part of her first collection, *Shu Shu Moko Jumbi, the Silent Dancing Spirit*, 1974, published by the Department of Pan-African Studies, Kent State University. Her 1978 collection is entitled *Palaver*, (Brooklyn: Downtown Poets Co-op). "Tropic Dimensions" is from the 1984 collection, *Two Faces*, and her third collection of poetry is entitled *Beyond Dreams: The Ritual Dancer*, 1989, both collections published in Monrovia, Liberia. She now lives in Switzerland.

Seketi (Suriname) is a poet with a strong commitment to women's social and political issues. The poem presented here appeared in *Creation Fire*, published by Sister Vision, Toronto, and CAFRA, Tunapuna, Trinidad-Tobago, 1990, and edited by Ramabai Espinet. The translation of "Poem" is by MJ Fenwick & Tracy Hudgins.

Olive Senior (Jamaica) has won several prizes as a poet, short story writer and playwright, among them: the Institute of Jamaica Centenary Medal, 1980, The Commonwealth Literature Prize, 1987, and the Musgrave Medal for Literature, 1988. "Amazon Women" and "Gardening On the Run" are from her latest collection, *Gardening in the Tropics*, 1994; "Colonial Girls School" is from her collection, *Talking of Trees*, (Kingston: Calabash, 1986). Among the many anthologies and magazines in which her work has appeared are *Over Our Way*, 1980, *Jamaica Woman*, 1980, *Focus '83*, 1983,

From Our Yard, 1987, *Voiceprint,* 1989, *Her True-True Name,* 1989, *Creation Fire,* 1990, *Green Cane and Juicy Flotsam,* 1991, *The Literary Review* special Caribbean issue, 1992, *Daughters of Africa,* 1992, *Savacou, Jamaica Journal, Arts Review* and *The Caribbean Writer.*

Sista Roots (Trinidad) is a poet, a visual artist and a children's story-teller. "The Great Escape" appeared in the anthology, *Watchers and Seekers,* (New York: Peter Bedrick Books, 1987) edited by Rhonda Cobham and Merle Collins.

Eintou Pearl Springer (Trinidad) is a performance poet, storyteller, playwright, and an award-winning actor with the Caribbean Theatre Guild. She is also well known as a cultural activist in Trinidad-Tobago and the Caribbean. She is presently the National Heritage Librarian of Trinidad-Tobago. Her work has been included in several literary magazines and anthologies, including *Daughters of Africa,* (New York: Pantheon Books, 1992) an international anthology of poetry and prose edited by Margaret Busby. "Freedom Child—Tilla's Lullaby" previously appeared in another important anthology, *Washer Woman Hangs Her Poems in the Sun,* (Trinidad-Tobago, 1990) edited by Margaret Watts. Her 1986 collection of poems is entitled *Out of the Shadows,* published by Karia Press, London. "The Speech Band Song" is from her 1991 collection, *Focussed,* (Oxford: Triangle). A third book, *Godchild,* (also by Karia Press, London) is a collection of stories and poems for children rooted in the oral traditions of Trinidad-Tobago and the Caribbean.

Lynn Sweeting is a Coordinating Editor of *WomanSpeak,* a creative publication of the WomanSpeak Collective of Nassau, Bahamas. "Prayer For the Nameless"and this new version of "Living on the Lee" are reprinted here with special permission from the author.

Elean Thomas (Jamaica) is a poet and novelist. She is degreed in history and political science from the University of the West Indies and has a strong commitment to the women's struggle in the Caribbean. "Before They Can Speak of Flowers" is the title poem from her 1988 collection, *Before They Can Speak of Flowers,* (London: Karia Press). "Litany of A Housewife" is from her first collection, *Word Rhythms* (London: Karia Press, 1986), an expression she has always used to describe her poems. Her novel titled *The Last Room,* published in 1991 by Virago Press, London, merited the Ruth Hadden Memorial Prize.

Patricia Turnbull is a prize-winning poet born in St. Lucia and now a resident of Tortola, Virgin Islands. She has two collections of poetry, *Late Blooming* and *Rugged Vessels* (Archipelago Press, 1992), in which "Corpus Christi" appeared. She received the Cedars Prize for Contemporary Poetry in 1991 and the James Michener Fellowship in 1993. Her work has been anthologized in *Caribbean New Voices*, 1995, edited by Stewart Brown and published by Longman Caribbean Writers, and *Moving Beyond Boundaries*, edited by Carole Boyce Davies and Molara Ogundipe-Leslie and published by Pluto Press, 1995. She has also published in *The Caribbean Writer*. The poems presented here are reprinted with special permission from the author. "... the rugged beauty of each piece / holds my primordial sense / to make and multiply / to fill, to store, to know / to keep, to carry, to show ..." (from *Rugged Vessels*)

Miriam Ventura-Medina is a poet and journalist from the Dominican Republic. She is a member of the literary group, the first Círculo de Poetas Dominicanas, and currently lives in New York. Her first collection of poems is *Trópico acerca del otoño*, published in 1987. "On the One Hand Daphne, On the Other My Wounds" is from a new collection, *De cartas y sentencias* (unpublished), and is presented here with special permission from the poet. The translation is by Daisy Cocco de Filippis.

María del Carmen Vicente is from the Dominican Republic. Her first poetry collection is entitled *Territorios verticales*, 1983, in which "Abril" appeared. Her work is anthologized in *Sin otro profeta que su canto*, 1988, edited by Daisy Cocco de Filippis. The translation here is by Tracy Hudgins.

Sherezada Vicioso (Dominican Republic), known as **Chiqui**, is a widely acclaimed poet in both the Dominican Republic and the U.S. She is degreed from Brooklyn College in Latin American History and Sociology and from Columbia University in Education. She was founder of the writers group Círculo de Mujeres Poetas, organizer of the first Concurso Nacional de Décima y Poesía de la Mujer Campesina and organizer of an homage to poets Aída Cartagena Portalatín, Carmen Natalia Martínez Bonilla and Julia de Burgos. Among the many anthologies in which her work has appeared are *Sin otro profeta que su canto*, 1988, edited by Daisy Cocco de Filippis, and *Poemas del exilio y de otras inquietudes / Poems of Exile and Other Concerns*, 1988, edited by Daisy Cocco de Filippis and Jane Robinette. "Doña Mariana" is from her collection *Viaje Desde el Agua*, (Santo Domingo: Visuarte, 1981), "Un extraño ulular traía el viento" is the title poem of her 1985 collection *Un extraño ulular traía el viento*, (Santo Domingo: Editora Alfa y Omega), and "Reykjavik"is from her newest manuscript, *Wish-Ky Sour*, 1996. Her other books are *Bolver a vivir: Imágenes de Nicaragua*, (1986), *Algo que decir: ensayos sobre literatura feminina*, (1991) and *InternAmiento* (1994). She was the recipient of the prestigious Anacaona de Oro en Literatura award and of the Medalla de Oro. The poems are reprinted here with special permission from the author. The translations are by Rosabelle White and MJ Fenwick.

Margaret Watts is a poet and a long-time resident of Trinidad-Tobago. She is on the faculty of the University of the West Indies, St. Augustine, and the editor of an excellent anthology of poetry by women of Trinidad and Tobago titled *Washer Woman Hangs Her Poems in the Sun*, 1990. "To a Correspondent Who Thought Before Seeing Me I Was Black" is from her 1989 collection, *Chautauqua to Chaguanas*. "Washerwoman" is from her newest collection, *Occasional Light*, published by The New Voices, Trinidad-Tobago, 1996, and all are reprinted here with special permission from the author. *Black and White Ivory* was her first collection of poetry, published in 1980, and her work has appeared in *Creation Fire*, the 1990 anthology edited by Ramabai Espinet, in the special 1992 Caribbean issue of *The Literary Review*, edited by Pamela Mordecai and Betty Wilson, in *Arachne, Ariel II, Passage, The Caribbean Writer* and the *Atlanta Review*.

Patricia Bonnie Zamia was born in Basse-Terre, Guadeloupe. The poem presented here appeared in *Karukéra Anthologie*, published in 1983 by the Association Guadeloupéenne des Amis de la Poésie. The translation is by Raymonde Niel.

Publisher's Note: An exhaustive effort was made to locate all the authors. If any permissions have been omitted it is unintentional and forgiveness is requested. If notified, the publisher will rectify any omission in future editions.

Also By MJ Fenwick

For further readings by Caribbean women writers consult *Writers of The Caribbean and Central America*, a two volume bibliography by MJ Fenwick published by Garland Press, New York, 1992.

Other Titles Available from Azul's Caribfest Series

Countersong to Walt Whitman & Other Poems by Pedro Mir, translated by Donald W. Walsh & Jonathan Cohen. ISBN 0-9632363-3-4, $12.95, 179 pages (bilingual)

Yania Tierra by Aida Cartagena Portalatin, translated by MJ Fenwick, ISBN 0-9632363-9-3, $12.95, 196 pages (bilingual)

When the Tom-Tom Beats: Selected Poems & Prose by Jacques Roumain, translated by Joanne Fungaroli & Ronald Sauer, ISBN 0-9632363-8-5, $11.95, 96 pages (bilingual)

Azul Editions
7804 Sycamore Dr.
Falls Church, VA 22042
703.573.7866 FAX 703.573.7480
e-mail: azulpress@aol.com